Africa's Challenge

AFRICA'S CHALLENGE

USING LAW FOR GOOD GOVERNANCE AND DEVELOPMENT

Edited by
Ann Seidman
Robert B. Seidman
Pumzo Mbana
and **Hanson H. Li**

Africa World Press, Inc.

P.O. Box 1892
Trenton, NJ 08607

P.O. Box 48
Asmara, ERITREA

Africa World Press, Inc.

P.O. Box 1892
Trenton, NJ 08607

P.O. Box 48
Asmara, ERITREA

First Printing 2007

Book design: Saverance Publishing Services
Cover design: Dapo Ojo-Ade
Cover Maps courtesy of Outreach Program, Boston University African Studies Center

Library of Congress Cataloging-in-Publication Data

Africa's challenge : using law for good governance and development / editors, Ann Seidman ... [et al.].

p. cm.

Includes bibliographical references and index.

ISBN 1-59221-470-3 -- ISBN 1-59221-471-1 (pbk.)

1. Public administration--Africa. 2. Democratization--Africa. 3. Law and economic development. 4. Africa--Politics and government--1960- 5. Africa--Economic conditions--1960- I. Seidman, Ann Willcox, 1926-

JQ1875.A745 2006
320.6096--dc22

2006003190

Table of Contents

Acknowledgements

We would like to acknowledge the contributions of the many people who have helped to make this book possible, but that, in itself, would almost require another book. We hope that the many whom we do not mention here by name do, nevertheless, realize our gratitude. We especially want to express our deep appreciation to the authors for their chapters in Parts II and III. Grounded on the authors' own research and experiences in various countries, these illuminate the way, in the post-independence era, dysfunctional institutions inherited from the colonial past have perpetuated so many African countries' external-dependence, poverty and vulnerability. Those chapters comprise their authors' own on-going study, research and debates with colleagues, friends and students over the years—not only in Africa and the United States. They also reflect, at least in part, exchanges of information and experiences with counterparts in some 30 other developing and transitional countries who must struggle with similar problems (for these linkages, see www.ICLAD-law.org). These chapters offer valuable evidence of the need for a qualitatively new way of thinking about the potential of using law to facilitate democratic social change.

We particularly wish to thank Dr. Charles Stith, former US Ambassador to Tanzania, and now Director of Boston University's African Professors Archives and Research Center (APARC). He contributed to making this book possible in several ways. Under his guidance, in 2003-4 the Center invited former Zambian President, Kenneth Kaunda, to serve as its first Presidential Professor. The President's staff, especially Mr. Godwin Mfula, a leading civil servant during the first quarter of a Century of Zambia's independence, contributed valuable evidence at a series of workshops concerning the potential of Lucian Ng'andwe's proposed law to establish a Commission on Law and Integrated National Development in Zambia (see Chapter 6, Part III, of this book). In addition, the Center funded Mr. Ng'andwe's return to Zambia to 'workshop' his proposal with legislators, ministerial, and university personnel. Back in Boston, the Center hosted a symposium at which Boston area Africanist scholars, in light of their own research, made further useful suggestions. Dr. Stith also serves on the Board of Advisors of the International Consortium for Law and Development.

We wish, too, to thank Barbara Brown, Director of the Boston University African Studies Center's Outreach Program for giving us permission to use that Program's map on this book's cover. The map graphically illustrates that the African continent exceeds in size the combined territories of China, Europe and the United States (the original map is available on the Program's website, http://www.bu.edu/africa/outreach). That map graphically illustrates this book's theme: the paradox of Africa's great poverty in the midst of vast resources, perpetuated by the institutions its divided countries have inherited from their colonial past.

We thank Will Khouri, Director of the BU School of Law's Computer Services. Vivek J. Ashar and his colleagues were wonderfully helpful with our computer problems and especially in preparing this book's diagrams and maps. Finally, we wish to express our deep appreciation to Sue Morrison who, as always, has helped us with all the secretarial jobs required to keep the project underway, and in many other ways far beyond the call of duty. She is indeed the office administrator beyond compare.

The Editors, October 18, 2005

PART I

THE CHALLENGE

Chapter 1

Introduction

Today, almost half a century after most of Africa's new nations won political independence, the peoples of that vast continent remain among the world's poorest (*see* Table1-1, *infra*).

Table 1-1: Indicators of Poverty in Selected African Countries, Comparing Those Indicators to Those of All Sub-Saharan Countries, and the World's High Income, And Low & Middle-Income Countries, in 2004.

	Population (Millions) 2004	Gross national income (GNI)* US$ per capita 2004	PPP gross national income** US$ per capita 2004	Life expectancy at birth		Adult literacy rate% ages 15 and older 1998-2004
				Male years 2003	Female years 2003	
Ghana	21.1	380	2,280***	54	55	54****
Mozambique	19.1	250	1,160***	40	42	46
South Africa	45.6	3,630	10,960***	45	46	n/a
Zambia	10.5	450	890	36	37	68*****
Sub-Saharan Africa	719.0	600	1,850	45	46	61
World High Income	1,000.8	32,040	30,970	75	81	91
World Low & Middle Income	5,344.3	1,460	4,630	63	66	81

Source: The World Bank, *World Development Report 2005* 292-93 (2006).

* Calculated using the World Bank Atlas method. Gross national income (GNI – formerly gross national product or GNP), the broadest measure of national income, measures total value added from domestic and foreign sources claimed by residents. GNI per capita is GNI divided by midyear population.

** GNI converted into international dollars using purchasing power parity (PPP) conversion factors, because nominal exchange rates do not always reflect international differences in relative prices.

*** Estimate based on regression. Other PPP GNI numbers are extrapolated from the World Bank's latest International Comparison Program benchmark estimates.

**** National estimate based on census data.

***** National estimate based on survey data.

These statistics reflect resource allocation patterns shaped by economic, social and political institutions imposed during a century and more of colonial rule. For centuries, throughout the continent, colonial powers focused on developing export enclaves designed to produce crude mineral and agricultural raw materials to feed the rapidly growing manufacturing industries of Europe and America. Dependent on those overseas markets, each enclave typically remained economically cut off from the rest of the neighboring regions, effectively blocking the potential for economically-integrated continent-wide agricultural and industrial development. The primary links inserted by the colonial rulers between those export-dependent enclaves and neglected rural hinterlands comprised the hut taxes and other devices used to coerce young Africans – mainly male – to join the low cost labor force that built the railroads and roads, dug the ore from the mines, and harvested the crops that proved so profitable for colonial settlers and firms (*see* Figure 1-1, *infra*).

Figure 1.1: Model of Global Misallocation of Resources

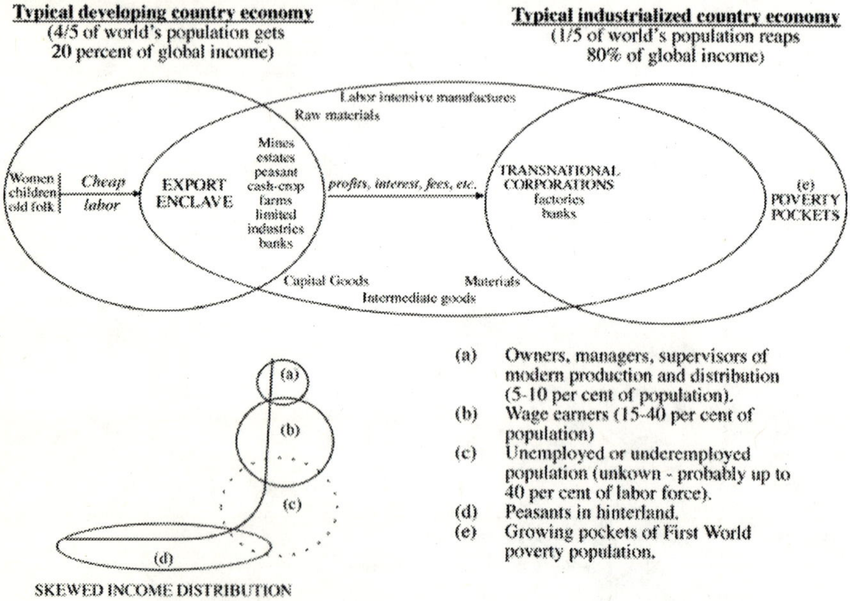

Over the years, historically-shaped political-economic institutions – settler farms, colonial mining and trading companies in East and Southern Africa, and colonial trading and mining firms in West Africa – perpetuated and expanded the distorted, externally-dependent mis-allocation of Africa's rich resources. After winning political 'independence,' Africa's newly-created nations' inherited institutions still focused government efforts on developing these narrow enclaves. Millions of African youths, seeking to escape rural poverty, typically ended up un- or under-employed, swelling the squatter townships dwarfed by steel-and-glass skyscrapers that dominated urban sky-lines. Global trade patterns still drained away the new countries' mineral and agricultural riches, along with the financial surpluses they generated: the billions of dollars-francs-pounds sterling these new nations required to provide increasingly productive employment opportunities and improved quality of life for all their citizens (*see* Table 1-2, *infra*).

Table 1.2: Balance of payments of selected African countries: current account summaries (in millions of dollars)

		Goods and Services			Current	Current
Country	Year	Exports	Imports	Balance on Goods and Services	Transfers (net)	Account Balance
Ghana	1990	983	-1506	-522	411	-223
	1995	1582	-2120	-539	523	-145
	1999	2473	-3926	-1453	620	-964
	2000	2441	-3350	-910	631	-386
	2001	2399	-3575	-1176	959	-325
	2002	2570	-3325	-755	900	-31
South Africa	1990	27742	-21016	6726	-321	2134
	1995	34689	-33373	1315	-645	-2205
	1999	33701	-30261	3440	-926	-640
	2000	36531	-33039	3492	-926	-575
	2001	35236	-31046	4191	-738	-296
	2002	35571	-32034	3537	-556	290
Zambia	1990	1360	-1897	-537	380	-594
	1999	879	-1176	-297	45	-386
	2000	871	-1318	-447	14	-553
Mozambique	1990	229	-996	-766	448	-415
	1995	411	-1055	-644	339	-445
	1999	579	-1496	-917	162	-912
	2000	689	-1492	-802	231	-764
	2001	976	-1616	-640	217	-657

Source: The World Bank, World Development Report 2003 (World Bank, 2003), Table 15 (Balance of Payments Current Account and International Reserves).

The chapters of this book explore the evidence from several countries to explain why – after decades of African liberation struggles to gain control over their countries' 'political kingdoms'[1] – their new governors seldom successfully exercised their state power through law (*see* Box 1-1, *infra*) to transform the inherited institutions that perpetuated their people's poverty and vulnerability.

Box 1.1: Law As Defined In This Book

Throughout this book, 'law' means a normative rule *promulgated by the state and ultimately implemented by state officials.* So defined, a law may take many forms: a statute, a local ordinance, subsidiary legislation, a ministerial rule, an administrative regulation, a military junta's decree.

Too often, instead, the new governors left those institutions intact, perpetuating growing unemployment and falling real incomes for the majority of their peoples. In that context, seeking to enhance their own wealth and power, not a few political leaders behaved corruptly. Tragically, some adopted policies that, aggravating ethnic and religious differences, culminated in devastating civil wars.

In Chapter 2 of this first part, the Seidmans review institutionalist legislative theory, especially its problem-solving methodology, as a potential guide to the use of law to facilitate democratic social change. They observe that law serves as government's primary tool for resolving social problems. They define that tool broadly to include legislation enacted by elected representatives; presidential decrees; ministry regulations, including all forms of subordinate legislation, and even local ordinances. They emphasize that, at all levels, law-makers should formulate, enact and implement legislation in accord with specified criteria and procedures designed to ensure non-arbitrary 'good governance:' That is, governance characterized by transparency, accountability, and, as far as possible, participatory processes. In that context, the Seidmans point out, governments can use law to help resolve social problems by changing the ***behaviors*** which, by definition, constitute ***the institutions*** that foster those problems. Self-evidently, laws cannot command distorted resources to reallocate themselves. The laws' detailed provisions can only prescribe new behaviors on the part of those who allocate resources. To ensure effective implementation, a law's provisions must specify government officials' behaviors more likely to facilitate people's efforts to reallocate their human, physical and financial resources in ways required to serve all the peoples' basic needs.

* * *

The chapters in Part II of this book offer three case studies of the way newly independent governments have failed to employ state power through law to transform inherited state institutions: The police force in Ghana, drafting institutions in Mozambique, and the relevant ministries responsible for facilitating development in South Africa. These examples illustrate the way inherited institutions too often have continued to foster the misallocation of Africa's valuable resources.

In Chapter 3, Raymond Atuguba analyzes how inherited police laws perpetuated the police's role in maintaining a *status quo* beneficial to the ruling elites. Like most former colonies, when it attained independence in 1957,

Ghana inherited a police force shaped during the British colonial government rule. Based on his Harvard University doctoral thesis, Atuguba describes the police as an institution deliberately designed to protect, not the people of the then-Gold Coast, but the colonial companies' export-oriented production and export of the territory's rich natural resources.

In every country the police provide an important forum for interaction between the state and its citizens; the behavior of the police projects the image of the way government treats its citizens. Atuguba summarizes the available historical evidence to show how, over more than a century, the colonial state employed the police as a key instrument to brutalize poor citizens and impose control over civil society. The British authorities used the police to arbitrarily enforce laws in broadly-defined areas of treason, arms and ammunitions regulation and public order to "maintain a political economy and social organization conducive to the colonial enterprise" (*see* ch. 3, at 7).

In the half a century since Ghana became the first sub-Saharan African country to win independence, successive democratic and dictatorial governments have seized the reins of power. None, however, have effectively restructured the police force. To mention two examples: To consolidate what he viewed as the political and economic freedoms of independent Ghana, President Nkrumah used the police to muzzle regional, tribal and religiously-based political parties. Decades later, President Jerry Rawlings' government, without altering the police force, merely strengthened its human, institutional and material resources.

In short, Atuguba graphically pictures the way, under post-independence governments, the Ghanaian police still interfered in many aspects of ordinary Ghanaian life, primarily to protect the rich and powerful. He emphasizes that the arbitrary use of this state institution has negatively affected Ghanaians' interactions with the state, thus undermining the rule of law.

Teodosio Uate's Chapter 4 offers an example to illustrate why drafters, functioning in the context of inherited drafting institutions, so frequently provide bills that prove ineffectively implemented. Like Atuguba, he draws on evidence he discovered while doing his doctoral thesis to describe in detail the causes of Mozambican legislative drafters' problematic behaviors. For a year and a half, these drafters worked on the bill enacted by the Mozambican Parliament as the Environmental Law of 1997. Nevertheless, despite those prolonged efforts, evidence demonstrates that the law they produced did not ensure transparent, accountable decision-making processes to enable Mozambicans to participate effectively in protecting their own environment. Ten years after the 1997 law's enactment, the designated implementing authority, the Ministry of Natural Resources refused to grant a non-government organization, LIVANGO, an opportunity to review the documents and facts on which it had granted a foreign firm permission to build a major dam. That dam seemed inevitably likely to affect the property and lives of thousands of Mozambicans. The Ministry's technical agency claimed, however, that the law had not specified the form for transmitting the information to LIVANGO, and that the Act granted each project sponsor discretion as to whether and how to submit it. A year later, under strong public pressure, the technical agency began a dialogue with the affected rural populations – but still refused to grant LIVANGO full access to its reports. Meanwhile, the dam's potential financers decided not to commit their funds until the government provided additional impact studies.

To explain the drafters' apparent failure to ensure the law provided the kind of transparent decision-making process required to ensure meaningful participation, Uate reports on his in-depth interviews with some of the drafters, as well as his detailed scrutiny of ministry files, including their drafts of the proposed law. He finds the explanation in part in the drafters' behaviors during the prolonged drafting process. Initially, following foreign consultants' advice and reviewing other Portuguese-speaking countries' and international 'model' laws, they sought to ensure public enjoyment of specified 'rights'-- to environmental education, to environmental information, to participate in environmental protection programs. They claimed to adapt these broad principles to Mozambique circumstances. Their past training, however -- as elsewhere, typically centered primarily on drafting techniques rather than Mozambique's social realities -- had not equipped them to gather and organize relevant evidence logically to defend their bill's detailed provisions against senior administrative decision-makers' objections. In particular, at the senior officials' urging, they substituted vague generalities for detailed measures required to facilitate stakeholder participation in environmental decisions.

Uate notes that at least some of the participants in the drafting process had actually studied institutionalist legislative theory and methodology. Nevertheless, when it came to actually drafting the bill, they had resorted to a focus on drafting techniques per se, rather than how to draft a law's detailed measures in a way likely to ensure the effective implementation of their substance.

In Chapter 5, Neva Makgetla investigates the way existing institutions shaped the patterns of post-apartheid South Africa's government policy making. As this book goes to press, South Africa's development path seems to lie at a crossroads. With the large number of its black majority living in abject poverty and the white minority still controlling most of the economy, the government still faces the challenge of creating an institutional framework likely to facilitate economic development to meet all South Africans' basic needs.

After taking power in 1994, South Africa's new government did act to replace the laws that openly maintained apartheid. The new laws did improve some aspects of life for those excluded from past South African 'development,' providing equal access to schools, health facilities, housing -- the social infrastructure essential to improving their quality of life – to those blacks who could afford to pay for them. The new laws did not, however, effectively transform the inherited socio-economic institutions that reduced, rather than expanded, available employment opportunities and perpetuated poverty-level living standards for almost half of all South Africans – especially most of the black majority.

The first section of Makgetla's chapter looks at the general reasons for the South African government's failure to use law to implement effective development policies. The African National Congress (ANC)-led South African government adopted policies, sometimes but not always in the form of laws, without attempting to win the support of stakeholders within the party like the Congress of South African Trade Unions (COSATU) and the South African Communist Party (SACP). Excluding these crucial stakeholders meant divorcing policy decisions from the concerns and inputs of the working class and the ANC's poor constituents. In adopting most of these policies immediately after democratization, Makgetla points out that the new government leaders apparently concluded they lacked capacity to conduct the necessary research and draft policy documents -- far less the legislation -- required to ensure their effective implementation. Instead, the government employed foreign consultants, most of whom neither grounded their proposals on research as to the nature and scope of post-apartheid institutional realities, nor sought inputs from those who, still suffering from those realities, might have contributed facts and ideas as a basis for policies more likely to change them. Makgetla concludes that those consultants "did not base their recommendations on appropriate or thorough research. They effectively excluded or largely ignored inputs from key stakeholders, especially organized labor and poor communities." Makgetla provides extensive statistical evidence to demonstrate that the first ten years of post-liberation government policies proved ineffective in achieving their declared goals; far less did they fully employ or fulfil the basic needs of South Africa's poor majority.

The South African Parliament did enact a law to establish a National Economic, Development and Labour Council (NEDLAC) to bring representatives of organized labour, government, the private sector, and civil society together in a consultative forum on development policy. NEDLAC initiated yearly summits where these stakeholders discussed and even reached agreement on crucial policy matters. Unfortunately, however, the law establishing NEDLAC included no provisions to require government agencies to implement the agreements reached at the summit. In the event, the responsible ministries too often simply ignored them.

Makgetla emphasizes that one of the challenges facing South Africa today remains that of making democracy truly participatory. The government still needs to ensure that the previously disenfranchised black and poor communities participate in the nation's policy decisions. Makgetla observes that, in the last decade, this proved difficult in part because some of the popular organizations that had led the liberation struggles failed to mobilize the population to influence the post-liberation government's policy decisions. Makgetla proposes using the institutionalist theory's model of decision-making processes to identify measures to ensure stakeholder participation in collecting relevant information, and providing inputs into the formulation of more effectively implemented policies.

Makgetla offers three case studies to illustrate the way inherited economic and financial institutions in the public and private sectors hindered the formulation and implementation of policies to meet the needs of all South Africans. The first two focus on institutions that shaped two essential government policy packages – the Growth, Employment and Redistribution (GEAR) strategy and the annual national budget. Her third case study analyses the way existing institutions tended to hinder formulation and implementation of an effective transformative industrial strategy.

In the first case, Makgetla shows that government ministry personnel – especially in the Ministry of Finance and Treasury – built GEAR along the lines recommended by international financial institutions according to the Washington Concensus. These not only failed to bring about promised economic development, but aggravated pre-existing social problems. Depending on the definition used, real unemployment soared to between 30% and 40% of the labor force. While making gestures to improve basic services, GEAR failed to deliver the economic growth required both to stimulate employment and provide the revenues needed to finance those services. Eventually, faced by the GEAR's failure to stimulate more equitable resource distribution, the government shifted its focus towards a Black Economic Empowerment Strategy (BEES). That strategy as commonly employed however, merely enabled a few blacks to join newly emerging wealthy public and private sector elites. It does little to improve most blacks' quality of life.

As the second case, Makgetla reviews the Treasury's historically-shaped decision-making processes. Operating in secret, these produced budgets that did allocate limited additional funds to expanded social services. However, they blocked the funds needed to restructure the nation's productive sectors in ways necessary to increase employment and output, and to generate the investible surpluses required to finance them. Only after the Treasury had made the key financial decisions behind closed doors, did Cabinet submit the – largely unchanged -- budget to the elected Parliament. MPs could question those decisions, but could not vote to alter them. As a result, through a process hardly characterized by the transparency, accountability and participation required for good governance, the Treasury exercised a powerful influence on government's policy formulation and implementation.

Magketla's third case focuses on industrialization strategy. Before liberation, the African National Congress called for restructuring the national economy to achieve more balanced, integrated production and consumption patterns to meet the needs of all South Africans. Yet only in 2002, a decade after attaining liberation, did the government publish its draft Integrated Manufacturing Strategy (IMS). Still unfinalized as this book goes to press, the IMS largely ignored key development initiatives recommended by NEDLAC, as well as other state and non-state efforts to implement more effective sectoral strategies. Makgetla provides the details to demonstrate that, to a significant degree, this reflected the existing institutionalized policy-making process's failure to provide an adequate framework for gathering and analyzing the relevant evidence required to resolve the stakeholders' deep-seated disagreements.

* * *

This book's Part III focuses on the factors that influenced Zambia's post-independence governments' efforts use law to foster people-oriented development. In some respects, the Zambian case starkly illustrates the paradox confronting almost all now-politically-independent African states. At independence, Zambia's average GDP per capita appeared among the highest on the African continent.[2] Today, as the new millennium dawns, only about 11 million Zambians – a smaller population than that of several countries' major cities -- inhabit a land area larger than England. During nearly half a century of 'independent' Zambian governance, real world prices for the copper exports – to which colonially-imposed institutions had geared Zambia's seeming prosperity – sharply declined. Unemployment soared to 40 percent of the nation's urban labor force. Zambians' per capita Gross Domestic Product (GDP - in dollar terms) plummeted to one of the world's lowest. Part III suggests the possibility of reshaping Zambian law-making institutions to produce legislation more likely to transform the inherited socio-economic institutions which, despite Zambia's rich human, agricultural and mineral resources, perpetuated and aggravated these harsh realities.

In Chapter 6, Lucian Ng'andwe proposes a bill to establish a Zambian Commission on Law and Integrated National Development which he, together with a group of colleagues, drafted.[3] If enacted, the law would establish a Commission to conduct research as a basis for designing and submitting transformatory bills to the legislature. Grounded in facts and logic, these bills would incorporate detailed provisions to alter Zambia's inherited socio-economic institutions which, to maximize profits for a handful of international mining companies, line-of-rail-settlers, and associated interests, continued to distort key sectors of the Zambian economy. The Commission would submit draft bills to the legislature accompanied by research reports to demonstrate the likelihood that their provisions would reshape the inherited institutions -- or create new ones -- to ensure that, in every sector, Zambia's resources would contribute to building an integrated national economy to meet all Zambians' needs.

Ng'andwe drafted the bill to establish the Commission primarily to encourage on-going discussion of the possibilities (and limits) of using law to transform the institutions that shape the role of major economic sectors in the development process of a country like Zambia. In the summer of 2004, Ng'andwe 'work-shopped' the bill and the accompanying research report in Zambia,[4] discussing it with government, parliamentary, university and NGO personnel. Using legislative theory's problem-solving method as a guide, his chapter comprises his report written to justify the proposed bill's detailed provisions. Essentially, the chapter demonstrates that the proposed Commission could conduct the necessary research, and organize it logically, to produce effectively implemented legislation to transform the institutions that have thwarted Zambian efforts to fulfil all Zambians' basic needs.

Ng'andwe's chapter's introductory section briefly reviews the inherited institutional context which contributed to the difficulties Zambian law-makers seemed to experience in their effort to formulate and implement legislation to restructure the Zambian economy. He points out that the first two post-colonial governments adopted seemingly diametrically-opposed development strategies: First, under President Kaunda, 'socialist humanism;' and then, under President Chiluba, that recommended by the 'Washington Concensus'. Neither worked.

In the chapter's second section, Ng'andwe describes the surface appearance of the specific problem the proposed bill targets: Essentially, the first 40 years of politically independent government did ***not*** lead to the exercise of state power through law to transform the dysfunctional institutions that, in every sector of the economy, still distorted resource use. Since law can induce institutional transformation only by altering the relevant problematic behaviors, Ng'andwe here analyzes *whose and what behaviors* – essentially, by definition, the 'institutions' – contributed to that problem:

(i) the post-independence *law-makers, including drafters and legislators,* who did not use their newly-acquired state power to formulate or enact legislation effectively to alter the main dysfunctional institutions; and

(ii) the government agencies' officials who, in implementing the new laws, operated within colonially-shaped institutional limits which hindered development of a more balanced, integrated national economy capable of providing increasingly productive employment opportunities and improving all Zambians' quality of life. For the most part, these comprised civil servants - especially in the ministries of finance, planning, industry and commerce – who did little or nothing to alter the way, in the sectors for which they held responsibility, inherited institutions fostered the distorted use of national physical, human and financial resources.

In the chapter's third section, Ng'andwe provides the available relevant evidence as to the causes of Zambian law-makers' and government officials' repeated failures to design laws competent to transform Zambia's inherited sectoral institutions. His analysis offers a sound basis in facts, logically organized, for designing the proposed law's detailed provisions to establish a Commission on Law and Integrated National Development.

In the fourth solutions section, Ng'andwe demonstrates that the detailed provisions of the proposed bill (see the appendix to Ch. 6) logically seem likely to ensure that the Commission will avoid the causes of Zambia's existing law-making and implementing institutions' officials' dysfunctional behaviors. Those should enable the Commission to create the conditions necessary to ensure that it employs and trains drafting teams which will more effectively design, enact and implement the necessary transformatory legislation for each major sector of the Zambian economy: mining, trade, finance, industry and agriculture, as well as the social and economic infrastructure. For each sector, Commission officials must introduce a transparent, accountable, and participatory research process for gathering the relevant information and designing appropriate legislation.

That process must empower those affected – especially the poor and vulnerable – to draw on their own experiences to provide the ideas and information necessary to understand the nature and causes of existing problematic institutional behaviors. That knowledge should enable the law-makers to design measures to restructure the relevant behaviors -- the institutions -- in each sector to foster effective self-sustainable development to serve all Zambians' needs.

Above all, as Ng'andwe's chapter emphasizes, the proposed law's detailed provisions specify criteria and procedures by which the Commission will decide on the detailed provisions of bills likely to transform the dysfunctional institutions in each sector of the Zambian socio-econmic structure.

To ensure that the Commission members ground their sectoral legislation on logically-organized facts, Ng'andwe's proposed law will require them to justify their prescriptions by an accompanying research report structured by legislative theory's problem-solving methodology. His chapter – itself essentially a research report -- underscores that the required report constitutes an essential quality control, especially for bills designed to transform basic societal institutions. In particular, that kind of report should provide logic and facts required for good governance by demonstrating that:

- the drafters of each bill really have considered all the relevant facts as well as the logic that underpins its details;
- the legislators can easily access those facts, as well as the drafters' logic, in order to determine whether the bill really will, in Zambia's unique circumstances, contribute to increasingly productive employment and improve all Zambians' quality of life;
- the general public, particularly those whom the bill's detailed provisions will likely affect, can determine if the reasons and experience behind the bill's details really will benefit all Zambians. If they have additional relevant evidence, they can submit it for the drafters and elected representatives' consideration.

Finally, as required by problem-solving's fourth step, the solutions section of Ng'andwe's chapter (his research report) explains that the proposed law's detailed provisions incorporate a feedback mechanism to ensure that, after the law's enactment, appropriate institutions exist to monitor and evaluate its implementation and social impact. This mechanism should provide feedback from those affected, not only to the Commission, but also to the elected members of Parliament who must decide whether and how to revise the law. Feedback proves an essential feature of the on-going process required to make and remake laws to foster effective economic transformation.

Skeptics of efforts to develop transformatory law as Ng'andwe proposes frequently object that the necessary evidence simply does not exist for each socio-economic sector of an economy like Zambia's. Christopher Annear's Chapter

7 reviews the abundant detailed and concrete evidence available that exposes how, over many decades, the colonialists' rapid expansion of the Zambian 'Copperbelt' fostered institutions that undermined and distorted the growth of the valuable and potentially sustainable fishing-industry in the neighboring province of Luapula.

In great detail, using evidence he obtained during his doctoral field research, Annear provides the facts to describe the nature and scope of the problematic behaviors – the institutions – imposed under colonial rule and perpetuated after independence. On the one hand, to provide foodstuffs for the copper mines' growing labor forces, the colonial governments – the British in Zambia and the Belgians in the Congo -- permitted major fishing companies to over-exploit the salmon and other fish in Lake Tanganyika. Although the post-independence Zambian government made some attempts to regulate this crucial industry, Annear argues that, for the most part, they merely altered the language of the laws without conducting the kind of research necessary to design legislative provisions likely to change the increasingly problematic behaviors. He suggests that law meant to regulate the economic and ecological well-being of the Mweru-Luapula fishery has perennially been penned at moments of crisis, and continues to be ill-suited to the long-term task of management—be it development or conservation. Unfortunately, Zambia's new governors made little effort to protect and foster the provincial fishing resources' optimal future development.

The fall of the world copper prices in the 1970s and 80s, especially after Zambian mines' re-privatization, led to mass unemployment in the entire region. Many former mine workers and their families returned to Luapula in search of an alternative livelihood. Desperate for new sources of income, they (illegally) used small-mesh mosquito nets to multiply their catch in the lake's shallows where the fish spawned – a strategy that threatened the potential for expanding future fish stocks.

Annear argues that, despite the declining fish catches, the Luapula fishing industry potentially remains a major provincial economic sector. As his evidence demonstrates, however, as long as the industry remains poorly regulated, as long as poor Zambians have no alternative other than fishing to survive, the industry will likely become increasingly unsustainable. Annear analyzes a bill, the Draft Fisheries Act of 2001. Based on extensive inputs from stakeholders, that bill – still subject to further debate -- purports to take into account Zambia's behavioral fishing patterns. Annear suggests that effective legislation to control and develop the fishing industry will need to incorporate detailed criteria and procedures for helping the fishers and traders to reconcile their potentially contradictory interests, and engage them in working together to protect and develop the fisheries.

In addition, it seems likely that Ng'andwe's proposed Commission on Law and Integrated National Development would need to conduct further research as the basis for further legislation to alter the producing and trading institutions' role in hindering the development of Luapula's other human and material resources.

Annear's chapter illustrates the availability of kinds of information that Ng'andwe's Commission would have to gather in every Zambian province. Detailed evidence as to each province's existing institutions' impact on its available human and material resources, organized logically according to problem-solving's four steps, could build a sound foundation for the design of legislative prescriptions for behaviors likely to ensure those resources' more productive employment. Over time, that legislation could facilitate provincial populations' efforts to create institutions likely to create a more balanced, integrated national economy. For example:

- The Agricultural Ministry might establish a rice-producing department to assist Zambian farmers in the vast Western Province to produce, mill, and market irrigated paddy rice,[5] not only contributing to needed food for all Zambians, but also earning incomes so they could purchase the fish and other consumer necessities Zambians elsewhere produced;
- A small farmers' government-operated Agricultural Extension Agency might assist unemployed Zambians, and those now employed for low wages on the line-of-rail estates owned by settler farmers,[6] to develop farming pursuits in other provinces by helping them acquire the necessary farm inputs plus knowledge of how to use them, as well as credit, transport and marketing facilities;
- A government cooperative and small enterprise support agency could provide training, access to technologies, materials, markets, and credit for potential micro-enterprise entrepreneurs, who, as individuals or in cooperatives, produce consumer necessities: farm equipment, bicycle repairs, clothing, tools of all kinds for household, farm, and small business, etc.;
- Government departments responsible for developing social and economic infrastructure could employ people to build or improve roads, schools, hospitals, providing them with incomes to buy consumer necessities

In short, Part III offers an example of one way to improve drafting capacity and strengthen law-making institutions effectively to foster good governance and people-oriented development: The establishment of a Zambian Commission on Law and Integrated National Development. Working together with university and research institute personnel, as well as engaging affected members of civil society, that kind of Commission could design detailed sectoral bills to transform the inherited sectoral institutions. These could then contribute to providing jobs and produce consumer goods for an expanding internal market. Over time, as Zambians learn how to draft more effectively implementable transformatory laws, they might begin to cooperate with other nations in the region to use law to strengthen regional institutions' contribution to using regional resources to increase productive employment opportunities to improve the quality of life of all the region's inhabitants.

* * *

This book's fourth Part, consisting of the eighth chapter, summarizes the editors' conclusions as to the implications of the evidence presented in the preceding three parts. Essentially, that evidence documents the way inherited government institutions – the repetitive patterns of government officials' behaviors – have perpetuated the deep-rooted social problems that plague many, if not most, African states. Unequipped effectively to exercise state power through law, too many of Africa's new governors have given up the effort to use law constructively to transform inherited dysfunctional institutions. Some have turned cynical, using their new law-making status, not to advance the public interest, but to enhance their own positions of influence and power.

That background, as well as the evidence relating to the Zambian experience, suggests the potential advantages of Lucian Ng'andwe's proposed Zambian Commission on Law and Integrated National Development. Essentially, he argues that the Commission could play an important role in filling a gap in the law-making process: Too often, law-makers rely on ill-equipped drafters to formulate laws to transform their nations' inherited institutions. Too often, those drafters lack a theory to guide them in designing new laws' detailed provisions based on the relevant facts about how to ensure their effective implementation in their own countries' unique circumstances. Instead, most simply copy laws from elsewhere regardless of their failure to conform to the requirements of their own country's circumstances; or adopt the pluralist notion that political bargains lead to the best possible legislation – a solution that inevitably serves the needs of the most powerful social groups; or criminalize behaviors that violate their laws' prescriptions.

This book offers evidence that suggests, instead, that law-makers and civil society advocates of democratic social change, good governance and development, can work together to use law to reduce their countries' external dependence, unemployment, and poverty. For that purpose, they need to learn institutionalist legislative theory, and methodology, as well as drafting techniques to draft and assess legislation that, grounded on logically organized evidence, will likely prove effectively implemented. Only that path seems likely to lead to the more effective exercise of state power through law to facilitate civil society's participation in newly-structured institutions to improve the use of available human as well as physical and financial resources to achieve democratic social change and development.

Notes

1. As a clarion call for liberation, Ghana's first post-independence President, Kwame Nkrumah, had declared, "Seek ye first the political Kingdom, and all else shall

follow." More than fifty years of African experience underscores that to realize this promise requires learning how to exercise state power through law.

2. The Seidmans taught and conducted research in the University of Zambia in the early 1970s, when independent Zambia's prosperity seemed at its height. Even then, in comparison with Tanzania where they had worked in the late 1960s, their trips through the countryside exposed the persistence of gross inequalities between life on the 'Copperbelt' and most rural Zambians' struggle for subsistence at or below poverty levels.
3. Ng'andwe worked in collaboration with a group of colleagues, several of whom had accompanied former President Kenneth Kaunda, who, in 2003-4, served as the first African president in Boston University's newly-established African Presidential Archives and Research Center (APARC). They included: Mr. Godwin Mfulu, a former senior civil servant in President Kaunda's government.
4. The Boston University APARC generously financed his trip, and, on his return to Boston, sponsored a symposium to facilitate further discussion with interested Africanist scholars – including some of the authors of the chapters in this volume – of the implications of his findings for the formulation and implementation of transformative law.
5. Thirty years ago, a Chinese rice expert estimated that, properly developed, the Western Province could provide enough rice, not only for all Zambians, but for export to meet the needs of all Africans. Interview with the Seidmans in Lusaka, 1974.
6. Today, white Zimbabweans are migrating to take over Zambian line of rail estates to grow tobacco for export. *See* Rachel L. Swarns, *For Zimbabwe's White Farmers, Time to Move On*, N.Y. TIMES, Aug. 4, 2002.

Chapter 2

Law, Social Change, Development: The Fatal Race – Causes and Solutions[1]

by Ann Seidman and Robert B. Seidman

The lawyer of yesterday was as a craftsman perfectly justified in treating his subject as a self-contained universe of discourse, since change in the constitution of human societies and consequently the change in Law ... were almost imperceptible. Under such conditions law codified or statutory, law customary and given in the precedent, could be treated on the principle of status quo. The whole work of courts, judges, and counsel ...moved within a well established reality which changed but little, and the foundations of which could be taken for granted. The lawyers of the older generation could...carry on their trade, accepting traditional data as something which need not be constantly revised.

When, however, the whole foundations of a craft or a practice, which is or ought to be an applied science, move and change in a well-nigh revolutionary manner, the relation between the craft and its doctrine, and the relation between that doctrine and the underlying reality, become a problem and an imperative problem at that....

In our modern world law also changes in consequence of new legal doctrines and theories, which in turn have to follow the new realities of culture. The industrial revolution with its needs of factory laws, trade union charters, the organization of trusts and the need of limiting these, has contributed towards our theoretical as well as practical insight into the nature of law....Law is but a part of social and cultural engineering. Today the questions about the limits of legislative action, about its relation to political force and economic efficiency, about its ability to create new types of man and new types of culture, are as practically cogent as they are theoretically illuminating...."

The question...whether law is omnipotent is as important to the modern jurist as it is interesting to the sociologist. There are limits to the lawmaker. These result from the relation between law and the existing order in society. To study this relation is, in my opinion, not only the central problem of the sociology of law, but also of the lawyer's own jurisprudence.

—Bronislaw Malinowski[2]

> *[L]aws are often ineffective, doomed to stultification almost at birth, doomed by the over-ambitions of the legislator and the under-provision of the necessary requirements of an effective law, such as adequate preliminary survey, communication, acceptance, and enforcement machinery.*
>
> — Anthony Allott[3]

INSTITUTIONS, SOCIAL CHANGE, AND THE LAW

Usually, as its underlying source, accounts of developing and transitional countries' poverty focus on inappropriate or dysfunctional resource allocations. In this chapter, we underscore the possibility that a polity can utilize the law to alleviate those kinds of social problems. In this first section we explain how law may thus facilitate social change: First, development—social change—*requires institutional change;* second, law constitutes government's indispensable tool for *transforming the institutions* that perpetuate the social problems which development processes must resolve; and, third, how, despite voices to the contrary, governments *can* use law to change those dysfunctional institutions.

Development implies social change, which in turn implies institutional change

Development comprises an on-going process of social change. Of necessity, that process requires *institutional* change appropriate to the changing circumstances that accompany it. By 'institution' we mean no more—and no less—than a repetitive pattern of social behaviors.[4] To describe a university as an institution one would describe, not its buildings, but what the various sets of actors within the university regularly do: From day to day, what the faculty does, what the groundskeepers do, what the staff does, what the students do, what the administration does. In developing countries, 'institutions' comprise a wide range of repetitive behavior patterns, for example:

- *Rural dwellers* who 'behave' as farmers, often only using hoes, to plant and reap crops for their daily subsistance, selling whatever surplus they can to buy a limited range of consumer goods.
- *Mine company managers and workers* who 'behave' by using modern mining equipment to dig out ores or pump oil for export.
- *Bank officials* who 'behave' by making loans, not to small African entrepreneurs, but to finance big transnational corporations, providing depositories for their profitable returns, and helping them to ship the major share to their home offices.
- *Trading company employees* who 'behave' by managing the import of consumer necessities and luxuries for sale in retail stores.

- *Government officials* who, in traditional bureaucratic fashion, frequently decide arbitrarily, behind closed doors, whether and how to implement proclaimed government policies.

The kind of institutions that exist in a country define its unique characteristics. To describe the difference between, say, Norway and Nigeria, one would describe their institutions: Their schools, banks, courts, hospitals, systems of real property, farms, factories—and a myriad more.

Although economists typically explain a country's relative poverty by describing its resource allocation, that explanation ignores the reality that resources do not—or cannot—'allocate' themselves: People, acting in institutions determine the use of a country's available human, physical, and financial resources. Disease does not of its own volition devastate a population. The same disease that in Norway would pass all but unnoticed may devastate Nigeria. The devastation that disease causes results not from the disease *simpliciter*, but because of what people in public health institutions do or do not do. How people behave in a country's governing institutions determine the quality of governance: Money does not jump from the giver to an official who takes bribes.

In short: If institutions describe a polity, and institutions consist of repetitive patterns of behavior, then its inhabitants' regular patterns of behavior describe the polity. That constitutes the most general and common statement of what makes an organized society: Its members' regular patterns of behavior. The overarching problems of the world's poorest peoples—living in former colonies and transitional countries—consist of poverty, vulnerability to disease, internal strife, natural disaster, and poor governance. They suffer these social problems because of persistent dysfunctional repetitive patterns of behaviors that constitute their institutions. ***Institutionalist legislative theory focuses on 'development' as the set of processes within which the state, using the law, deliberately transforms the country's institutions—existing repetitive patterns of behavior—in ways likely to help resolve those social problems.***

How can government use law to bring about the social change that comprises 'development'?

How government may deliberately induce social change through the instrumentality of the law

To bring about social change, government has no other instrument than the law, broadly conceived. When President Nkrumah declared, "Seek ye first the political power, and all else shall follow," he plainly believed that Africa's newly independent governments could wield state power to accomplish development. But to do that, the new governors had to transform their countries' institutions—and—as half a century of experience reveals—they had no other tool than the law.

To transform an institution that perpetuates a social problem, a government can only use law, for two reasons. First, in every government in today's increasingly complex societies, a very few elected and appointed officials, supposedly acting on behalf of all its citizens, must direct the behaviors of a host of state employees who, in turn, must influence the behaviors of an even larger numbers of citizens. To do that, a government must promulgate and effectively implement rules that, at every level, prescribe and contribute to shaping the relevant social actors' behaviors in desirable ways. Every rule promulgated and implemented by government, no matter at what level, comprises a 'law'. To ensure implementation of desired behaviors (institutions), a government has no choice but to use law and the legal order.

Secondly, governments (with or without a constitution) generally recognize the *ultra vires* rule as a key element of the rule of law: A government official has no power except what the law permits. Unless a government embodies a command in the form of a law, the *ultra vires* rule forbids an official of that government to obey it. Not only the necessities of governance, but the *rule of law* requires a government to prescribe its citizens' and officials' behaviors in the form of law.

Can government use the law deliberately to change behaviors?

After attaining independence, most new governments in Africa and elsewhere enacted laws a-plenty. With rare exceptions, however, those laws failed to transform the old institutions in beneficent ways. Almost everywhere, despite governors' promises, poverty, vulnerability, execrable governance—the trio of overarching social problems that plague most poor countries' inhabitants—persisted and even worsened. Too often, the populists—and the people—lost the 'fatal race.'

A clutch of scholars insist that reliance on law as a potential engine for social change inevitably produced that tragic result. Human behavior, some say, has so many interrelated complex explanations that one cannot isolate the law as a causative factor.[5] Unable to predict a law's probable behavioral consequences, a government cannot use it purposefully. Other critics maintain that as a text, a law's words always stand subject to the reader's deconstruction and reinterpretation in terms of that reader's own value-set; it may not induce a desired behavior because the social actor targeted does not understand the words as the drafter intended.[6] Still others claim that law constitutes an artifact of society; how can it change the fabric of the society that gave it birth?[7] Finally, some critics object that law in itself has no importance; only the political decisions behind the law count.[8]

These nay-sayers err. To refute the proposition that law can never change behavior requires only a single case in which law constitutes a clear 'but for' cause of changed behavior. Would anyone pay a tax, but for the law? Would anyone vote, but for the law? Plainly, although too often it does not do so, law can, and sometimes does, induce changed behavior. So why did populist governments the world around so often fail to use law to transform the institutions that perpetuated their countries endemic poverty, vulnerability, and poor governance?

WHY THE LOSS OF THE FATAL RACE? THE ROLE OF LEGISLATIVE DRAFTERS

Many actors' behaviors contributed to the loss of the fatal race. Here we focus on the drafters, as essential, but much-neglected, players in the law-making process. This Part first describes the drafter's role in the law-making process; second, it explains the importance of a bill's *design* in determining whether a bill will induce desired change; and finally it describes how, absent a legislative theory, drafters usually design a bill's detailed provisions.

The drafter's role in the law-making process

The law-making process conveniently divides into three segments. The first, *prioritization,* determines what social problems government prioritizes for drafting and enactment. The second, *bill-creating,* includes all the steps by which an idea about legislation proceeds from idea to a bill and its introduction in the legislature. The third, *law-enacting,* encompasses all proceedings after the bill's introduction into the legislature. Here, we focus on bill-creating, in which drafters play a central role.

For the legislature to enact a law requires successful completion of all three segments of the law-making process. Government must prioritize a legislative solution for the social problem at issue, and instruct the relevant line ministry to develop the necessary 'policy'.[9] The line ministry must then begin the bill-creating process that ends with a finished bill. Typically, a centralized drafting office drafter (sometimes in the Ministry of Justice, sometimes attached to the President's office) gives the bill a final cut before presenting it to Cabinet. Cabinet must approve and the legislature enact (and in many countries, the President must also approve) the bill.

In all this, as illustrated by the following anecdote from China,[10] the drafter's role seems critical. The consultant for a bill on that nation's diminishing supply and increasing pollution of underground water reported that the Ministry of Hydrology officials knew the location and chemical composition of every cubic meter of underground water in the country. The drafters in the central drafting office knew how to draft a bill in proper form. Yet, alone, neither had the skills required to design a law likely to change the behaviors—the institutions—that threatened water supply. Guided by institutionalist legislative theory, and working together with the ministry personnel, however, the drafters did design a bill to begin the on-going process of reducing underground water pollution.

Everywhere, people claim, 'we have good laws, but they are badly implemented.' That seems an oxymoron—a contradiction in terms: Unhindered by the law's 'good' wording, existing institutions perpetuate the unwanted social problem. Unless the drafter designs a bill susceptible of effective implementation—that is, one likely effectively to induce appropriate behaviors—the legislature cannot enact a law likely to ameliorate the social problem addressed. Over time—unable to keep their promises—populist governors too often lose , not only their legitimacy, but also the fatal race.

In the China case, drawing on the ministry's knowledge of the difficulties hindering the existing implementing agency from preventing pollution, the drafters designed a bill that prescribed detailed behaviors to help that agency's officials effectively change the polluters' polluting behaviors.

Given drafters' crucial importance, we focus here only on their role in the process by which a government bill typically proceeds from someone's bright idea[11] into a full-dress bill ready for Cabinet scrutiny and ultimately for submission to Parliament.

In the vast majority of developing countries, almost all bills originate not (as they do in the United States) in the legislature, but (as they did in the former colonies of Africa) in government. Mozambique's bill-creating processes, described in this book in Theodosio Uate's chapter, typifies the process.[12] In Mozambique, the majority party in the legislature forms the Government (i.e., the Cabinet). As an important part of its task, Government designates the bills for enactment into law by the legislature in its legislative program.

Whatever the source of an idea for a bill, some official in a line ministry does some preliminary work, and prepares a memorandum generally outlining the bill. That memorandum (in the British tradition, called a 'layman's draft,' sometimes accompanied by a draft bill prepared by the relevant ministry's lawyer) then goes to the central drafting office (frequently a department of the Ministry of Justice). After discussions of varying degrees of detail with the instructing ministry officials, that office's drafters produce the draft bill's final form.

The central drafting office drafters—almost always lawyers—typically view their own role as quite limited: To translate Government 'policy' into the language of the law, and to fit the new law seamlessly into the country's corpus of the law. As a kind of mantra, they assert, 'We have no role in 'policy;' we only decide on a bill's form.'[13] That assertion, however, ignores the critical importance of the design of a bill's *details* in the process of bill-creation and indeed in the whole law-making process.

A bill's *details*' critical importance

A bill's 'design' determines the substance of its detailed provisions. Typically, the political authorities who decide on a drafting proposal inform the drafters of the bill's purpose in terms, not of the social problem, but the title of bills they want them to draft: In Afghanistan, for example, "A bill to prevent forced marriages;"[14] in Vietnam, "A bill to reduce road traffic accidents;"[15] in Mozambique, "A bill to help individuals disabled by land-mine explosions."[16] The policy-makers may provide a few details, but they usually leave the task of formulating the details to the drafters.

As a leading legislative drafting textbook explains,

> Legislative policy is not the same thing as the legislative plan [what in this book we denote as 'design'—editors]. . . . For example it may be laid down as a policy that certain grants are to be paid to a class of persons under specified conditions. In order to give effect to such

> a policy the draftsman needs to know that his statute must, among other things, specify the amount of the grant and the conditions under which it may be paid, and provide authority for the payment out of the Consolidated Revenue Fund, for suspension for breach of conditions and for recovery of unauthorized payments, for application, decisions and awards, for penalties for misrepresentation or other wrongful conduct. In the case of an amending statute, the draftsman must decide what statutes are to be amended, what sections, and in what manner.[17]

In reality, those 'details'—not the instructions that originate from the ministry --inevitably define the policy's specific features. As an analogy, suppose a family determines on a family policy: To build a new house. Asked to define the word 'house,' the family can only give a general answer. At that point, the family's 'policy' amounts only to a prioritization of a problem, their discontent with their present housing. The family then talks with an architect about their budget; the number of rooms needed, and their functions (bedrooms? playroom? living-room?); the style of architecture; a site for the house—a long list of substantive 'details'. The architect produces a blueprint and specifications. Now if one asks the family to define the word 'house,' the family points to the plans and specifications. Who formulated the policy? the family (the nominal 'policy-maker)? the architect (who in theory 'merely' translated the family's policy into concrete reality? or both?

By analogy, drafters play the role of the architect to their ministerial clients. In designing a bill by formulating its detailed substantive provisions, the drafters may make key decisions in determining the bill's details—the essential content of its 'policy'. Indeed, the final bill may seem far removed from the original specification of the 'policy'. In the Mozambique bill mentioned above,[18] for example, the drafters finally produced a bill for a state-subsidized factory to manufacture wheel chairs—seemingly a long distance from the original instruction.

In many newly independent countries, the drafters too often designed bills that proved ineffectively implemented, and failed to help resolve the social problems targeted. The following section offers an explanation.

WHY SO OFTEN LAWS SEEM TO FAIL TO FACILITATE DEVELOPMENT?

In this section we describe what most drafters actually did in designing laws, and suggest explanations for those behaviors.[19]

Drafters' behaviors: Their methodologies for designing a bill

In practice, by telling the drafters little more than the goal of the bill they should draft, policy makers really specified what John Dewey calls a 'generalized end.'[20] That left the drafters broad discretion in designing the detailed provisions needed to resolve the underlying social problem. Everywhere, the drafters tended to do what their country's drafting institutions made easy. Most often, both in developed and developing countries, they either adopted one of several 'entropic'[21] practices, or resorted to trial-and-error . We briefly review each of these approaches.

'Entropic' practices: 'Entropic' practices tend to fall into four categories:

- Following an interest-group contestation theory, drafters frequently tried to incorporate into their bills provisions based on a (generally implicit or hypothetical) variant of what pluralists characterize as an interest-group bargaining process. In the bargaining process, however, those with power and wealth too often predominate. In Uate's Mozambique case, for example (see Ch. 4 below), the senior ministry officials apparently sought to retain their power—and the drafters accommodated their claim.[22] As Schattschneider observed, "the flaw in the pluralist heaven is that the heavenly chorus sings with a strong upper-class accent."[23]
- Not infrequently, drafters merely sought to criminalize unwanted behaviors. To deter widespread corruption, for example, many countries' drafters frequently proposed bills that imposed increasingly severe criminal sanctions. That implied that, as self-interest comprised the only significant explanation for corrupt behaviors, a law could best counter it by severe punishment. Corruption, however, results as much from weak institutions as weak people.[24] (Detection of a crime ordinarily requires a victim willing to report the crime to the authorities—but who has a motive to report an instance of government corruption?) Experience demonstrates that legislation that institutionalizes enhanced transparency and accountability will likely prove more effective than criminalization in reducing corruption.[25]
- Other drafters, sometimes seemingly blindly, simply copied foreign law—ignoring their own country's very different circumstances. Bhutan, for example, copied the U.S. Uniform Commercial Code, including sections dealing with transactions involving railroad carloads of goods, but mountainous Bhutan had no railroad within its boundaries. Sometimes, drafters copied another country's law without realizing that the originating country's drafters had introduced significant changes. The US State of Colorado, for example, published for public comment proposed new regulations to protect mining environments against pollution. After they received public comments, the Colorado drafters amended almost every section of the original draft. Meanwhile, however, Russian drafters simply copied the original draft, unchanged. The list of these 'hasty transplants' seems endless.[26]
- Some drafters drafted bills that prescribed behaviors in terms so general as to negate any real possibility of effective implementation. Indonesia's law devolving power to the Regencies (or Provinces), for example, simply listed the regency governments' new duties, providing little or no details as to either the agencies that should undertake the required new tasks, or the training those agencies' personnel required to implement them. No wonder that it took years to start up regency government!

To design a bill's *details*, which crucially determine its effectiveness, a drafter must examine the country's specific constraints and resources—including the law's provisions—which influence how a law's addressees decide how to behave. Yet none of the entropic methodologies advised the drafter to study the unique country environment in which the proposed law would function. Small wonder that bills drafted by using any these 'entropic' methodologies rarely either induced the behaviors prescribed by the new law, or significantly helped to resolve the targeted social problem.

Trial-and-error approaches to drafting

Less often, drafters adopted a pragmatic trial-and-error methodology. Rather than facilitating institutional transformation, the authors of this approach argued that, given the uncertainties inherent in developing or transitional country contexts, it seemed safer to use law to make only incremental changes. Some texts explicitly recommended a kind of trial-and-error methodology.[27] Others seemed to endorse an ends-means approach.[28] In either case, if the initial laws failed to resolve the social problems targeted, they simply advised law-makers to try again by enacting new laws. In the event, these methodologies proposed using law, not to fundamentally transform dysfunctional institutional behaviors, but only to make incremental changes. Without any viable alternative in conditions of uncertainty, this approach at least seemed to urge the necessity, after the law's enactment, of monitoring and evaluating its social impact. It did not, however, contribute much to the essential institutional change required for effective people-oriented development.

Why drafters relied on these methods?

Drafters seemed to follow 'entropic' practices, or to adopt a trial-and-error methodology, for some or all of three sets of reasons—institutional, ideological, and their own lack of capacity to do otherwise.

In the first place, drafting institutions rarely provided detailed guidance to a drafter engaged in designing a bill. Many governments introduced rules to detail the path that a bill must track from ministry to central drafting office to Cabinet to Parliament, frequently specifying required intervening steps. Drafting offices' internal regulations typically specified the bills' formal technical features: The width of margins, the size of type, the content of a long title, the use of marginal headings (or catch lines) for sections of a bill. A few departmental handbooks prescribed substantive standards, for example, that drafters should avoid drafting clauses that might impair vested rights in property, or impose disproportionate criminal sanctions. In no jurisdiction that we have studied did the law-making institutions introduce rules that required drafters to use a specific methodology for deciding a bill's detailed provisions; typically, they left drafters to use their own discretion.

Several ideological elements influenced drafters to adopt an 'entropic' or trial-and-error methodology. As noted earlier, drafting tradition told them to pay no attention to a bill's substance, but to deal solely with its form. Powerfully directing their attention away from their bills' likely social impact, that tradition seemed to justify adopting any of the entropic methodologies outlined above.

The still-popular nineteenth century jurisprudence, analytical positivism, furthermore, suggested that law should principally guide, not relevant actors' behaviors, but dispute-settlement. To guide judges in deciding cases, drafters need only write laws to declare the relevant actors' rights and duties.[29] That reinforced the presumed advantages of copying law: What counts as justice in one place must surely count as justice in another. In addition, if law's underlying objective centers on justice, by definition, it must rest on 'values.' Since, like taste, values remain non-commensurable, then interest-group bargaining seems as good a way as any to determine what provisions to incorporate in a bill. Finally, if law aims at dispute-settlement (rather than changing behaviors), stating the law in vague general terms permits a judge to decide a given case in terms of equities; in a particular case, a vague law may serve justice better than a tightly-crafted rule whose very clarity may give the judge no alternative but to decide unjustly.

Thirdly, most drafters' training focused on drafting techniques related to the bill's ***form,*** how to chain words together:[30] Draft in the present tense; draft in the active voice; draft in the positive; draft in the singular; beware 'squinting' modifiers—the list goes on. Drafters learned precious little about a theory or methodology likely to guide them in *conceptualizing and designing* a bill's substantive detailed provisions.

Working within drafting institutions' rules, influenced by prevalent ideologies, trained in the use of techniques, not the broader skills needed for designing a bill's substantive details: It seems little wonder that most drafters fell back on widely-used entropic methods. What else could they do?

The remainder of this chapter outlines an institutionalist legislative theory and methodology. Experience in several countries[31] suggests that these offer a more useful guide for drafters seeking to design the substantive details of transformative bills likely to prove effectively implemented to help overcome the institutional obstacles and achieve good governance and development.

AVOIDING THE FATAL RACE: USING THEORY AND METHODOLOGY TO GUIDE THE DRAFTER IN DESIGNING A BILL'S SUBSTANTIVE DETAILS

Time and resources for conducting research and designing a bill always come in short supply. Drafters require a theory and methodology to guide them in identifying fertile fields of relevant evidence, and organizing those facts as a logical basis for conceptualizing the detailed provisions required for an effectively implemented law. Otherwise, almost inevitably, they fall back on customary practice, on entropic or trial-and-error methods.

The first section sketches the way institutionalist legislative theory serves as a guide for designing and justifying an institution-transforming bill. The second section discusses that theory's methodology for deciding and justifying a bill's detailed provisions. To explicate that methodology, it outlines the structure of a report on the research required to justify a bill's details.

A theory for designing a law in aid of development: why do people behave as they do in the face of a rule of law?

Institutionalist legislative theory centers attention on the potential of using law as government's primary tool for resolving social problems. In particular, it focuses on the design of detailed rules to facilitate the transformation of the historically-shaped dysfunctional institutions which, in Africa and elsewhere, have tended to thwart good governance and effective development.

To help understand the nature and causes of the relevant social actors' problematic behaviors, institutionalist legislative theory draws on three interrelated jurisprudential and philosophical foundations: Legal realism, [32] sociology of law, [33] and problem-solving[34]. Legal realism contributes a recognition of a deep-seated reality: The law-in-action never appears the same as that prescribed by the law-in-the-books. Drafters must aim to reduce the gap between the law's reach and its grasp, between the words of the law and the behaviors that result, between the law-in-the-books and the law-in-action. To achieve that aim, a drafter must find an answer to the question, Why do people behave as they do in the face of a rule of law?

To answer that question, institutionalist legislative theory proposes a set of categories of data that a drafter should examine to ascertain the probable causes of behaviors in the face of existing law as a logical basis for assessing a new law's likely behavioral consequences. That answer rests on two principal pillars: The sociology of law, and the pragmatic school of philosophy's problem-solving methodology.

First, sociology of law contributes indispensable insights into the essential understanding of why people behave as they do in the face of a rule of law. Institutionalist legislative theory offers a simple diagram to facilitate analysis of the causes of particular sets of 'role occupants'[35] problematic behaviors in the face of a rule of law (*see* Fig. 2.1).

Figure 2-1 illustrates what Kelsen taught[36]: A law always targets two sets of role occupants: (1) the social actor in civil society (a 'primary role occupant'); and (2) the agency (sometimes called the 'secondary role occupant') whom the law directs to implement its provisions aimed at inducing the primary role occupant to conform to the behaviors the law prescribes. (A simple example illustrates this proposition: A law prohibits the operator of a motor vehicle from exceeding 65 m.p.h. on a freeway. Either the same law or another commands a policemen, who observes a car traveling on a freeway in excess of that speed, to arrest the operator. The same law or another commands a judge, if it appears before the judge that the operator violated the rule addressed to the primary role occupant, to impose a stated sanction.)

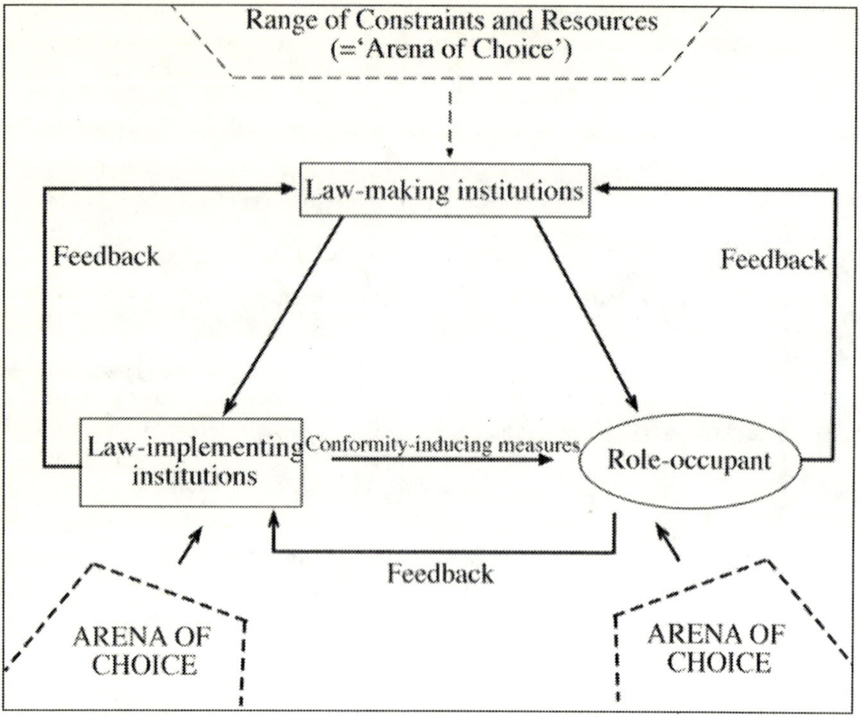

Figure 2.1 A Model of a Legel System

Sociology teaches that a person behaves by making *choices* within the arena of constraints and resources within which that person chooses. [37] As Fig. 1 shows, in making that choice in the face of a rule of law, a role occupant—the relevant actor—considers three categories of factors: (i) the rule itself; (ii) the expected behavior of the implementing agency, and (iii) the manifold objective and subjective *non-legal* factors that comprise the particular country- and location-specific circumstances.

This model shouts one message loud and clear. If a law's behavioral response depends in large part upon the specific conditions of the addressee's environment, then a law copied from some other jurisdiction will induce the same behaviors that it did in the law's original home *only if* its new environment contains constraints and resources similar to those in the law's original environment. That may happen—but rarely. Save in the broadest outline, no country resembles another. A country, therefore, cannot copy another's laws, and confidently expect it to induce similar behaviors in its new home as in the old.

As stated, the three categories enumerated above remain *too* all-inclusive—especially, the last one, the *non-legal factors* likely to influence behaviors. An all-inclusive category does not serve its function of directing the drafter to the *specific* sets of evidence required to design a law's detailed provisions. (Institutionalist legislative theory proposes a way to disaggregate these categories—see pp. 35-37 below.)

In addition to the the substantive theory suggested by Figure 2.1, institutionalist legislative theory includes a variant of the problem-solving methodology

Why a legislative theory must facilitate decision-making in terms of facts and logic

Preliminarily, this section explains why a legislative theory, despite its normative thrust, must rest solidly on a methodology that guides a drafter to design and to justify the bill in terms of facts and logic, of 'reason informed by experience'; that is, in terms of *publicly stated reasons that appear consistent with the available evidence.*

Here, the word 'fact' refers not to a raw 'fact', in itself, but a *proposition* about what is the case, derived from an observation of the relevant circumstances, usually presented in the form of data or a description. The validity of a 'fact,' so stated, reflects the extent to which it accurately measures or describes—that is, proves consistent with—the relevant available evidence. [38] Like any other hypothesis, a statement of fact always remains subject to further observation, more appropriate data, better description of the relevant details. Typically, lawyers' training enables them to understand and engage in the discourse of legal doctrine, law's prescriptions as to how people ought to behave. Social scientists, in contrast, devote a great deal of effort to improving techniques designed to ensure that propositions of fact as to the nature and causes of 'behaviors' in society prove consistent with reality.

To draft (or assess) a law in terms of whether it will likely to prove effectively implemented to change problematic behaviors, law-makers must learn to assess the validity of propositions concerning the available facts as to why people behave as they do in the face of a law.

An adequate theory of legislation must guide drafters in justifying a bill's detailed provisions in terms of facts and logic. To do that, the theory must serve three subsidiary functions which provide:

1. a series of steps that, if followed, tend to produce implementable laws with a high probability that, once implemented, will help overcome the targeted social problems;
2. an outline for a written report to inform legislators and stakeholders about the propositions and evidence which underpin the bill's details; and
3. a justification for the bill likely to persuade, not only to the bill's sponsor's political allies, but also a reasonable skeptic on the other side of the aisle.

Together, these three functions add up to a unified theory and methodology. First, take the requirement that the theory provide a way of justifying the bill 'across the aisle.' A justification might persuade a 'rational skeptic'[39] either by appealing to its *opponents,*' as well as its *proponents*' 'values'; or by resting on relatively incontrovertible propositions like those offered by the social and political sciences, mathematics, history and other fact-based disciplines.[40]

Yet, as a practical matter, no such thing as universal 'values' exist—at least not on a level of specificity sufficient to tease out of them universally-agreed legislative provisions. People learn 'values' in the course of growing-up and acculturation, usually not through explicit instruction, but by absorbing those in their environment, as it were, through their shoulder blades. In every country, people grow up in different environments. The environment in which a Ghanaian civil servant, the child of upper-level civil servants—living in an elite neighborhood in Accra, educated in Achimota School[41] and the University of Ghana, who then earned a graduate degree at Oxford with more graduate study at Harvard—fundamentaly differs from that of a farmer from Northern Ghana with at most a few years of school who migrated south to cultivate cocoa beans for export on the global market. The civil servants' and the sharecroppers' values inevitably must differ as much as the environments in which each grew up and works.

How, then, to justify a proposed law—invariably, a value-soaked proposition? Drafters have no alternative but to justify a bill in terms of facts, logically organized: "*Reason* is the keystone of deliberative discourse."[42] If a bill's proponent can ground a bill on facts and logic—on 'reason informed by experience,' or, in John Rawls's vocabulary,[43] 'public reason'—in principle that should persuade the bill's opponent.[44] Drafters cannot legitimate their bills by the drafter's status; their bills must stand or fall on their face, or on the justification the drafter provides. To persuade the 'rational skeptic', that justification must employ the discourse of 'public reason.' The drafter has no other choice.

To guide the formulation of an adequate justification, legislative theory must serve two additional functions: Provide an agenda of logically-organized steps which a drafter can follow to design an implementable bill likely to reduce the targeted social problem; and a checklist of the kinds of information a drafter should offer at each step to enable legislators and others to assess whether the bill's detailed provisions will likely 'work' to help resolve the problem targeted.

Long centuries of human experience teach that to design a law—as in designing a solution to any of the complex problems in today's world—facts and logic produce better results than throwing the bones, consulting a madwoman's bablings at the Oracle of Delphi, reading the entrails of a chicken, or following the *diktat* either of a sacred text, a Great Leader or a Great, Overarching Value. The rest of this chapter aims to demonstrate that institutionalist legislative theory's problem-solving methodology offers drafters an outline of the steps required to ensure that their bills' design rests on the relevant available facts, logically-organized. Those steps guide drafters in gathering the relevant information, needed both by legislators and by those the law will likely affect, to assess whether a proposed bill will likely prove effectively implemented, and resolve the problem it addresses in the *public* interest. In other words, the problem-solving methodology offers both law-makers and stakeholders a kind of *quality control* over a proposed bill's substance.

HOW THE PROBLEM-SOLVING METHODOLOGY GUIDES THE USE OF FACTS, LOGICALLY, TO JUSTIFY A BILL

A series of steps—that is, a *methodology*—for using facts and logic to conceptualize a bill's details simultaneously offers an outline for *justifying* that bill. Institutionalist legislative theory's problem-solving methodology proposes four steps for gathering and logically organizing the available relevant evidence to justify a new law to alter a set of problematic behaviors (a dysfunctional institution) that persists under existing law: (1) Describe the social problem, including the behaviors that comprise it, which the proposed law aims to resolve; (2) identify the causes of those problematic behaviors; (3) show that logically the bill's detailed provisions will likely overcome those causes and induce new, more appropriate behaviors; and (4) incorporate in the bill a monitoring and evaluation process by which, after the law's enactment, those affected—especially the poor and vulnerable—can provide additional evidence as to the new law's social impact, laying a basis if necessary for improving it.

An adequate description of the relevant evidence at each of these four steps should demonstrate the likelihood that the bill's detailed provisions logically will help to resolve a particular social problem. That constitutes the main argument for recommending that drafters accompany every important bill by a research report that tracks these four steps.[45] The report should contribute the facts, logically organized—the 'reason informed by experience'—necessary to persuade a 'rational skeptic' that the bill probably will contribute to transforming the institutions and help to resolve the problem it targets. The outline for a research report that follows adapts that four-step methodology to the task of justifying a bill.

A well-drafted research report[46] serves three functions. First, in preparing it, a drafter—or team of drafters—must think through how the available evidence, logically organized, contributes to demonstrating that the proposed bill's detailed provisions will likely prove effectively implemented and help to resolve the social problem the bill targets. Second, a well-prepared research report serves as an educational document, providing the evidence legislators need to understand the nature and causes of the social problem addressed, and assess whether the available evidence, logically organized, tends to prove the proposed law will in reality 'work' as its proponents claim.[47] Third, an adequate research report should provide the facts and logic the general public needs—particularly, those affected by the social problem addressed—to participate knowledgeably in debates concerning the bill, using their own experience as evidence for assessing its detailed provisions' probable advantages and disadvantages. In that sense, accompanying a transformatory bill by a well-drafted research report should foster the increased transparency and accountability essential for meaningful community participation in the law-making process.

JUSTIFYING A BILL IN TERMS OF FACTS AND LOGIC: AN OUTLINE

A *law* constitutes a normative document. Some 95% of a law's sentences consist of commands, prohibitions and permissions. As its principal task, a research report should justify those commands, prohibitions and permissions by demonstrating that each one will likely contribute to helping to solve the specified social problem. For this reason, in part, a research report appears somewhat different from most didactic writing. In the following section, therefore, the outline of the report appears in *italics*. Given the report's presumed educative role, the commentaries on specific parts of the outline (which appear in brackets in small type), explain the reasons for including those parts.

This section provides a *default outline* of a research report to justify a bill's detailed provisions. It comprises a default outline in this sense: Unless compelling reasons dictate otherwise, it provides a sufficient guide for organizing the available relevant evidence to demonstrate that the bill's detailed provisions will likely prove effectively implemented, and help to resolve the social problem the bill targets.

Part I: *Introduction*

'Grabber' paragraph: A striking anecdote or startling statistic may illustrate the importance of using law to tackle this particular social problem.

[This kind of paragraph may help to 'grab' the busy reader's attention.]

A. *A one-paragraph statement describing the social problem the proposed bill aims to target; and a brief summary of the bills' proposed solution.*

[By summarizing at the outset what social problem the bill targets, and how it aims to help resolve it, the report here provides information that enables the busy reader decide whether to read the full report.]

B. *A brief review of the country-specific circumstances in which the targeted social problem arises enables the reader to understand the reasons for enacting a well-conceived and effectively-implemented bill addressed to that social problem now as part of a more complete legislative program for dealing with that larger context.*

[A specific social problem always nestles within another, somewhat larger social problem. Here describe the larger social problem and, if the connection does not seem obvious, explain how the narrow social problem addressed relates to the larger problem identified.]

C. *A description of the logic of problem-solving's four steps and how they serve to structure the rest of the research report's remaining parts.*

[Following the problem solving methodology's four steps, this 'table-of-contents' paragraph should explicate the logic that under-girds the research report's main parts: (i) The narrow problem's surface appearance, and whose and what behaviors comprise it; (ii) an analysis of the causes of each of those behaviors; and (iii) the solution (the bill's provisions) designed to alter or eliminate those causes, inducing behaviors likely to help resolve the problem, and providing a mechanism for monitoring and evaluating the law's social impact after its enactment.

[To justify the claim that the bill rests on facts and logic, each of the report's three main parts must (a) incorporate adequate connectives—mini-introductions and mini-conclusions[48]—to remind the reader how that part logically fits into the report's overall argument; and (b) provide the relevant evidence to warrant its descriptions of the problematic behaviors (institutions), the explanations for their causes, and the assessment that the bill's benefits will likely outweigh its costs.]

Part II: *The social problem the bill targets*

A. *The nature and scope of the social problem's superficial manifestations.*

[Frequently, the social problem manifests itself as a problem in resource allocation, for example, as underground water pollution, unemployment, inadequate public transportation or insufficient rural clinics. This section of the research report should describe the nature and scope of the resource *mis-allocation*, and provide the relevant facts. Drafters will likely discover those facts in the relevant ministry files; university and independent research institutions' reports; studies on the Internet of other countries' experiences with efforts to implement similar laws; and concerned community organizations' findings.

[Depending on which aspects of the particular social problem seem important, the available facts might include quantitative data --statistics—as to the geographical regions, numbers of people, the particular social groups it affects, and other aspects that seem relevant for understanding the problem's significance.

[Some social problems, however—for example, corruption constitutes a serious one[49]—defy statistical analysis. In these cases, the drafter(s) should at least provide *qualitative* information, essentially, verbal descriptions of examples of the problematic behaviors: anecdotes, or stories reported in the press, in hearings, in focus group discussions, or observed by researchers in the field (see the *Drafters' Manual,* Ch. 6, on the possibilities of gathering quantitative as opposed to qualitative evidence; and the issues involved in assessing their utility)].

B. *Whose and what behaviors constitute the identified social problem?*

[Law can only 'work' by prescribing changes in the repetitive patterns of behavior (the institutions) that comprise a specific social problem, and ensuring those prescriptions' effective implementation. As noted above, many social problems appear in the first instance as resource allocation problems. In some cases, however, the problem appears in the first instance as a problem of behaviors—for example, unfair trade practices, domestic violence, motor vehicle traffic problems or dishonest banking or corporate practices. In those cases, the drafter may combine step II-A with this step, II-B.

[Legislative theory underscores the importance of describing ***two sets of relevant role occupants' problematic behaviors,*** and showing how they relate to each other:

(i) The ***primary role occupants*** whose behaviors the bill's detailed prescriptions aim to change; and

(ii) the ***officials of the agency***—governmental, semi-governmental, even a private one under contract to the government—designated by the existing law as ***responsible for implementing its conformity-inducing measures.***

[The world around, complaints about existing law focus on the designated institutions' ineffective implementation as a common cause of transformatory laws' failure. The more complex the social problem a bill targets, the more difficulties a drafter may have in describing the relevant, often complicated, institutional relationships of the implementing agency. Nevertheless, here, in section II-B, the drafter must describe the responsible implementing agency system and how it functions now, under existing law, to permit the primary role occupant to behave in ways that perpetuate the social problem. Only on that basis can the drafter design—and ultimately can legislators and the public assess—the likelihood that the bill's provisions will likely change those behaviors to ensure the law's effective implementation.

[In describing the role occupants and their behaviors the drafter should differentiate between the several sets of role occupants. For example, in discussing surface water pollution, rather than lumping the people who put pollutants in streams and lakes in one group, the drafter should separate them into different sets: Farmers, who permit the run-off of heavily fertilized fields to drain into nearby streams; industrial users, who dump wastes into those streams or flush them into underground waters; householders, who get rid of household wastes in the same places. The interacting causes of each of these sets of actors' behaviors inevitably differ. Since, in problem-solving, solutions must logically alter or eliminate those causes, the drafter must identify the different causes for each set, and decide whether, logically, to specify different detailed prescriptions to change each set of role occupants' problematic behaviors.

[Again, the files of investigators in ministries, and university and research institutions may already include valuable evidence about the relevant sets of social actors' problematic behaviors. Less commonly, some may have explored that evidence to identify those behaviors' causes. Even if they have not done so, engaging those investigators in gathering and presenting relevant evidence for the preparation of a research report to justify a proposed bill may stimulate them to look for additional information as a sounder foundation for translating policies into effectively implemented transformatory laws.]

[**C.** *The country's history of dealing with the social problem; and* D, *comparative law and experience.*

[Both the history of a country's past efforts to resolve a social problem, and comparative law and experience, may constitute treasure troves of human experience that drafters ignore at their peril. The former may provide insights into the problem's changing manifestations, and the causes of past efforts' failure to solve it. As to the latter, each country's unique realities make it impossible for drafters to copy another country's law and expect similar results in their own. Nevertheless, drafters may learn a lot from analyzing the originating country's ***experiences*** under that law; their new insights into aspects of a social problem, and the behaviors that comprise it, may enable them to formulate more fruitful descriptive hypotheses to guide the search for useful relevant evidence in their own country.

[Depending upon the drafters' conclusions as to the implications of the social problem's history in their own country, or other countries' experiences in using law to try to resolve it, they may find it useful to include one or both kinds of information at whichever places in the research report they deem appropriate.]

E. *Identify which social groups currently benefit and which suffer from the problem's social impact.*

[A significant part of the social cost-benefit analysis of the preferred solution—that is, the proposed bill's social impact—will focus on the new law's probable social consequences, compared with the current situation, for different groups in society. Identification of the existing law's impact on these groups will help to lay the necessary foundation for making that cost-benefit assessment.]

Part III. *Explanations of the behaviors that comprise the social problem addressed*

A. *Explanations for the first set of problematic behaviors identified in II-B: Role occupant 1, behavior #1:*

1. An agenda of possible explanations; an introductory note:

[In institutionalist legislative theory's problem-solving methodology, a research report's Explanations Part comprises a crucial step. It centers attention on the evidence necessary to show why each separate set of relevant role occupants behaves problematically; that is, it provides evidence to warrant the drafters' ***hypotheses as to the causes*** of that set of role occupants' problematic behaviors. Once drafters show that their statements (hypotheses) as to the causes of existing problematic behaviors prove consistent with the facts, they can with some confidence design the bill's provisions in a way that logically seems likely to 'work' by altering or eliminating those causes, and inducing new behaviors to help resolve the targeted social problem.

[a. Behavior results from many interacting causes; this gives rise to many possible interrelated explanations. Institutionalist legislative theory offers drafters a simple checklist of possible categories of explanations. (The acronym 'ROCCIPI' offers a mneumonic to help remember them.[50] These letters stand for **R**ule, **O**pportunity, **C**apacity, **C**ommunication, **I**nterest, **P**rocess, and **I**deology.) Following the ROCCIPI check list, a drafter should explore the implications of each category for suggestions as to possible explanations (that is, explanatory hypotheses, or 'educated guesses') for each set of role occupants' problematic behaviors, considered separately.

[b. To ensure that a new law probably will change a problematic behavior, drafters should, as far as possible, consider the available evidence to assess *all the possible, often interrelated, hypotheses,* suggested by the ROCCIPI categories, to explain why role occupants behave problematically in the face of the existing law. On that basis, they can design a bill's detailed prescriptions in ways logically likely to alter or eliminate those causes, and induce new behaviors to help resolve the targeted social problem.

2. *Possible hypotheses inspired by each ROCCIPI category:*

[***R*ule** refers to existing laws (defined broadly, see above, Box 1-1, p.4)—in reality, the 'cage' of laws—which purport to prescribe specified sets of role occupants' behaviors. No matter what social problem arises, always, somewhere, some existing rules bear on it. These rules'[51]prescriptions may appear either in a specific law (or regulation), or the laws and regulations that deal with related issues. To formulate hypotheses as to how the existing 'Rule' might influence a set of role occupants' behaviors, drafters must review all the relevant laws and regulations: How, specifically, do they require the role occupants to behave (or not to behave)? Do their words prescribe those behaviors clearly, precisely and non-ambiguously? Or do they permit the role occupants to exercise discretion in deciding what to do, leaving room for the non-legal 'OCCIPI' factors to influence their behaviors?]

[***O*pportunity** and ***C*apacity** comprise two closely-related *objective* non-legal categories: Does the specified set of role occupants have the Opportunity, either granted by the Rule, itself, or as a result of external non-legal country circumstances, to behave (or not to behave) as the Rule requires? Does that set of role occupants have the skills and resources to obey the Rule's requirement, or to respond to other non-legal factors like self-interest or ideology, regardless of the Rule's possible sanctions?

[***C*ommunication** generally refers to whether the appropriate authorities have informed the relevant role occupants of the Rule's requirements: Do they know and understand what they shall, may, or shall not do? (For government officials, this category of *objective* causal factors usually remains an 'empty box.' Bureaucratic authorities usually do inform their subordinates of their responsibilities under the law—although sometimes they neglect adequately to tell local government personnel, especially in remote areas, about new laws' substantive prescriptions. More important, even if the authorities do inform local officials, they may fail to ensure those officials acquire the **Capacity** (the necessary form of training) to implement the tasks prescribed by a new law.

[*I***nterest** constitutes a broad category of ***subjective*** causal factors. These may include everything the specified set of role occupants consider important to their own well-being, from financial incentives (salaries and rewards, or even benefits reaped from corrupt behaviors) to the public's well-being, or potentially-enhanced personal power (nepotism, improved job opportunities). Some academics—especially market-oriented economists—tend to attribute all role occupant behaviors to *I***nterest**, thereby neglecting important ***objective*** factors—like **Capacity**—that may constitute equally or more important causal influences.

[***P*****rocess** refers to the ***objective*** characteristics of the *processes* within which a set of role occupants must make decisions in complex organizations: non-government organizations, like trade unions, cooperatives or corporations; or—especially significantly for the law-making enterprise—the agencies a law assigns to implement its detailed provisions. Indeed, ***Process*** may prove the most important category of possible explanations for implementing agencies' problematic behaviors. Here, drafters should examine the criteria and procedures which specified sets of role occupants (whether company or coop managers, or implementing agency executives) may employ in choosing the 'inputs' into the decision-making process: what range of ideas and information, and who provides them? In reaching their decisions, do the role occupants take those inputs into account secretly, or in an open, transparent form, reporting to the public on the reasons and facts they have considered? What kinds of 'feedback' mechanism do they use to learn of that decision's social impact (and whose and what feedback do they consider in deciding whether to revise their decisions)?

[*I***deology** refers to *subjective* 'cultural values', traditions, attitudes, or beliefs which may influence role occupants' behaviors. Too often neglecting the persistent ***objective*** factors that determine behaviors, many sociologists and anthropologists perceive **Ideology**, thus defined, as the primary factor likely to influence individuals' and small groups' behaviors.]

B. *If, as almost always proves the case, more than one role occupant's behaviors contribute to the social problem specified, repeat the preceding step for each set of role occupans' behaviors*.

[To induce the relevant sets of role occupants to behave in ways more likely to help resolve the targeted problem, the proposed law's detailed prescriptions must aim to alter or eliminate the causes of each of their relevant problematic behaviors. Therefore, as far as possible, the drafters must specify, in as much detail as they can, ***the causes of each set of role occupants' behaviors that, under the existing law, contribute to perpetuating the problem.*** Once the drafters have identified those causes (and provided sufficient evidence to show their explanations prove consistent with the country-specific realities), ***logically*** they can design detailed prescriptions which, incorporated into the proposed law, seem likely to alter or eliminate those causes. ***Only then can they claim that their prescriptions, taken as a whole, will likely induce new, more appropriate behaviors to help overcome the problem specified.]***

C. It proves especially important to repeat the steps outlined in 'A', above, to explain, given the existing law, the problematic behaviors of each set of implementing agency officials.

[**1.** To one degree or another, almost without exception, implementing agency officials' problematic behaviors comprise a factor that, in deciding how to behave, a primary role occupant takes into account. Implementing agency officials behave in the face of rules and regulations addressed to them (see Fig. 2.1) much like any other set of role occupants. An explanation for an official's behavior follows the same general structure as an explanation for all primary role occupant behavior. Because an implementing agency always constitutes a complex organization, drafters usually can find useful explanatory hypotheses by examining the category, **Process.** In fact, many implementing agency officials' problematic behaviors, at least in part, appear rooted in the criteria and procedures which govern the agency's decision-making processes. The drafters might well begin by asking whether those processes conform to the fundamental characteristics of good governance: Transparency, accountability, and, as far as possible, participatory?

[**2.** Drafters, of course, also must demonstrate that their hypotheses as to the causes of implementing agency officials' problematic behaviors prove consistent with the available evidence. For that purpose, they should first explore the available facts as to the nature of the objective factors they have hypothesized as causes of the officials' seeming failure to implement the law's prescriptions. What facts can they find as to whether the prevailing circumstances ensure that the officials do know about the law's detailed prescriptions directed to them? Do they enjoy both the Opportunity and the Capacity to obey those prescriptions? Here. government reports on the numbers, qualifications, and financial resources of the agency's personnel may prove helpful. Perhaps university students could work with a concerned faculty member to survey carefully-selected samples of relevant role occupants to determine whether and to what extent the officials really do, or do not, know about the law; and whether they do, or do not, have the necessary resources, tools and skills to behave in conformity with its prescribed commands. Informants with knowledge about the particular sets of social actors the proposed bill targets may provide the drafters with facts to warrant their initial explanatory hypotheses as to the objective causes for those actors' problematic behaviors.

[It may prove more difficult to get evidence as to whether the **Process** by which a set of role occupants make decisions seems transparent, accountable and participatory. Too often, that **Process** remains hidden behind closed doors. Here, as did Theodosio Uate in his chapter in this book, an investigator may interview those involved, or gain access to minutes of relevant decision-making meetings. The more information drafters obtain about these kinds of objective causal factors' probable effects on particular sets of actors' dysfunctional behaviors, the more possible will they find it to design legislative provisions likely to alter or eliminate those causes.

[Drafters should also search for the available facts to test hypotheses suggested as to *subjective* factors' influences on implementing officials' behaviors: their **Interests** and **Ideologies**. Since, as noted above, academic researchers tend to focus on these as the causes of behaviors, they already may have unearthed useful relevant information. Drafters should scrutinize that evidence, however, to ensure that it derives, not from general assumptions drawn from preconceived models, but from actual observations of how those causal factors may influence officials' behaviors in their own country's unique context.]

Part IV. *The proposed 'solution' (a bill's detailed provisions)*

A. *List alternative proposals for solutions that logically seem likely to alter or eliminate the causes of the behaviors that comprise the targeted social problem.*

[1. The drafters' research report should aim to persuade a hypothetical 'rational skeptic' that the proposed bill's details result from rational choices grounded on evidence. For that purpose, the solutions part must provide a list of the alternative solutions which, based on available facts, seem logically possible. Drawing on these, the drafters must design and incorporate in their bill detailed provisions likely to prove most cost-effective in helping to resolve the problem addressed.

[2. Drafters may discover ideas for alternative solutions from a variety of sources: Discussions with country experts familiar with the problem addressed, as well as stakeholders—especially the poor and vulnerable—who know their own resources as well as what factors constrain their own efforts to find solutions; examination of relevant ministry files, library histories, and internet reports of their own and other countries' experiences in using law to try to resolve the problem; the relevant legal and professional literature; and ideas the drafters, themselves, may generate as they study the problem and its causes.]

B. *Describe the bill's provisions in some detail, including the proposed prescriptions requiring implementing agency officials to behave in new ways.*

[The drafters should specify in detail the bill's provisions for changing each set of role occupants' problematic behaviors. The devil lies in the details: Carefully formulated, the details of these provisions must prove so clearly stated that the drafters can easily translate them into the wording of the bill's prescriptions to specify how each set of role occupants, especially the implementing agency officials, must behave to help resolve the problem.]

C. *Demonstrate how the proposed bill's detailed prescriptions logically seem likely to alter or eliminate the causes of the problematic behaviors under the existing law.*

[In effect, drafters should use the ROCCIPI categories as a checklist predicting the relevant role occupants' (including the implementing agency officials') behaviors in the face of the bill's new prescriptions. In other words, the drafters must show that each of the bill's provisions contribute to altering or eliminating the causes identified in Part III for role occupants' existing problematic behaviors. Only then can the drafters claim that, logically, the bill will likely ensure that those role occupants will behave as the new law prescribes to help resolve the problem.]

D. *Demonstrate that the proposed bill's probable economic and social benefits will likely outweigh its probable economic and social costs.*

1. *Economic costs and benefits.*

[Whether measured in dollars, kwacha, pesos, yuan—whatever currency the country uses—drafters can work with government financial officers to estimate the immediate economic costs of implementing the bill. It will likely prove more difficult to estimate the potential longer term economic costs and benefits to the community. Involving those affected, however—especially the poor and vulnerable—may prove helpful in making these estimates.]

2. *Non-quantifiable social costs and benefits.*

[It will likely prove even more difficult to estimate the non-quantifiable social costs and benefits—the impact of the new rules in changing the relevant role occupants' life patterns. Nevertheless, involving those involved in making those estimates should help ensure consideration of all the relevant factors, as well as persuade those affected of the legitimacy of the government's efforts in seeking to introduce laws to resolve the problem in the public interest.]

3. *Social impact statement.*

[Drawing on the economic and social costs and benefits estimates, the research report should provide a summary statement of the bill's detailed provisions' impact on different social *groups, especially women, children, the poor, minorities, and on valued interests not usually well represented in the halls of power (e.g. environment, human rights, the rule of law, the prevention of corruption).*]

4. *Provisions to ensure monitoring and evaluation of the implementation the bill's implementation and its social impact.*

[The problem-solving methodology requires that the drafters incorporate a provision for a 'feedback mechanism' in their bill: A system for monitoring and evaluating the law after its enactment, both as to its effective implementation, and its social impact. This holds true for two reasons. First, a bill's drafters may find it difficult to gather all the evidence required to validate their descriptive and explanatory hypotheses, and their cost-benefit estimates. If, for any reason, they neglected important facts as to a significant aspect of a problematic behavior or its causes, or underestimated the costs of effectively implementing its proposed solution, their bill's provisions might not 'work' as anticipated. Second, in the nature of the development process, the world 'out there' always remains changing. The consequences of enacting the new law, itself, may change the factors that influence the relevant social actors' behaviors in unexpected ways. The proposed new law's feedback mechanism may also provide new evidence to identify causal factors that the drafters may not previously have understood, as well as new, unanticipated conditions. This new information may lay a new basis in facts, logically organized, for amending the law to make it more effective. In that sense, law-drafting, -enacting, and -implementing constitutes an interrelated, on-going process, always subject to improvement in light of new evidence. Again, that underscores the vital necessity of ensuring all those affected—especially the poor and vulnerable, as well as often-neglected community interests—an opportunity, drawing on their relevant experience, to provide inputs and to assess proposed further changes in the new law.]

THE BILL'S FORM: LEGISLATIVE DRAFTING TECHNIQUES

When lawmakers failed to enact laws to transform the inherited institutions that perpetuated most poor nations' poverty, vulnerability and poor governance, the people bore the brunt of losing the fatal race. To a significant degree, that loss reflected the drafters' failure to supply bills for the legislators to enact to effectively alter the problematic behaviors that comprised those dysfunctional institutions. Too often, the drafters drafted in out-moded, entropic ways: They copied law, they compromised between competing interests, they criminalized behavior, they drafted in vague and empty sentences.

The institutionalist legislative theory and methodology outlined above offers drafters a guide for designing bills more likely to prove effectively implemented to help overcome the institutional obstacles that thwart good governance and development in Africa, as well as the rest of the world. The rest of this chapter emphasizes the symbiotic relationship between the substance of a bill's detailed provisions, and the techniques used to draft those details: the bill's form.

Every legislative drafting text proclaims that a drafter's task consists of translating 'policy' into the language of the law. Traditionally, drafters viewed their task as simply drafting the commands, prohibitions and permissions that comprise a law's ***form***.

Old institutions die hard. Most drafters learned their craft by an apprenticeship system, working with senior drafters in their country's central drafting office or ministries. Some attended workshops and seminars, often sponsored by their country's former colonial power, on drafting techniques. Drafters in the former British colonies frequently interned in the Chief Parliamentary Counsel's offices in London, or in the similar office in Australia or Canada, learning from older drafters who themselves had served as apprentices in London. There, they learned to chain words together in the traditional technical form imported from abroad—in Africa, mostly imposed by the former colonial power, usually British, French, Portuguese, or Spanish.

The British tradition aimed to persuade drafters they should draft bills to guide a judge in settling disputes in court. In most systems, after all, neither the drafters' nor the legislators' intended meaning counts. Instead, the tradition focused on the proposition that how a judge construes a statute gives that statute its enforceable meaning. The drafter's task, they learned, consisted in communicating government policy in a form that a judge would construe as the drafter intended.

Latent in that tradition lies the notion that form and substance exist in different spheres. [52] If, however, one perceives the law as an instrument to channel behaviors, rather than as an instrument for dispute-settlement, form and substance appear as two closely-related sides of the same coin. A drafter must not merely anticipate how a judge might construe a bill, but draft that bill in ways that communicate to its addressees the bill's commands, prohibitions and permissions in a form that leads to understanding and hence more likely to conforming behavior. In Jamieson's words, [53]

> The linguistic universe in which we live does not begin to manifest itself until we cease to mistake for a real distinction what we think to be a mere linguistic vehicle for the illusory substance of communication.

For law to serve as an instrument of social change, it must induce conforming behavior. Drafters must draft bills in a form readily usable by a bill's audience, a form that, clearly, precisely, unambiguously, and understandably, commands, prohibits or permits the relevant role occupants to behave as specified. For that, drafters must not only learn how to work with policy- and law-makers in designing a bill's structure to center attention on the role occupants whose behaviors it proposes to change; they must also learn new ways of drafting a bill's detailed sentences that prescribe how the relevant sets of role occupants—including implementing agency officials—may, must, or may not behave to help resolve the social problem the law targets.

Unlike the relatively under-researched state of legislative theory and methodology, considerable scholarly work exists on 'plain language' drafting. [54] We do not visit that scholarship here. Suffice to close with an injunction to drafters that derives from the central message of this chapter: A drafter must design and draft a bill so that its prescriptions, if obeyed, will likely tend to resolve the social problem addressed—and make it likely that relevant actors will obey. ***For that, the drafter must perceive form and substance as one, so that, just as choices as to substance dictate choices as to form, so choices as to form dictate the substance of a bill.*** A bill's words comprise both its form and substance. The drafters' choices about a bill's words necessarily imbricate both.

SUMMARY AND CONCLUSION

In most of Africa, as throughout most of the world's developing and transitional countries, populist governments—whatever their policy claims—too often lacked the capacity to draft, enact, and implement laws capable of transforming their countries' inherited problematic institutions. Far too often, the people still suffered poverty, vulnerability and poor governance; in some countries, their conditions grew worse. Their populist leaders apparently had lost the first round of the fatal race. From time to time in every country, however, populist governments return to office—and, once again, have a newopportunity to win the fatal race.

That race's outcome crucially turns on how effectively the new governors use law as an instrument of social change. As the great legal anthropologist, Bronislaw Malinowski, held more than a half century ago,[55] learning how so to use law proves the great challenge of the age.

Institutionalist legislative theory and its problem-solving methodology offer a guide for designing legislation, grounded on logically-organized country-specific facts, to facilitate institutional transformation leading to more productive employment opportunities and a better quality of life. That theory emphasizes that law-makers must learn to use law as their primary tool for changing the repetitive behaviors—the inherited institutions—that thwart their efforts to achieve good governance and development. That calls for an understanding of how law influences human behavior, and a methodology that both facilitates designing a bill's substantive details, and provides an outline for a research report to justifying them.

Substantively, institutionalist theory argues that relevant actors decide how to behave by making choices shaped by their particular country's constraints and resources: the law itself, the expected behavior of the relevant implementing agency, and the non-legal factors inherent in the environment. ***Procedurally***, legislative theory offers a four-step problem-solving methodology to guide law-makers in gathering the relevant facts to

- Describe the nature and scope of the social problem of concern, and the behaviors that comprise it;
- Validate their explanations for the causes of social actors' problematic behaviors by proving their explanatory hypotheses consistent with the available evidence;
- Logically derive detailed, cost-effective legislative provisions likely to alter or eliminate the causes identified; and
- After the law's enactment, monitor and evaluate the facts as to the effectiveness of its implementation and its social impact.

To facilitate an on-going, people-oriented development process, law must alter the behaviors that comprise dysfunctional institutions. To change problematic behaviors, the drafter must begin, not with visions of what might be, but with a careful study of what *is* the case. From that examination, drafters can construct cost-effective legislation to transform the behaviors (the institutions) that perpetuate a global system which condemns four out of five of the world's inhabitants, receiving a fifth of the world's output, to a daily struggle for bare survival.

Too long and too often have well-intentioned, populist governments lost the fatal race. They seem likely to win it when they learn how, with popular participation, to manage the reins of government through law to discipline and direct state power to fulfill the majority's basic needs. That constitutes the minimum demand for democratic social change.

Notes

1. Portions of the first Part of this Chapter are taken from an earlier paper of ours, Ann Seidman & Robert B. Seidman, *Beyond Contested Elections: The Processes of Bill Creation and the Fulfillment of Democracy's Promises in the Third World*, 34 HARV. J. LEG. 1 (1997), and from Ann Sidman & Robert B. Seidman, "Law in Aid a=of Development: 'Hasty Legal Transplants' and the Fatal Race," International J. Comp L., forthcoming.
2. Bronislaw Malinowski, *A New Instrument for the Interpretation of Law—Especially Primitive*, 51 YALE L.J. 1237, 1246 *et seq.* (1942).
3. ANTHONY ALLOTT, THE LIMITS OF LAW 287 (Butterworths, 1980).
4. GEORGE C. HOMANS, THE NATURE OF SOCIAL SCIENCE 50-51 (Harcourt, Brace & World, 1967); *cf.* NORMAN UPHOFF, LOCAL INSTITUTIONAL DEVELOPMENT: AN ANALYTICAL SOURCEBOOK WITH CASES 9 (1986). This definition is contested. *See* Sven-Erik Sjöstrand, *On Institutional Thought in the Social and Economic Sciences*, in INSTITUTIONAL CHANGE: THEORY AND EMPIRICAL FINDINGS 3, 9-12 (Sven-Erik Sjöstrand ed., Armonk, 1993). 'Institution' means "a human mental construct for a coherent system of shared (enforced) norms that regulate individual interactions in recurrent situations"; 'institutionalization' means "the process by which individuals subjectively approve, internalize and externalize such a mental construct." *Id.* at 9.; Douglass C. North, *Institutional Change: A Framework for Analysis*, in INSTITUTIONAL CHANGE, *supra,* at 36 ('Institution' consists of "formal rules, informal constraints (norms of behavior, conventions and self-imposed codes of conduct) and the enforcement characteristics of both." 'Organizations' consist of "groups of individuals engaged in purposive activity. The constraints imposed by the institutional framework (together with other constraints) define the opportunity set and therefore the kind of organizations that will come into existence." Id. "The agent of change is the entrepreneur, the decision-maker(s) in organizations." *Id.* at 37.); HARRY M. JOHNSON, SOCIOLOGY: A SYSTEMATIC INTRODUCTION 22 (Robert K. Merton, ed., Harcourt, Brace & World 1960) ('social institution' means a "complex normative pattern that is widely accepted as binding in a particular society or part of society.")

   For analyzing the law-making enterprise, a behavioral definition seems more useful: Law can only change resource allocations by changing the behaviors—the institutions—that allocate them. Problem-solving holds that the key question becomes, why do those behavioral patterns exist? A drafter ought to count as important not merely the clarity and elegance of a bill's words, but also their likely effectiveness in bringing about the prescribed behaviors, and those behaviors' effectiveness in resolving the social problem at which the law aims. To serve a drafter's needs, the definition of 'institutions' ought to reflect the requirement that a bill should not merely change the rules, but change behaviors.
5. *See* ROBERT L. KIDDER, *CONNECTING LAW AND SOCIETY: AN INTRODUCTION TO RESEARCH AND THEORY (Prentice Hall, 1983).*

6. **Joseph Singer,** *The Player and the Cards: Nihilism on Legal Theory*, **94 Yale L. J. 1, 60 (1984).**
7. *See* **David V. Williams,** *The Authoritarianism of African Legal Orders: A Review and Critique of Robert B. Seidman's The State, Law and Development,* **5 Contemporary Crises 255 (1980).**
8. *See* **John Griffiths,** *Is Law Important?* **54 N.Y.U.L. Rev. 339 (1976).**
9. Perhaps the most probable hypothesis to explain populist governments' failure even to commission a ministry to formulate a policy to resolve a development-related social problem lies in their leaders' insufficient understanding of law's potential development function.
10. For a general report on the Chinese drafting project, which included preparation of this bill , *see* Ann Seidman, Robert B. Seidman & Janice Payne, Legislative Drafting for Market Reform: Some Lessons from China (Macmillan, 1997).
11. That bright idea may stem from a community group's concern with a social problem like that of polluted water; or from a legislator's reaction to scientific studies that expose an emerging danger, like that of a diminishing supply of underground water; or from a government ministry's recognition, for example, that, unless government takes appropriate action, the available water supply—essential to human life -- may become unusable or diminish below levels required for sustainable urban living. Whatever the source of the idea, however, the drafter (or perhaps a drafting team) must assume responsibility for formulating the detailed proposals for overcoming the problem, including specification of who must do what to ensure those details' effective implementation. *See generally* Ann Seidman, Robert B. Seidman & Nalin Abeyesekere, Legislative Drafting for Democratic Social Change: A Manual for Drafters (Kluwer Law Int'l, 2001) [hereinafter the "Drafter's Manual"].
12. *See also* Robert B. Seidman, *Law, Development and Legislative Drafting in English-Speaking Independent Africa*, 19 J. Modern African Studies 133 (1981); Ann Seidman & Robert B. Seidman, *Beyond Contested Elections: The Processes of Bill Creation and the Fulfillment of Democracy's Promises in the Third World*, 34 Harv. J. Leg. 1 (1997); the Drafter's Manual, at 21 *et seq.* Without further attribution, we have freely incorporated in this Chapter sections of these articles and books.
13. In Britain, the first Chief Parliamentary Counsel, Sir Henry Thring, adopted that stance as a defense against other ministers' fear that his new office -- established in 1869—posed a threat to their prerogatives. He insisted that, as drafter, he had no concern with 'policy,' but only with a bill's 'form'. Over the years, that assertion hardened into the central ideology of drafters in the British tradition. Alec Samuels, *Henry Thring: The First Modern Drafter*, **24 Stat. L. Rev. 91, 91 (2003).**
14. In local custom in parts of Afghanistan, rival clans may settle feuds by providing that a daughter of one clan marry a man from the other. The female involved has no choice in the matter. *Karzai Calls For End to Injustices Against Women,* Daily Times (Pakistan), May 12, 2004.
15. Traffic accidents constitute a leading cause of death in Vietnam. *See* http://travel.state.gov/travel/cis_pa_tw/cis/cis_1060.html (last accessed on Oct. 15, 2005).
16. Mozambique had one of the world's highest percentage of people disabled by explosions of landmines (left over from its ruinous civil war between FRELIMO and

RENAMO). *Landmine Survivors Rehabilitation Services Database: Mozambique*, available at http://www.lsndatabase.org/country_text.php?country=mozambique (last accessed on Oct. 12, 2005).

17. E. A. Driedger, *The Preparation of Legislation*, 31 CAN. BAR. REV. 33, 39 (1953).
18. *See supra* note 16 and accompanying text.
19. *See* ch. 4 of this book, *infra*, which offers an excellent illustration of these drafting behaviors in the context of Mozambique's drafting institutions inherited from that country's Portuguese colonial rulers.
20. *See* JOHN DEWEY, THEORY OF VALUATION 43-45 (University of Chicago Press, 1939).
21. 'Entropy' means "a state of disorder or disorganization, as in a social system, or a hypothetical tendency toward such a state." RANDOM HOUSE WEBSTER'S COLLEGE DICTIONARY (Robert B. Costello, et al., *eds*. 1995). As used here, it refers to the practices that, in the absence of a theory for designing a bill's details, most drafters in fact follow in translating policy into law.
22. *See* ch. 4 of this book, *infra*.
23. ELMER E. SCHATTSCHNEIDER, THE SEMI-SOVEREIGN PEOPLE: A REALISTS VIEW OF DEMOCRACY IN AMERICA 35 (1960).
24. *See generally* Robert Klitgaard, Controlling Corruption (1988).
25. *See* DRAFTER'S MANUAL, at ch. 14.
26. *See generally* Wade Channell, *Lessons Not Learned: Problems with Western Aid for Law Reform in Post-Communist Countries,* available at http://www.carnegieendowment.org/files/CP57.Channell.FINAL.pdf (visited Oct. 15, 2005).
27. *See* Brian Z. Tamanaha, *A Pragmatic Approach to Legislative Theory for Developing Countries*, in ANN SEIDMAN, ROBERT B. SEIDMAN & THOMAS WAELDE, MAKING DEVELOPMENT WORK: LEGISLATIVE REFORM FOR INSTITUTIONAL TRANSFORMATION AND GOOD GOVERNANCE 145 (Kluwer Law Int'l, 1999).
28. *See* Edward L. Rubin, *Legislative Methodology: Some Lessons from the Truth-in-Lending Act*, 80 GEO. L.J. 233 (1991); B. R. ATRE, LEGISLATIVE DRAFTING: PRINCIPLES AND TECHNIQUES 88 *et. seq.* (Universal Law Publishing, 2001); *see also* G. C. THORNTON, LEGISLATIVE DRAFTING (4th ed., Butterworth, 1996) (stating, without further elaboration, that "A drafter needs ... to study most rigorously the practical aspects of the legislation proposed and be satisfied that the scheme will work, that the machinery proposed is practical and that the legislation is capable of enforcement.")
29. *See* Driedger, *The Preparation of Legislation*, *supra* note 17, at 296 ("A drafter should always ask 'What will courts say?" If the draftsman succeeds in writing his statute so that the courts are left in no doubt as to its meaning, it is altogether likely that the persons at whom it is directed and the persons who have to administer it will also understand it.")
30. *See* DRAFTER'S MANUAL, at Part III.
31. For examples, *see* the website of the International Consortium for Law and Development (ICLAD), http://www.ICLAD-law.org.
32. Karl Llewellyn, *Some Realism about Realism: Responding to Dean Pound*, 44 HARV. L. REV. 1222 (1931).

33. Fredrik Barth, Models of Social Organization (Royal Anthropological Institute Occasional Paper 23, Glasgow Univ. Press, 1966); WILLIAM J. CHAMBLISS & ROBERT B. SEIDMAN, LAW, ORDER AND POWER (Addison-Wesley, 1969).
34. *See generally* DEWEY, *supra* note 20; EUGENE J. MEEHAN, VALUE JUDGMENT AND SOCIAL SCIENCE: STRUCTURES AND PROCESSES (Dorsey Press, 1969).
35. A set of 'role occupants' refers to the addressees of a law, a particular group of persons for whom the law prescribes a specified role. Self-evidently, everyone may simultaneously perform many 'roles' in life, as a parent, a spouse, a child, a consumer, a worker, a manager. Legislative theory, however, centers attention on a person's (or set of persons') role as the object of a law's prescriptions. *See* DRAFTER'S MANUAL, at ch. 1.
36. *See* HANS KELSEN, GENERAL THEORY OF LAW AND STATE 58 (A. Wedberg *trans.*, Russelll, 1961).
37. Barth, *supra* note 33. Some scholars object that most people behave out of habit, not by choice. Using the law for social change, however, concerns laws that require its addressees to change their behavior. In the face of a law requiring a person to change behavior, self-evidently a person must *choose* whether or not to obey.
38. *See* Section III-B, *supra*. Chapter 6 of the DRAFTERS' MANUAL (pp. 167-186) reviews some of the issues drafters and legislators must consider in assessing whether the available facts really do warrant their authors' propositions as to their significance.
39. A 'rational skeptic' may express doubts as to whether the bill will 'work' as its sponsors claim, but agree to review the available evidence (including new 'facts' not incorporated in the research report) to determine whether, logically, the bill's detailed provisions seem likely to alter or eliminate the existing causes of the problematic behaviors targeted, and induce new ones that help to resolve it.
40. John Rawls, *The Idea of Public Reason Revisited,* in JOHN RAWLS, COLLECTED WORKS 596 (Harvard Univ. Press, 1999).
41. An elite Ghanaian secondary school modeled on a British Public School.
42. Jay Bregman, *Theoretical Frameworks of Deliberative Democracy*, available at http://cyber.law.harvard.edu/projects/deliberation/theory (last accessed Sept. 28, 2005).
43. Rawls, *supra* note 38.
44. JÜRGEN HABERMAS, LEGITIMATION CRISIS 108 (T. McCarthy trans., Beacon Press, 1990) ([in the ideal deliberation], "no force except that of the better argument is exercised.")
45. In many countries, existing 'law on law' does require that drafters accompany an important law with a 'memorandum of law' or its equivalent. Too often, however, these memoranda merely restate, in non-legalistic language, the law's main provisions. Seldom do they provide country-specific evidence to justify the bill's detailed provisions (*see, e.g.*, Uate's chapter in this volume). In contrast, as outlined in the DRAFTERS' MANUAL, at 118-22, a research report structured by the problem-solving methodology at each step must provide the available relevant evidence, logically-organized.
46. *See* ch. 4 of the DRAFTERS' MANUAL, and particularly the 'checklist' for a research report at 118-22. We have unblushingly copied large portions of this section from that checklist.

47. *See* Assessing Legislation: A Manual for Legislators, available for downloading free of charge from the website http://www.ICLAD-law.org, which shows how the problem-solving methodology can help a legislator—presumably acting as a 'rational skeptic'—to ask for information required to assess whether a particular bill in a particular country's unique circumstances will likely resolve the problem it addresses.
48. For details, *see* DRAFTERS' MANUAL, at 190-93.
49. As a problematic behavior without a victim, corruption, like prostitution, remains difficult to expose; absent some type of reward, none of those involved will complain.
50. *See* DRAFTERS' MANUAL, at 92-99. ROCCIPI constitutes a mnemonic, formed by the first letters of the name of each category to help drafters (and assessors) to remember all seven categories of possible causes for role occupants' behaviors in the face of the law. The order of the categories listed reflects only the necessity of including them all in an easily remembered form. (The translation of the Drafters' Manual into many languages—Vietnamese, Russian, Bahasa Indonesia, etc—has revealed a difficulty in using ROCCIPI as a mnemonic: Most categories' names in these different languages begin with a different letter than they do in English. Some translators have tried to order the different letters into a different mnemonic; others have left it as ROCCIPI.)
51. *See id.* at 12.
52. *See* Driedger, *supra* note 17.
53. N. J. Jamieson, *Towards a Systematic Statute Law*, 3 OTAGO L. REV. 342, 343 (1976).
54. *See e.g.* Ruth Sullivan, The Promise of Plain Language Drafting, 47 McGill L.J. 97 (2001).
55. *See* Malinowski, *supra* note 2.

PART II

AFRICA'S INHERITED DYSFUNCTIONAL INSTITUTIONS: SOME CASE STUDIES

Chapter 3

Ghana: Changing Our Inherited Police Institutions

Raymond Atuguba

At 8:00 AM, Tuesday, 8th February, 2005, radio Joy FM announced that the Accra Metropolitan Assembly (AMA) had voted for a city 'decongestion exercise,' backed by 350 police, to oust over 10,000 hawkers from the Accra city streets. The next day, the Daily Graphic described the scene as the exercise continued 'under heavy police protection':

"People, including children under 12 years, who slept on street corners and pavements, were seen quietly watching as the exercise went on.

"Others folded their sleeping mats in their armpits, perhaps waiting to bolt in case of any eventuality.

"An elderly man who was sleeping on a pavement near the Rawlings park cursed and hurled insults... .

"Some of the market women, who sat moodily in groups, did not believe that the AMA could sustain the exercise. Consequently, they said, 'time will tell.'"[1]

An Accra metropolitan Assembly official reportedly declared, "AMA has no obligation to look for markets for ***these women."***[2] *During the Parliamentary debate on the President's Sessional Address, the Honourable Mahama Ayariga, MP for Bawku Central, sought to raise issues related to AMA's 'exercise' on the floor of the House, but it seems that the House leaders prevailed on him to withdraw his questions.*[3]

A week later, apparently emboldened by the 'decongestion' exercise's enforced success, another Assembly meeting requested 500 policemen to help relocate the Kasoa Market "under heavy security". The Assembly unanimously agreed that there would "be no time to allocate all traders from the existing market places before the relocation exercise...."[4]

On the same day, a Daily Guide headline reported, "AMA Boss Escapes Death By the Skin Of His Teeth." Nevertheless, the following week Kaneshie Market 'decongestion' would start and extend to Kwame Nkrumah Circle. The police arrested and prosecuted any who tried to stay. Two days later, the Daily Graphic reported that 29 petty traders, caught still hawking in the streets, had been sentenced to a fine of ¢1,000,000 or 2 months in prison.[5] *The Kumasi Metropolitan Assembly (KMA) also called on hawkers in the metropolis voluntarily to vacate unauthorized places by March 7, 2005, or face forcible ejection.*

Although Ghana had won independence almost half a century earlier, these police actions seemed reminiscent of the colonial era—nor did they appear as isolated incidents. Five years earlier, in May, 2001, a funeral took place at the Awudome Cemetery for some of the 126 people who died in a stampede at the Accra stadium, 33 came from Nima, Mamobi and New Town.[6] *The police had been publicly blamed for throwing teargas into the crowds at the stadium, causing the stampede. After the funeral, many young people headed home on motorbikes. Near the Nima Police Station, the police stopped them and detained one. More youths, arriving on foot, joined in the riders' verbal exchanges with the police. The youths became increasingly rowdy. The police fired a warning shot. Gathering in larger numbers around the police station, the youths attempted to vandalise the Nima Police Station. The police called in the military who succeeded in tactfully moving the youths away from the station. Later, however, some youths returned and did vandalise both state and private property in and around the police station. These events strained the relationships between the police and the communities. Community members feared to seek police assistance, and, fearing for their lives, the police no longer came into the community to prevent crime, apprehend offenders and perform other police duties. In Nima those days, people asked, "'Abotchie' where is my Police?"*

A last story suggests the possible causes that spurred these growing tensions. About 20 years ago, the Government of Ghana initiated proceedings to compulsorily acquire a large tract of land in one of the best residential areas in a major Ghanaian town. It never completed the process, but occupied the land for several years before apparently leaving it to the original community owners. Nevertheless, a number of persons, highly placed in the town, parcelled the land out to and built expensive houses on it for themselves as private owners. Although the community members complained, the police never attempted to prevent this encroachment on their property rights. On the contrary, any time the members of the community attempted to exercise even incidental rights over parts of the land, like fetching clay for building purposes, the big new houses' owners reported them to police who harassed and even arrested them. The lawyers whom the community asked to take their case experienced pressures to withdraw. What can a poor struggling lawyer do who receives a call from a minister of state to back off? Finally, in January 2005, the community asked the Legal Resources Centre (LRC), a human rights organisation made up primarily of lawyers and community organizers, to take their case. Perhaps, they had heard that that the LRC takes on 'unpopular causes'.....

THE ROOT CAUSES OF CIVIL-POLICE UNEASE

As the new millennium opened, these stories, appearing almost every day on a smaller or larger scale in Ghana, looked like a replay of the days of the "Riots of 1948" that presaged the Gold Coast's mounting struggle for indepen-

BOX 1: "Ghana: A Fragile Success in Africa"
– A New York Times editorial, Apr. 25, 2005

"Ghana has taken up the mantle of what passes for a success story in Africa. It is the new darling in the halls where donors like the World Bank, the International Monetary Fund, the United States and Britain talk about making sure foreign aid does not end up in the hands of corrupt regimes....

"But for all the talk of what a model African country Ghana is, it is still, literally, dirt poor, a fact of life that demonstrates just how removed Africa is from the proverbial rising tide of the global economy that is supposed to be lifting all boats. Ghana has a per capita income of $421 a year; most people survive here on $300 to $400. Ten-year-old girls still run barefoot up to stopped cars in the sweltering midday heat trying to sell anything they think will bring in money – from oranges to cell phone batteries to toilet paper. Street children still sleep on the median separating highway lanes.....

"Child mortality rates, already high, increased in 2004; nobody seems to know why. A huge gender gap remains in primary-school education: far more boys make it to school than girls. Almost half of Ghana's national budget comes from foreign aid; Britain is its largest single -country donor. But the size of the country's budget, a scant $3 billion, supporting some 20 million people, is testament to just how far Ghana still has to go, and how much more it needs to climb out of poverty."

dence from British rule. Today, the symptoms of an increasingly uneasy relationship between the police and the citenzenry reflect deep fissures between the two sets of institutions. This chapter aims to expose the underlying root causes of the unease in civil-police relations, to analyse the history of their birth and nurturing in today's Ghana.

Traditionally, people everywhere tend to view as the police's role the 'maintenance of law and order'—but those words remain empty categories, leaving the authorities to fill them with their own preferred substance. Not too long ago in countries as different as the United States of America and South Africa, the 'law' simply ignored black persons' rights and well-being. In erstwhile apartheid South Africa, the maintenance of 'order' served as an excuse for opening fire on unarmed school children engaged in peaceful demonstrations. Over time, leaving the definition of 'Law' and 'Order' as open, loosely monitored categories has proven fundamentally dangerous.

This chapter briefly reviews how, over the last 176 years, the changing faces of those exercising state power in Ghana have filled the seemingly-empty categories of "law" and "order" with particular forms of political-economy that have worked for their particular ends. They have assigned to the police the task of maintaining law and order that operated along the Atlantic corridor of West Africa as they have defined it. Analysis of this history helps to understand the underlying institutional relationships between the police and the political

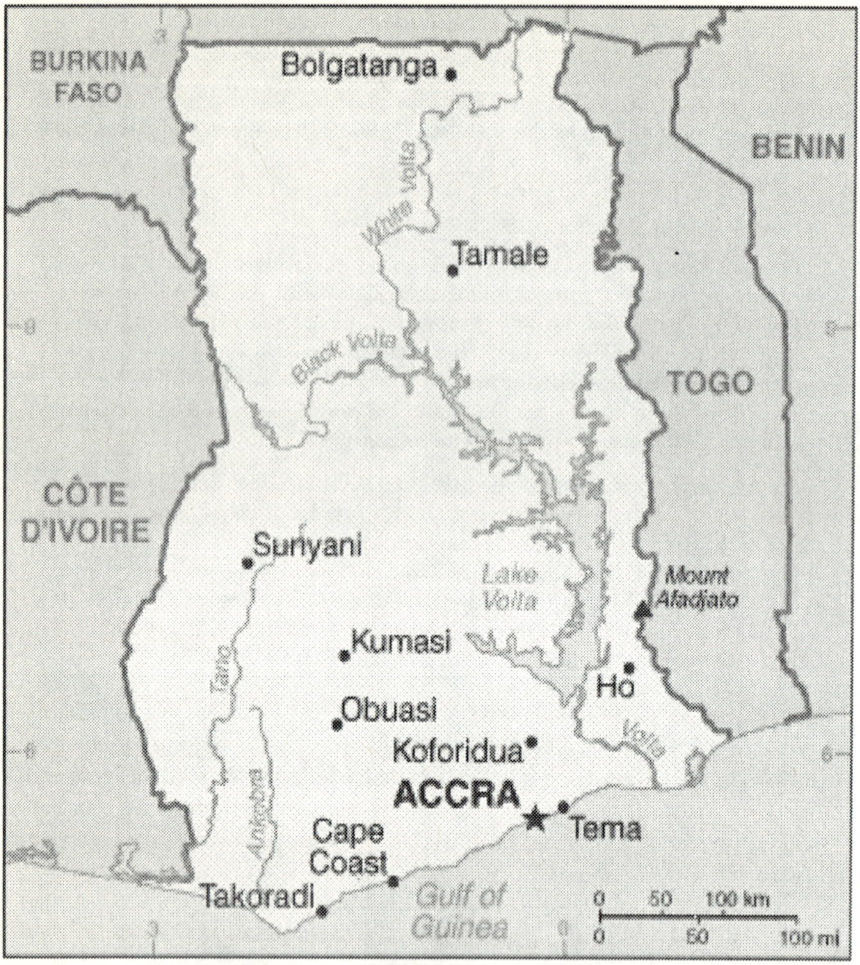

Ghana

economy. The concluding section suggests that those seeking to reform the Ghanaian police should consider using institutionalist legislative theory as a guide to design the details of legislation to ensure new police behaviors more likely to serve the needs of all Ghanaians.

THE POLICE AND THE POLITICAL ECONOMY OF GHANA: 1829-2005

History "matters not just because we can learn from the past, but because the present and the future are connected to the past by the continuity of a society's institutions. Today's and tomorrow's choices are shaped by the past. And the past can only be made intelligible as a story of institutional evolution."[7] To fully understand the relations between the "police and the political economy of Ghana" requires analysing their growth and development beginning back in the colonial rule of the then-Gold Coast.

As David Bayley[8] has argued, the police generally have not served as independent actors, but rather as instruments of those wielding political power: "[P]olice forces are the creatures of politics." As elsewhere, the colonial regime planted the roots of the police force to ensure the effective implementation of its colonial policies.[9]

A brief review of the last 176 years[10] suggests that the basic characteristics of Ghana's police force as an institution have changed little despite seven seemingly-different phases of government:

1. The period of conquest and 'legitimate trade' from about 1830 to 1900;
2. The period of political domination and intensive exploitation of natural resources from about 1900 to the mid 1940s;
3. The tumultuous period of transition to independence, beginning in the mid-1940s, through the attainment of independence in 1957;
4. The Nkrumah period, from 1957 to 1966;
5. The period of economic downturn and political uncertainty that, between 1966 and1981, witnessed the rise and fall of five military regimes and two democratically elected constitutional governments;
6. The Rawlings era and the period of the Economic Recovery Program (ERP) and the Structural Adjustment Program (SAP), 1982-2000; and
7. The current period, 2001 to date.

As background, this chapter's next part first describes the pre-colonial community policing system; summarizes the changes introduced by the British colonialists to protect their commercial investments; and, finally, reviews the post-independence governments' failure to exercise state power through law to restructure the police force to meet the needs of the Ghanaian people.

THE PRE-COLONIAL PERIOD, UP TO THE FORMAL END OF THE SLAVE TRADE IN ABOUT 1830

In the territory now called Ghana, pre-colonial societies had long maintained their own policing systems. They did not establish a centralized and formal body of trained officers with specific policing duties. Instead, in the traditional system, when necessary, some people undertook police duties. The community as a whole acted in concert in response to an alarm, for example, to catch a fleeing offender or search for one in hiding. Bands of adult men would also lie in wait to apprehend thieves[11] or patrol the village. The Paramount Chief sometimes gave specified Messengers of the Chiefs oral warrants to arrest offenders or patrol the village.[12]

In short, pre-colonial Ghana had well-developed institutions for maintaining social order and bringing under control behaviors that threatened the stability of an ordered society. Tribal elders, chiefs, and their ruling councils derived this power of social control from religious norms and beliefs, which permeated the fabric of pre-colonial society in Ghana.[13] Norm violation brought shame not only to the offender but also to his or her extended family and kin group. The extended family brought collective pressure to ensure the compliance and conformity of its family members.[14] These interrelated policing systems served many functions, from crime control to the maintenance of order, to the reaffirmation of secular and religious authority.[15]

The advent of colonialism wiped away most of these pre-existing systems. The British explicitly sought to incorporate elements of the village or native policing institutions as part of their broader design of indirect rule. In reality, however, the so-called 'native authority' police had lost their independence; they operated as little more than junior appendages of the Gold Coast Police Force. Even in respect of these forces, the colonial government set out to introduce a completely new form and purpose of policing in the Gold Coast. In the grinding words of a British colonial official,

> The customs of the savage and barbarous native states have left no mark on modern organisation or methods, for the Native Authority Forces of today are copies of the Government Police rather than survivals of indigenous methods of Peace preservation.[16]

As the next sections suggest, the British apparently considered the pre-existing indigenous systems of policing inappropriate for their unfolding exploitative agenda.

THE PERIOD OF COLONIALISM 1830 TO 1957

The British introduced rules to establish their political and legal authority over the Gold Coast. Treaties, however tenuous; laws on treason, sedition and other crimes against the state;[17] arms and ammunition regulations;[18] laws on public order[19]—all aimed to secure British political authority. In subtle but critical and effective ways, laws on property, tax, and liquor licensing also influenced the distribution of economic and social power. The entire gamut of these laws constructed the social reality by regulating the interactions of the colonized in a capacity subordinate to the colonizers—and even, in some cases, to their fellow colonized. The colonizers called on the police to enforce these laws to maintain a political economy and social organization conducive to the colonial enterprise:

> The baseline is that policing the empires developed largely in response to several imperial demands, the most important of which was the global expansion of capitalism, particularly in the nineteenth century, and the need to control international markets in raw materials as well as outlets for Europe's industrial goods....[T]he police forces that eventually emerged in the colonies were essentially 'hybrids', with many having characteristics that did not mirror police models in the 'mother-country' but were shaped by colonial events and needs....

...

> [T]he use of the colonial police forces generally to maintain unfavourable colonial tax and labour policies earned them the reputation of being nothing but instruments of state coercion, representing an unquestionable political authority and existing only to serve the political and economic interests of the colonialists. Incidents of police brutality, corruption, violence, murder and abuse of power punctuated almost every decade of colonial police history. The political image of the colonial police was most visible during the period of decolonization when development in colonial policing shifted rapidly towards political policing against the 'enemies' of the colonial states.[20]

As its primary task, the professional Gold Coast police force served to protect representatives of trade companies, supervise convict labor on plantations, maintain the peace and security necessary for the extraction and export of agricultural and mineral products, and maintain the colony as a market for European goods by protecting trade routes.[21]

Thus, the British created the police, not primarily to preserve law, order, peace and security for all in the colony, but rather to protect the persons, territory and the economic interests of the British companies—the United Trading Company (UTC), the Imperial British East African Company, and the Royal Niger Company—then operating along the Atlantic corridor of West Africa.[22] The British viewed the professional police as directly linked to the commercial interests of their capitalist expansion in search of new markets and resources. As they pacified the interior and expanded trade, "some kind of armed constabulary was required for the protection of British traders, missionaries, and officials and for the support of friendly tribes."[23] The colonist police force, driven by the economic imperative of safeguarding and enhancing exploitation through trade and control of a low-cost, compliant labor force, remained inextricably linked to the new era of Victorian capitalism and imperial legitimation.[24]

The British success in this enterprise reflected, in part, the police force's effective brutalization of the citizenry. Consequently, although the police included a significant number of Ghanaians, the population generally conceived of it as an intrusive alien force.[25] Civilians repeatedly complained about the brutal character, not only of the Hausa Constabulary, but also the Gold Coast Regiment.[26] In 1886 in Accra, "a large part of the population stoned the civil police."[27] They viewed them as traitors to the native African community.[28] In 1885, the Police Commissioner had written: "The Force is unpopular with the natives and the great majority of the natives would rather do anything than become a constable."[29]

A South African observer described the rank and file of the Native Police as

> [T]he most worthless body of men on the coast ... recruited from among the worst classes of West African native-Sierra Leone Niggers and the lazy, good-for-nothing ignorant slum blackguards who

> imagine the duties of a Policeman to consist in wearing a uniform and getting drunk-the Policeman on the coast is a disgrace to his cloth.[30]

He added that West Africans attached more disgrace to the calling of a Policeman than to that of a convict or ex-convict: "[T]he latter receives sympathy for having been unfortunate enough to have been found out, but everyman's hand is against a Policeman who is looked upon as a traitor to his race."[31]

In the rural areas, too, the people feared and disliked the Native Authority Police. Poorly trained and irregularly paid, the police often acted on their own in carrying out assignments and making arrests. Another commentator noted:

> Very often, the Native Authority Policemen whose province has not been determined, used any amount of force within their power to bring offenders to Court even on a very minor charge.
>
> It was a common thing to see people being beaten and dragged along by these officers. Many were disgusted with the overbearing manner by which these officers went about their duties....[32]

In 1882, the Gold Coast Times declared the Ada police as "useless; they are generally seen sitting outside grog-shops and strive to escape work".[33]

In the events leading up to the fall of empire, more than any other government agency, the police had to deal directly with the forces of nationalist politics and anti-colonial protest. After the wars of conquest and the consolidation of their rule in the Gold Coast, and before the 1940s, the British had usually limited police work to local issues, tribal clashes, boycotts, de-stoolment disputes, and opposition to taxation. For these tasks, a small number of policemen had almost always appeared sufficient.

After a century of colonial rule, however, organized opposition to the colonial government finally emerged in the context of the liberation struggle. Popular opposition to the police force became an inextricable by-product of opposition to the entire British imperialist architecture. The 28th February 1948 social movement targeted the Governor as representative of the British Crown. A police attempt to prevent a march on the Governor's office led to a showdown. The resulting chaos, widespread rioting and looting, closely related to nationalist activities, caught the colony and its police force unprepared.[34] The years 1948-1951 saw mounting unrest, lawlessness, rapid changes of policy, and turbulence. Nationalist militants heralded challenges to the colonial government and its laws as patriotic.

Under the pressure of these crucial years, the colonialists attempted a rapid expansion and reform of the police. The government imported troop-carrying vehicles, signals equipment, riot equipment, as well as twenty former gazetted Palestine Police officers experienced in police mobile force work—and, as a final dressing, added an armored car unit. In the following months, the military held exercises in crowd control and anti-guerrilla techniques. In 1949, with warnings of Positive Actions already in the air, the government decided to form a third battalion and expand the armed forces as a back-up to the police. To deal with serious disorders beyond the resources of the regular police, it established a Voluntary Police Reserve which quickly could call out over 2,000 Africans, Asians, and Europeans.[35] Thus, faced with renewed violence, the government dramatically expanded the police force, made it more paramilitary in character, developed more centralized command systems, and established special branches.

In effect, the1948 riots proved a catalyst for police reform, forcing the Gold Coast Government to create an increasingly militaristic police force, better organized and equipped, and, on command, ready to descend upon the citizenry. Unfortunately, the political protests of the time provided fodder for police brutality.

To summarize: The British originally set out to establish the Gold Coast Police Force for obvious reasons: The conquered peoples, whose chiefs had unwillingly or strategically signed peace treaties and treaties of protection with the British, remained restless. To govern, the political class—the Governors and their officials—established the Gold Coast Police Force to ensure needed security. They sought to preserve peace and security for 'legitimate trade'[36] in imported European goods and increased exports of agricultural and mineral production to feed the people and industries of Europe. The police maintained the essential law, order, peace and security by enforcing the 'rule of law'. In performing these tasks, the police implemented other laws, including eviction and property laws, to facilitate imperial economic expansion.

To conquer and pacify backward peoples; to protect and keep the wheels of capital moving; and to discipline the nascent working-class to ensure the stability of the social relations of production: Policing lay very much at the centre of the ideology as well as the practice of an imperial rule that fostered political domination as well as economic and social construction. When private policing increased the trade companies' costs, the government nationalized their policing institutions and transferred the cost from the private to the public sector financed by colonial tax revenues.

In short, policing in the Gold Coast changed drastically from the pre-colonial to the colonial era, from the enforcement of moral and religious order to the protection of political and commercial interests. Unfortunately, however, as demonstrated in this chapter's next parts, Ghana's victorious post-independence governors failed to exercise state power through law significantly to alter the police force as an institution.

THE NKRUMAH ERA: 1957-1966

After independence, as during the colonial era, the police remained central to the maintenance of the political economy of neo-colonialism—and continue to do so in the era of 'post-modern colonialism' today.[37] The nationalist leaders still employ the police as instruments for national integration and protection of their so-called 'modern, developmentalist' state. As one observer notes:

> [T]he colonial policing legacy did not disappear in the developing world after independence, even in those post-colonial states that adopted anti-colonial revolutionary governments. Many post-colonial states continued in the colonial tradition of political policing, using the police as the most visible symbol of political power and control, to legitimize and entrench largely authoritarian governments. Thus, in many respects, the post-colonial police forces, like their colonial predecessors, are still misused and abused....Various accounts of the police in Africa continuing in the colonial tradition as agents of the state against trade unionists, students and political opponents, persist....In a nutshell, the strategic position that the police occupied in the colonization process together with their operation as an arm of authoritarian governments ever since have enabled them to consolidate their position as an instrument of the central state which functions to perpetuate existing power relations in the interest of the different factions of the post-colonial political classes.[38]

Two main challenges faced President Nkrumah's immediate post-independence political administration: First, consolidation of the new nation's hard-won political and economic freedom while building the necessary infrastructure for economic and political development; and, second, creation of the new social institutions necessary to foster the integration of diverse ethnic and clan groups into the process of nation-building and development.

To achieve these two objectives, Dr. Nkrumah called on the strongest institution of coercion and governance the colonial regime had constructed: the police. He sought to use the police to shore up his fragile regime and to keep political opponents at bay. At the same time, because he mistrusted independent sources of power, he tried to maintain strict political control over the police; when he sensed police disloyalty, he divested them of several powers .

In the political sphere, for instance, the first years of independence witnessed a series of constitutional and legislative measures aimed at reducing potential ethnic conflict and, simultaneously, stifling political opposition to the Convention People's Party (CPP). The Avoidance of Discrimination Act in late 1957[39] forbade the existence of parties on a regional, tribal, or religious basis. These obviously affected both the Ashanti-based parties and the Northern Peoples Party (NPP). To get around the law, several opposition forces, originally formed on ethnic lines, came together to form the United Party (UP). The Preventive Detention Act of 1958[40] gave the government the right to detain persons without trial for up to five years.[41] The 1960 Constitution, the first republican constitution that replaced the independence constitution of 1957, created the position of Executive President, a position Nkrumah filled. The new Constitution, which gave the president many powers, did not contain an actionable and enforceable bill of rights.[42] Then in 1964, Ghana became a one party-state. These measures aimed to introduce a new era, based on a consistent, centralized government.

Nevertheless, agitation against the Nkrumah government persisted. The Ga people in Accra, the national capital, felt frustrated and overwhelmed by others who, as part of continent-wide urbanization trends, moved into their midst. Many complained that the C.P.P. and Nkrumah failed to repay them for their pre-independence support. As early as July 1957, some organized the Ga Shifimo Kpee (the Ga Standfast Organisation). On his return to Accra from a Prime Ministers' Conference in London, former supporters, now waving protest banners, hurled epithets at the President. Marches and demonstrations turned bloody as the police intervened. By late August police began to make arrests, though not exclusively of opposition figures. The Ga Shifimo Kpee complained the police closed their eyes to C.P.P. 'terrorism', unfairly arresting opposition supporters, offering false testimony in court, and refusing them permits for public meetings or rallies.[43]

Ashanti had had a long history of opposition to rule from Accra, whether colonial or indigenous. In the immediate post-independence era, the National Liberation Movement waned everywhere, but even at its peak, few government supporters had appeared in Ashanti. While the authorities dared not act against the Asantehene, they had no such trepidation in regard to other leaders, like those in Kumasi's Muslim community. In the summer of 1957, the government ordered the police to serve deportation orders against two of these leaders, although both held Ghanaian citizenship. This fueled public disorders in both Kumasi and Accra—and the police bore the brunt of the people's anger. In Ashanti as in Accra, people protested that the police hindered the newly-formed United Party's efforts to hold rallies. Then, in the fall of 1958, the police carried out four more deportations despite a court order delaying their action to ensure clear determination of the men's nationality. These actions generated even more large-scale hostility toward the police.[44]

In the Volta Region, political and economic issues aggravated friction with the Nkrumah regime. Some 'Voltarians' wished to merge the region with what soon would become an independent Togo. Others urged all Ewes in Eastern Ghana to join their brothers in the new nation-state across the border. Yet others wished to keep and strengthen ties to Accra.[45] On the economic front, a long-standing, lucrative smuggling operation between Ghana and Togo appeared endangered for the first time.[46] Nkrumah's government again sought to use the police to integrate these varying peoples and corresponding interests.

In sum, the evidence suggests that, in a bid to establish centralized control over the new nation-state, Nkrumah's government employed the police to shore up his fragile regime and to keep political opponents at bay. Many voices expressed obvious displeasure. Some charged the police with being impolite, using harsh methods, telling plaintiffs or witnesses to 'go and come' no matter how many miles they had to travel, spontaneously altering complaints against those accused, behaving in authoritarian ways that brooked no opposition, locking people in cells and trying to force confessions, jailing people who complained for making false accusations, and generally beating, detaining, and bullying individuals. Many Ghanaians considered it unwise to help the police track down criminals, or to go to court, or to get mixed up in any way with police officers.

Rural communities tended to view the regular police with even greater suspicion. A member of the Legislative Assembly declared:

> The Policemen are a terror in the rural areas....The Policemen do not in fact respect the views of the common people, and in my own constituency, a Policeman...will never respect whatever views are put before him."[47]

The Nkrumah government apparently never really tried to use law to transform the institutions of policing to ensure they worked more closely to help those living in the poorer communities resolve their own concerns.

In 1966, after a military coup[48] ousted President Nkrumah, Ghana experienced a decade and a half of economic downturn and political uncertainty that witnessed the rise and fall of five military regimes and two democratically elected constitutional governments. None of these governments made any serious attempt to reconstruct the police force as an institution. Essentially, as before, the police served, not the majority of the urban or rural poor, but the ruling elites of the day. Then, in 1981, yet another military regime, headed for a second time by a military man, Flight Lieutenant John Jerry Rawlings took over, and some people voiced renewed hope for real change. Instead, for the next quarter of century in the midst of emerging new social problems, the dominant police 'behaviors' remained essentially unchanged.

FROM THE RAWLINGS ERA TO THE CURRENT PERIOD: 1981-2005

In the mid-1980s, under the tutelage of the World Bank and the International Monetary Fund (IMF), a second Rawlings government initiated the Economic Recovery Programme (ERP) and Structural Adjustment Programme (SAP). To date, under different names and with minor substantive changes, first the Rawlings and then the Kufuor administrations continued to implement these same programs. In terms of understanding Ghana's political economic context, this seems to justify treating the Rawlings and Kufour eras together.

The second Rawlings military regime took over the reins of government on 31st December 1981. The government inherited a weak, debt-ridden economy, largely thanks to global market forces that prolonged low world prices for Ghana's main export: cocoa. At first, Rawlings called for moving the country ideologically to the left, but not for long. Dry national coffers, the depletion of the nation's foreign reserves, a mounting debt service burden, shortages of essential commodities, drugs and equipment, and on top of all this, severe drought, caused the Rawlings regime to rethink its strategy. In less than two years, the government requested food aid to deal with the threat of famine. Immediately, the World Bank and the IMF offered tempting assistance—if the regime would divest itself of its leftist ideological trappings. Internecine conflict within the leadership of the regime led to a purging of the regime's ultra left-wing guard, and the assumption of full control by the moderates joined by new centre and right-wing recruits. Thus dawned a new era of liberalism—what some call 'post-modern colonialism.' The government adopted the usual fine-sounding code names for their new programs—'Economic Recovery,' and 'Structural Adjustment.' From time to time, over the Rawlings era and in the present, these program's titles changed, but, essentially, guided by the same tutors (the World Bank and the IMF), they retained the same characteristics.

What then characterizes the political economy of post-modern colonialism,[49] which others term the 'Washington Consensus'? In general, it reflects strong globalizing pressures that, at once, demand strengthening state power, in the form of enforcement of the 'rule of law' and the fight against crime; and weakening state power in areas involving economic regulation and welfare policies. The post-modern colonialism project incorporates four seemingly contradictory dimensions: a neo-liberal economic consensus; a weak state consensus; a liberal-democratic consensus; and a consensus on the rule of law and the role of courts.

In this context, the Rawlings regime attempted two seemingly contradictory reforms of the inherited institutions that comprised the police force. First, it introduced a leftist approach of decentralizing policing functions and involving non-police officers in the policing system. Second, it purchased more hi-tech equipment to strengthen the police force's capacity to protect the new elements of the neo-liberal post-modern colonial era. The first set of reforms, involving the use of community-based 'Revolutionary Defence Committees' to perform various police duties,[50] crumbled with the marriage of the regime to the International Financial Institutions (IFIs), and altogether ceased by 1988. The second set of reforms endured, and has continued to date. In effect, over the last two and a half decades the reigning governments thus preserved the police force, basically in its inherited form, while strengthening its human, institutional, and material resources. This reflected the underlying reality of the coincidence of the tenets of the colonial and post-modern colonial agendas, which both required a similar type of police officer. Today, under the tutelage of the World Bank, the IMF and the World Trade Organization (WTO), the police serve primarily to implement and police Ghana's neo-liberal-integration into the world economy.

During the period of military rule, and—despite constitutional guarantees—in the period afterwards, the Rawlings regime used the military and the police to suppress dissent, initially expressed in the form of severe, if muffled, opposition to the regimes' sudden marriage to the IFIs. They arrested and imprisoned the few who voiced their opposition openly; many claimed the police tortured them.[51]

In 1996, just three years into the new democratic dispensation, the Rawlings government[52] set up a high level commission of inquiry into the police service. The commission presented its report in March, 1997. The terms of reference of the commission, its methodology, and its conclusions, proved consistent with the post-modern project that required a hi-tech police force to protect the political class, ensure peace and security for economic exploitation, and enforce a rule of law whose interstices were populated with the agenda of post-modern colonialism.

Thus, two centuries after the beginning of colonial rule, and half a century after that rule had formally ended, the Gold Coast Police Force—now called the Ghana Police Service—retained the same basic objectives. As created during colonial rule, the institution has endured, still patterned after the British imposed police system and enforcing laws inherited from British colonialism.[53]

Still used mainly for the protection of the political class, the police's stated aim became that of providing peace and security to attract foreign investors. The police still enforce a whole range of laws, including those evicting poor and powerless people, to create space and wealth for the powerful and the rich.[54] That the police behave in repetitive patterns shaped by almost two hundred years of history comprises yet another illustration of the theory of institutional continuity.[55] Unless a nation's new governors learn how to exercise state power through law to transform the institutions inherited from the colonial past, those institutions—like the Ghanaian police—will likely perpetuate the socio-economic circumstances that coerce the majority of Africans to struggle for bare survival.

Bankole Cole's observations clearly fit the Ghanian case:

> Although many post-colonial countries have, since independence, experimented with different types of governments, most of them have preserved in their new political structures several features of the colonial state, some practically in their original forms. This is particularly true of policing.[56]

In Ghana, as illustrated by the case of the New Patriotic Party v. Inspector General of Police [1993-94] 2 GLR 459, the role of the police as an arm of the regulatory state soon came into conflict with the 1992 Constitution's new human rights guarantees. In this case, the presidential candidate of Ghana's future governing party, the New Patriotic Party (NPP), serving as plaintiff, complained that the government's requirement of a police permit to hold rallies or demonstrations thwarted democratic participation.

In a succinct, very short two-paragraph opinion, Edward Wiredu, Justice of the Supreme Court (as he then was), declared in part:

> The police permit has outlived its usefulness. Statutes requiring such permits for peaceful demonstrations, processions and rallies are things of the past. The police permit is the brainchild of the colonial era and ought not to remain in our statute books.[57]

While striking down some of the provisions of the law as unconstitutional, the Chief Justice went further by calling on the legislature to act beyond the court orders:

> I would urge that the whole of [the Public Order Decree] should be reviewed and modernised in its entirety to enable the Police Service

to carry out its duties effectively without contravening any provision in our current Constitution, 1992.[58]

On 7th January 2001, the majority of Ghanaian voters elected John Agyekum Kufuor to replace Rawlings as President, ushering the New Patriotic Party into the seat of Ghanaian government. In his inaugural speech, Kufuor promised an era of 'positive change' in everything throughout the country. Would that 'positive change' include the police?

The NPP governors did pay more attention to the police. They ordered new vehicles and other equipment for the police force, recruited thousands of new policemen, appointed two new Deputy Inspectors General of Police, and generally talked of making the force more capable of maintaining effective law and order. Various NGOs (non-government organizations) piggy-backed on this initiative, focusing on monitoring police performance and police reform.[59] These efforts by the government and the NGOs to reform the police continue today. Unfortunately, however, the government merely seemed bent on fully implementing the recommendations of the Presidential Commission on the police, appointed by the Rawlings government in 1996. In his state of the nation address to Parliament, 3 February, 2005, the new President once again promised still more high tech equipment for the police.

The roles of the Gold Coast police in 1830 and the Ghanaian police today have hardly changed. Perhaps, as the main difference, instead of providing physical protection to the colonial Governor and other officials of the Colonial Office, the police now protect a President and Ministers, mostly trained in London, Europe and the United States, who have returned home (perhaps temporarily) to 'lead' the country for a political term; instead of the British Trading Companies the police preserve law and order for foreign investors and Ghana Club 100;[60] and, instead of importing the Rule of Law from the Colonial Office in London, Ghana now imports the Rule of Law from the World Bank, IMF and WTO offices in Washington, DC and Geneva.

Many Ghanaians have expressed deep mistrust of the nation's police force. Surveys taken as far apart as 1974[61] and 2001/2003[62] showed that many still considered it the most corrupt institution in Ghana. Serious confrontations between members of the public and the police have led to riots, street battles, loss of property and even lives. In 2002, a commentator noted that "the burning and seizing of Police Stations and equipment, and killing of police personnel...is gaining currency in the country nowadays."[63]

The police remain under strict political control. The Police Council, a body mostly appointed by the President, supervises the Inspector General of Police (the chief executive and administrator of the Service), appointed by the government of the day. Ministers of State and their deputies, the Speaker of Parliament, judges and other political appointees today may have one or two policemen (sometimes a whole platoon) at their service, paid for out of tax revenues. Meanwhile, wealthy individual citizens buy private security from private security companies, while the poor must try, as best they can, to establish their own systems of private security in the form of land guards or vigilante groups.

Box 2: A Note on "Illegal Security Operatives"

Only the so-called 'illegal security operatives' appear capable of creating new institutional forms to deal with the globalizing forces of post-modem colonialism. Falling outside the purview of formal state statutory regulation, these shadowy institutions may involve chiefs, headmen, earth priests, and other holders of traditional authority, or modern 'opinion leaders', grassroots-level political operatives, and bands of rich and poor, educated and uneducated, young men—all of whom engage in critical but non-public aspects of the security sector. They have survived the constricting forces of colonialism and post-colonial states' modernization programs, not only because of their adaptability, but also because of their strategic, but often hidden, alliances with emerging power centers.

Part of their success appears to lie in their capacity to mobilize and reinvent themselves in multiple ways as necessary to deal with the new and constantly changing technologies of power mobilized by globalizing forces. The processes by which these operatives align themselves with public and private institutions, shifting micro level political and economic relations to maneuver around the law and state power, illustrates their capacity to open up new and fluid opportunities to advance themselves. Typically, they remain quite invisible, undocumented, under-documented, and un- or under-researched. When they finally seem documented and coalesced into observable patterns of alternative institutional ordering, the globalizing forces of postmodern colonialism too often capture and transform them.[64]

The police still appear most brutal when engaged in their traditional functions of protecting the dominant political elite, preserving the regime in power and the resources of the economically-powerful. As they implement that form of the 'rule of law,' they most clearly reveal the historically-shaped institutional continuities.

What has all this to do with police reform?

POLICE REFORM IN GHANA: SOME PRELIMINARY THOUGHTS

There exists today a growing pressure to reform the Ghana Police Service, rather like the rush to reform the Ghana Police Force that began in 1948 and ended up high-teching and militarizing an already brutal force. Today, many call for extending the tentacles of the National Governance Programme (NGP) to the police.

Overwhelmed by the symptoms of the problem, most reform agents call only for changing the individual—often brutal, unfriendly and corrupt—police officer. Virtually no one talks about reforming the institutions—the repetitive patterns of behavior that shape the police's role in today's neo-liberal, postmodern colonial world.

Beginning in the 1980s, the neo-liberal agenda in Africa started with economic reform:[65]

1. Tighten the national budget to service the national debt;
2. Devalue the national currency to sell more exports and attract more foreign tourists;
3. Retrench (assumed excess of) government workers and charge fees for government services;
4. Abolish agricultural subsidies, which the government cannot afford;
5. Sell state owned enterprises to multi-national companies to ensure greater efficiency.

Emboldened by the alleged 'successes' of economic reforms, again prompted by the World Bank, Ghana's government began flirting with institutional reform. But, although to introduce economic liberalism seems easy, its after-effects indeed proved enduring. Governments need to regulate the new economic regimes. The architects of neo-liberalism assumed that they could use the same toolkit to reform governance institutions that they had employed for economic reform.

But reforming institutions of governance seems a different ball-game altogether, perhaps more so in Africa because of its complex history. From the colonial era to date, the police in Africa have combined aspects of the roles of Politician (District Commissioner), Prosecutor, Magistrate, and Policeman. As their chief complaints against the police today, people say they remain too politicized, too powerful, too brutal, and too corrupt. These persist as direct features of the historically shaped role of the police. All stakeholders seem to agree on the need to reform the police, but few agree on how to tackle that reform.

Neo-liberalism seeks to resolve problems like those involved in police reform at very high levels of abstraction, aided by abstract, fluid, and manipulable concepts: 'Human rights', 'public sector reform', 'national institutional renewal', 'public order', 'rule of law' 'governance' and the like. Too often, however, the interpreters of those fluid and manipulable categories ultimately interpret them to exclude innovative institutional reform alternatives.

Box 3: Human Rights vs. Institutional Change

Instead of designing detailed laws to restructure dysfunctional institutions, human rights activists too often call for implementation of 'global human rights standards' and the 'Rule of Law'—leaving those vague concepts' precise interpretation to those responsible for implementing them. Too often, the interpreters—implementing agencies, the police, the courts—assign meanings that, instead of fostering radical change, perpetuate the **status quo.**

Historically, the demand for 'human rights' arose as a cry of the oppressed. In contrast, when law-makers seek to protect those rights, they have the option of exercising state power to require officials to provide effective protection. To do that, however, they must enact and implement laws that prescribe the officials' required behaviors—institutions—in detail. To ensure police officers respect human rights, law-makers must adopt laws that specify what a **police officer must, may, or may not** do; that is, they must impose specified limits on police officers' behaviors. For example:

*'A police officer may not torture arrested or detained persons;'

*'Without authorization of a court, pursuant to procedures specified in Article X, a police officer may not take action to require street traders to leave areas for which city authorities have previously granted them a licence to trade;' or

*'Without authorization of a court, pursuant to procedures specified in Article Y, a police officer may not force a person to desist from using communally owned property.'

Given a law that prescribes precisely what a police officer must, may, or may not do, a person who claims an officer has violated those prescriptions may bring an action to a court for damages, or for an injunction to prevent future violations. The law's detailed prescription leaves the court no discretion: If, based on the facts, a judge decides that the police office violated a detailed prescription specified in the law, that judge shall award damages or impose an injunction.

CONCLUSION: THE NEED FOR LEGISLATION

In sum, this chapter underscores several points:

First, many problems—like those plaguing the Ghanaian police force—seem merely simple issues of institutional dysfunction that need reform. In reality, an in-depth, historical review demonstrates that those institutional problems prove linked to trajectories rooted in intense contestations between the forces of colonialism (past and present) and those of the colonized, and their respective agents, allies and sympathizers.

Second, available evidence reveals that problematic institutions structured in long years of colonial rule, like those of the police, have survived the turbulent half century since Ghanaians won their independence. Those institutional continuities persist, not merely because of inertia, or the series of new governors' seeming lack of capacity to govern. New structures, interests and patterns of resource control have emerged that, coinciding with those of the colonial era, foster the institutions' perpetuation. Thus, this institutional inertia—half-hearted reforms; closure of the imagination to different normative forms of institutional ordering; discouraging and preventing the proliferation of alternatives for institutional design—all serve a purpose: neo-liberal engineering for the maintenance of the status quo.

Not comprehending the fundamental logic of institutional continuity, all across the African continent frustrated persons and groups have attempted to institute institutional reform. Authoritarianism, heady revolutions, assassination of ruling elites—all have occurred in a desperate search for solutions to the persistent complex issue of institutional malaise, but to no avail. Condemnations of neo-colonialism and of the unfair world political and economic order, accompanied by exhortations to make a clean break from them, have proven unsuccessful. Today, high-sounding human rights refrains, human rights and public interest litigation, and templates for magical institutional reform, marketed by consultants of international financial institutions and their local governmental and non-governmental associates, have fared no better.

On a personal note, in search of a more productive solution, I chose to research the police. Established as an essential aspect of the colonial enterprise, the government has perpetuated and expanded the police to protect those presiding over the national political economy in the post-independence era. Effective police reform, it seems to me, must comprise an integral feature of the reform of the full range of inherited political economic institutions—some more dysfunctional than others—which successive Ghanaian governments have repeatedly called on the police to protect.

In reality, the bulk of this chapter's evidence, a summarized version of the findings of many years of doctoral research,[66] broadly describes **the problematic behaviors that comprise the existing Ghanaian police force as an institution.** To alter those behaviors, the many social elements of Ghana's society today have to learn **to work through their government to use its primary tool for effectively making reforms of any kind: the law.**

As a first step, I propose the establishment of a Commission, broadly representative of all the affected societal groups, to conduct the necessary further research and design the detailed legislation required to transform Ghana's police force so that it contributes effectively to national development to fulfil the basic needs of all Ghanaians. Using institutionalist legislative theory as a guide, the Commission should accompany the proposed law with a research report that provides the relevant available country-specific facts, organized logically, to demonstrate that the bill's detailed provisions will likely alter or eliminate the problematic behaviors that comprise the Ghanaian police force today. Structured by legislative theory's problem-solving outline,[67] Box 4 provides an outline of the kinds of evidence, logically organized, which that kind of report should provide. Since a law can only try to resolve problems by changing behaviors, the draft report should focus on formulating possible hypotheses to identify and explain the problematic behaviors which, as this chapter has shown, still characterize the Ghanaian police force as an institution. That would help to ensure that, as its primary task, the proposed law would aim to change those behaviors, laying sound foundations for a police force more likely to serve the basic needs of all Ghanaians.

Box 4: Draft Outline of a Research Report to Justify the Details of Legislation to Transform the Ghanaian Police Force

[**Note**: *To prepare a research report grounded on logic and facts, a drafter must first formulate relevant hypotheses ('educated guesses' based on the drafter's knowledge of the existing situation) about the social problem and the problematic behaviors that comprise it. Then, at each step required by problem-solving's logic, the drafter must gather the relevant evidence to demonstrate that those hypotheses prove consistent with all the available data. (Of course, if an hypothesis appears inconsistent with the available facts, the drafter must reject it, or revise it until it does appear consistent; that constitutes the essential premise for a drafter to claim the bill's detailed provisions—designed to alter or eliminate the causes of the problematic behaviors—rest on facts logic.)*][68]

Introduction: A few sentences summarize the social problem posed by the behaviours of the existing police force, and the proposed solution: the creation of community-based police. The rest of the Introduction informs the reader that the proposed bill, as part of a larger, on-going legislative program to transform other inherited dysfunctional Ghanaian institutions, aims to transform only one: the police force. A final paragraph outlines the report's table of contents, showing the reader how these conform with institutionalist theory's problem-solving logic.

Step I: Provides hypotheses, accompanied by the relevant evidence, that describe the surface appearance of the social problem posed by Ghana's police force today, and the problematic behaviors that comprise it:

i. [*This chapter provides ample evidence as to that social problem's surface appearance; the research report should summarize enough of that evidence to show the necessity of changing the behaviors that comprise it*];

ii. Analyses the evidence as to the existing Ghanaian police force as an institution, and the relevant societal actors and their problematic behaviors. Depending on further analysis of the available evidence, these might include:

(1) police officers—whose behaviors this chapter has described above;

(2) local police chiefs—who instruct police officers as to their duties. Since the chapter does not describe these chiefs' role, this section may require further analysis of available evidence.

(3) the national Inspector General of Police - responsible for supervising national police behaviors; again, an adequate description may require gathering further evidence as to the Inspector General's role in the police force's decision-making process.

(4) elected legislatures - responsible for overseeing how the police implement the existing law; this too may require reviewing further facts.

Step II: Using the ROCCIPI agenda,[69] this step involves formulating hypotheses and providing the available evidence as to the interacting, country-specific non-legal, as well as legal factors which, in the face of existing law, seem to cause each set of problematic behaviours.

i. Consider *separately* each set of actors' problematic behaviors (identified in Step I), since the circumstances in which they live and work likely may influence their behaviors in very different ways.

[*Note: Analysis of the criteria and procedures in the existing law (including departmental regulations) that govern the relevant actors' decision-making, especially those, like the officials, who act as members of the police force as an implementing agency, proves very useful in understanding how the non-legal causal factors may influence their behaviours in the face of the existing law*].

ii. Once formulated, these explanatory hypotheses serve to guide identification of the relevant available facts required to prove those hypotheses consistent with the available evidence.

Step III: Formulate hypotheses as to 'solutions'—the bill's detailed prescriptions

i. Demonstrate that the proposed detailed prescriptions logically seem likely to alter or eliminate the legal and non-legal causes of the existing problematic behaviors, and therefore to induce behaviors to help resolve the social problem.

ii. Consider available evidence as to alternative possible solutions;

a. Decide on the 'best' detailed provisions in terms of their do-ability, given existing physical and human constraints and resources;

b. Demonstrate that those provisions' social and economic benefits outweigh their social and economic costs.

Step IV: Formulate hypotheses as to the kind of feedback mechanism which, incorporated into the proposed bill, will likely ensure that the law-makers learn whether, after they enact a law, that law's detailed provisions do prove effectively implemented and really help to resolve the social problem—that is, make the police as an institution function more effectively to ensure good governance, and contribute to development directed to fulfilling the basic needs of all Ghanaians.

i. Specify criteria and procedures for ensuring that those affected—especially the poor and vulnerable, based on their own experience—can and do provide inputs (facts and ideas) into the evaluation of the law's implementation and its effect in altering police behaviors.

ii. Provide detailed provisions to ensure law-makers take this feedback into account in designing new legislation in the on-going process of improving the behaviors of the police force as an institution.

Notes

1. DAILY GRAPHIC (Accra, Ghana), Feb. 9, 2005, at 1 and 3.
2. *Id.* at 3 *(emphasis added).*
3. Interview with the Honorable Mahama Ayariga, Member of Parliament for Bawku Central, at the Faculty of Law, University of Ghana (Feb. 9, 2005). *See also* 49 PARLIAMENTARY DEBATES, OFFICAL REPORT (THE HANSARD) (Feb. 9, 2005), at 458-461.
4. THE INDEPENDENT NEWSPAPER (Accra, Ghana), Feb. 15, 2005, at 1.
5. DAILY GRAPHIC, Feb. 17, 2005, at 29.
6. Thirty-three of the 126 came from nearby Nima, Mamobi and New Town. For a description of the May 9 Stadium Disaster, *see* ALEX AKURGO & CAMILLUS ABONGO, MAY 9 AT ACCRA STADIUM: A GRIPPING STORY OF A DISASTER THAT TURNED ORDINARY PEOPLE INTO HEROES (Blue Volta Associates, 2001).
7. DOUGLASS C. NORTH, INSTITUTIONS, INSTITUTIONAL CHANGE AND ECONOMIC PERFORMANCE vii (1990).
8. Quoted in Richard B. Kranzdorf, The Military and Police in the Gold Coast/Ghana Through February 1966: A Study of Limited Institutionalization 20 (1973) (Ph. D. dissertation, University of California at Los Angeles)(on file with the Department Of Political Science, UCLA).
9. *Id.* at 63.
10. For details, *see* Raymond A. Atuguba, Institutional Continuities: The Police in the Regulation of Public Order and Alcohol in Ghana (Jun. 2004) (Doctor of Juridical Science dissertation, Harvard Law School).
11. S. K. ANKAMA, POLICE HISTORY: SOME ASPECTS IN ENGLAND AND GHANA 22 (1983). Ankama does not discuss the role of the police during the era of slave raiding and trading. This is probably because slave raiding was a military and not a police function in pre-colonial Ghana.
12. *Id.* at 20-26.
13. John A. Arthur & Otwin Marenin, *British Colonization and the Political Development of the Police in Ghana, West Africa,* in COMPARATIVE CRIMINAL JUSTICE: TRADITIONAL AND NONTRADITIONAL SYSTEMS OF LAW AND CONTROL 165 (Charles B. Fields & Richter H. Moore, Jr, eds. 1996).
14. *Id.* at 166.
15. *See* M. FORTES AND E. E. EVANS –PRITCHARD, AFRICAN POLITICAL SYSTEMS (1958).
16. *See* W.H. GILLESPIE, THE GOLD COAST POLICE: 1844-1938 1 (1955).
17. Criminal code of Gold Coast, 1832 (CAP 32).
18. Arms and Ammunition Ordinance of Gold Coast, 1922 (CAP 253).
19. Public Meetings and Processions Regulations of Gold Coast, 1926 (No. 10 of 1926).

20. BANKOLE A. COLE, POLICING ACROSS THE WORLD: ISSUES FOR THE TWENTY-FIRST CENTURY 100-02 (R. I. Mawby, ed., 1999).
21. *Id.*
22. John A. Arthur & Otwin Marenin, *British Colonization and the Political Development of the Police in Ghana, West Africa,* in COMPARATIVE CRIMINAL JUSTICE: TRADITIONAL AND NONTRADITIONAL SYSTEMS OF LAW AND CONTROL 163, 167-8 (Charles B. Fields & Richter H. Moore, Jr., eds., 1st ed., Waveland Press, 1996).
23. Mike Brogden, *An Act to Colonise the Internal Lands of the Island: Empire and the Origins of the Professional Police,* 15 INT'L J. THE SOCIOLOGY OF L. 179, 205-06 (1987).
24. *Id.* at 202-05.
25. David M. Anderson & David Killingray, *Consent, Coercion and Colonial Control: Policing the Empire, 1830-1940,* in POLICING THE EMPIRE: GOVERNMENT, AUTHORITY AND CONTROL, 1830-1940 1, 6 (David M. Anderson & David Killingray, eds., Manchester Univ. Press, 1991).
26. David Killingray, *Guarding the Extending Frontier: Policing the Gold Coast, 1865-1913,* in *id.*, at 119-20.
27. *Id.*
28. *See* Mathieu Deflem, Law Enforcement in British Colonial Africa: A Comparative Analysis of Imperial Policing in Nyasaland, the Gold Coast, and Kenya, 17 POLICE STUDIES 45 (1994). Also on the World Wide Web at: http://www.cla.sc.edu/socy/faculty/deflem/zcolpol.html (last visited on Oct. 26, 2003).
29. GILLESPIE, *supra* note 16, at 34.
30. *Id.* at 12.
31. *Id.* at 38.
32. S. K. Ankama, The Police and Maintenance of Law and Order in Ghana 163-164 (1967)(Ph D. Dissertation, University of London), quoted in Richard B. Kranzdorf, The Military and Police in the Gold Coast/Ghana Through February 1966: A Study of Limited Institutionalization 20 (1973) (Ph.D. dissertation, University of California, Los Angeles)(on file with the Department Of Political Science, UCLA).
33. EMMANUEL K. AKYEAMPONG, DRINK, POWER, AND CULTURAL CHANGE: A SOCIAL HISTORY OF ALCOHOL IN GHANA, C. 1800 TO RECENT TIMES 52 (Heinemann, 1996).
34. *See* F. M. BOURET, GHANA-THE ROAD TO INDEPENDENCE 1919-57 157ff. (1960), for political context of the riots.
35. Kranzdorf, *supra* note 32, at 173.
36. The legitimacy of this trade has been highly controversial.
37. Susan S. Silbey, Let Them Eat Cake: Globalization, Postmodern Colonialism, and the Possibilities Of Justice, 31 L. & SOC'Y REV. 207 (1997).
38. *See* COLE, *supra* note 20.
39. Avoidance of Discrimination Act, 1957 (No. 38 of 1957).
40. Preventive Detention Act, 1958 (No. 17 of 1958).
41. *Id.* at § 4.

42. As interpreted by the Supreme Court in the case of RE AKOTO [1961] 2 Ghana Law Reports (GLR) 525.
43. Kranzdorf, *supra* note 32, at 253-55.
44. *Id.* at 255-56.
45. *Id.*
46. FRANCIS AGBODEKA, AFRICAN POLITICS AND BRITISH POLICY IN THE GOLD COAST 1868-1900: A STUDY IN FORMS AND FORCE OF PROTEST 62-76 (1971).
47. *Id.* at 196.
48. Reports suggest that in that process, still shrouded in mystery, the military cum police regime that overthrew Nkrumah (and its immediate successor in office, the government of the Progress Party) utilized money from the US Office of Public Safety (OPS) Program for internal security purposes that barely met the OPS program's formal requirements. See the following documents for hints at this. UNITED STATES DEPARTMENT OF STATE, TERMINATION PHASE-OUT STUDY: PUBLIC SAFETY PROJECT GHANA (United States Agency for International Development, Washington D.C., March 1974); UNITED STATES DEPARTMENT OF STATE, GHANA POLICE ASSESSMENT: SUMMARY OF FINDINGS, CONCLUSIONS, RECOMMENDATIONS AND EQUIPMENT SPECIFICATIONS, SEPT. 12-OCT. 23, 1968, reviewed and declassified by John Weiss, OPS, Feb. 24, 1975. In reality, it appears that, under cover of anti-communist rhetoric, US Government assistance strengthened Ghana's ruling class' efforts to bolster their fragile positions and silence dissent.
49. The term 'post-modern colonialism,' which I have borrowed from Susan Silbey, *Let Them Eat Cake: Globalization, Postmodern Colonialism, and the Possibilities of Justice*, 31 L. & SOC'Y REV. 207 (1997), is apt here because it captures the theory of historical continuity which I have endeavored to establish in this chapter, by drawing the linguistic relationship between colonialism and post-modern colonialism.
50. John A. Arthur & Otwin Marenin, *British Colonization and the Political Development of the Police in Ghana, West Africa,* in COMPARATIVE CRIMINAL JUSTICE: TRADITIONAL AND NONTRADITIONAL SYSTEMS OF LAW AND CONTROL 163 (Charles B. Fields and Richter H. Moore, Jr., eds., Waveland Press, 1996).
51. *See* Raymond A. Atuguba, Institutional Continuities: The Police in the Regulation of Public Order and Alcohol in Ghana, ch. 3 (Jun. 2004) (Doctor of Juridical Science dissertation, Harvard Law School) (on file with Harvard Law School).
52. "Rawlings regime" refers to the military rule of Jerry John Rawlings as Head of State between Dec. 31, 1981 and Jan. 6, 1993; "Rawlings government" refers to the democratic constitutional rule of Jerry John Rawlings as President between Jan. 7, 1993 and Jan. 6, 2001.
53. Mathieu Deflem, *Law Enforcement in British Colonial Africa: A Comparative Analysis of Imperial Policing in Nyasaland, the Gold Coast, and Kenya*, 17 POLICE STUDIES 45 (1994). Also available at: http://www.cla.sc.edu/socy/faculty/deflem/zcolpol.html (last visited on Oct. 26, 2003).
54. *See, e.g.,* Issah Iddi Abbas and 10 Others v. ACCRA Metropolitan Assembly and the Attorney-General, Suit No. Misc. 1203/2002, where the Center for Public

Interest Law (CEPIL) contested one such eviction in court. *See also* CEPIL's website http://www.cepil.org for information on the case.

55. Others have called this the theory of institutional reproduction. *See* ROBERT B. SEIDMAN, STATE, LAW AND DEVELOPMENT, *passim* (St. Martin, 1978).
56. *See* COLE, *supra* note 20, at 96.
57. *Id.* at 477-78.
58. *Id.* at 466.
59. *E.g.,* these NGOs include Africa Security Dialogue and Research, Center for Democratic Development, and the Legal Resources Centre.
60. Ghana Club 100 is the Ghanaian equivalent of the Fortune 500—the 500 leading global corporations.
61. FINAL REPORT OF THE COMMISSION OF INQUIRY INTO BRIBERY AND CORRUPTION, 1974, popularly called the 'Anin Report on Corruption.'
62. Ghana: Police-Community Relations in an Emerging Democracy (CDD-Ghana Research Paper 2003-12)(Aug. 2003).
63. J.B. POKOO-AIKINS, THE POLICE IN GHANA 1939-1999 10 (2002).
64. *See* Atuguba, *supra* note 51.
65. DYING FOR GROWTH, GLOBAL INEQUITY AND THE HEALTH OF THE POOR, *passim*, esp. ch. 5 (Jim Yong Kim, et al., *eds*., Common Courage Press, 2000).
66. *See* Atuguba, *supra* note 51.
67. *See* ch. 2 of this volume, esp. pp. 31-41.
68. *See* ch. 2 in this volume for an explanation of institutionalist legislative theory's underlying premises. For more detailed analysis, *see* DRAFTERS' MANUAL, at ch. 4 (esp. 118-122) & ch. 5.
69. *See* ch. 2 of this volume; *see also* DRAFTERS' MANUAL, chs. 4 & 5.

Chapter 4

Implementing Environmental Policies Through Legislation in Mozambique

by Teodosio Uate[1]

On August 22, 2003, LIVANINGO, a Mozambican non-governmental environmental organization, complained to the President of the Assembly of the Republic[2] that—despite repeated requests—the Ministry of Natural Resources had not sent the assessments made by the relevant technical agency (UTIP)[3] concerning the probable environmental impact of constructing a proposed dam at Mpanda Ncua on the Zambezi River.[4] Required by the Environment Law (Law 20/97)[5], those assessments should have enabled LIVANINGO and other concerned members of civil society to determine the project's probable impact on public interest issues the Ministry might have overlooked,[6] including population displacement,[7] compensation for the displaced people,[8] job creation,[9] and the expected benefits from the dam-generated electrical energy.[10] In response,[11] the technical agency had claimed that the law had not settled the question of the medium for the transmission of data;[12] and that its wording did not impose duties on project sponsors.[13] A year later, LIVANINGO claimed that, only as a result of "a strong public pressure and denunciation,"[14] the technical agency, UTIP, had finally begun a dialogue with the affected rural populations.[15] Potential financiers apparently decided not to commit their funds until after the government had undertaken additional impact assessment studies.[16] Yet UTIP still continued to deny LIVANINGO full access to its reports.[17]

INTRODUCTION

The Ministry of Natural Resources' refusal to provide information to LIVANINGO, a non-government organization, as to the proposed Mpanda Ncua Dam's probable social and environmental impact denied the public the facts they needed to assess the project's likely effect on their lives. Despite Mozambique's constitutional guarantees of freedom of information, the Ministry's technical agency officials referred to the law's vaguely-drafted provisions to justify their refusal to release the environment-related information LIVANINGO had requested. This illustrates the way drafting legislation in vague 'rights' language—rather than specifying detailed criteria and procedures—may endanger a law's effective implementation.

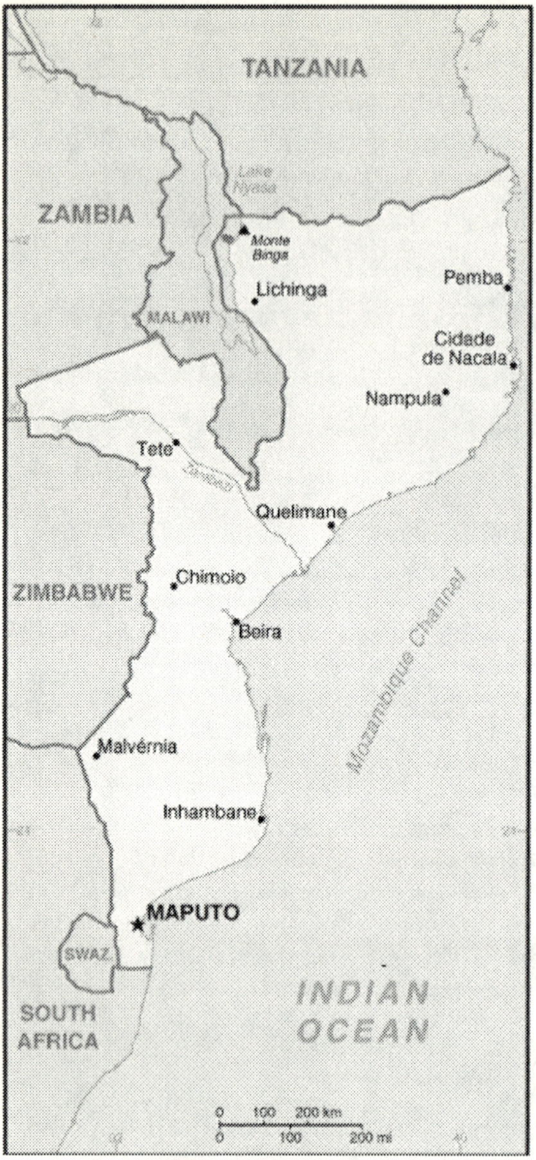

Mozambique

It may help to review the LIVANINGO case in the larger Mozambican context. The Mozambican liberation movement won political independence from Portugal in 1975. Fearing that Mozambique's freedom would spur the South African liberation fighters to greater efforts to topple their regime, South Africa's then-apartheid rulers financed a counter-revolutionary army. The devastation of the resulting decades-long civil war inevitably had detrimental consequences for Mozambique's environment. After South Africa's African National Congress won the 1994 elections, the warring Mozambican parties negotiated a peaceful settlement. After almost two years of a behind-the-scenes drafting process, the new Cabinet proposed and the Parliament enacted the Environmental Law of 1997. Nevertheless, the responsible authorities apparently refused to comply with the law's stated aim of ensuring publication of studies as to the likely social impact of the Ncua Dam project on the environment.

Analysis of the prolonged drafting process that preceded enactment of the 1997 Environmental Law reveals how inherited drafting institutions may influence drafters to shape legislation in ways that actually thwart efforts to foster transparency, accountability and participation—all the features that today most authors agree comprise essential characteristics of good governance.

This chapter provides detailed evidence as to the factors that contributed to the drafters' performance during a two year process in which they drafted and redrafted three versions of the environmental bill. They completed the first by November 27, 1995, the second by December 11, 1995, and the third by February 1996. Then the Cabinet submitted the version to Parliament. In turn,—without making any significant changes—the Parliament enacted that version into the law that went into force on December 7, 1997, as the Environment Law (Law 20/97).[18]

Cabinet's initial policy document explicitly aimed to:

- ensure the Cabinet played a central role in coordinating the responsible environmental agencies' implementation of its environmental policies;
- incorporate a rights-based approach to induce public participation in promoting environmental values; and
- define the rules for the design of future administrative regulations to foster the national environment's sustainable development.

This chapter first describes the Mozambique Cabinet's policies which initiated the new law's enactment; second, summarizes the drafters' acceptance of the notion that they should adapt into the Mozambican bill the 'universal principles' found in other countries' legislation and international model laws; and, third, focuses on the way, as the drafters drafted and redrafted the bill, they sought to ensure its provisions conformed with the three criteria specified by Cabinet.

A detailed scrutiny of the available evidence reveals the factors that influenced the drafters as they worked over the environmental bill's three drafts. All of them had received training in Western European drafting traditions. The existing drafting institutions did not require them to ground their bill's provisions on Mozambican evidence. Nor did any of them have a theory to guide them in examining the available evidence as to the Mozambican circumstances in a way likely to ensure effective implementation of the government's declared policies. Nothing in the Mozambican drafting process required them to consider inputs of facts or ideas from the public, in particular from the poor and vulnerable, as to the nature and causes of environmental degradation's impact on their lives. Instead, as enacted, the 1997 Environmental Law seems mainly to reflect, not an in-depth analysis of Mozambique's environmental problems and the behaviors[19] that contributed to them, but the (implicit) values and concerns of the senior officials in charge of the drafting process.

GOVERNMENTAL ENVIRONMENTAL POLICIES AND THE ADOPTION OF THE ENVIRONMENTAL LAW

In 1995, the Mozambican Council of Ministers (the Cabinet) published a document stating governmental policies in the environmental field.[20] Subsequently, the Ministry for the Coordination of Environmental Action (MICOA) reprinted an edited version of that policy document under the title "Programa Nacional de Gestão Ambiental"[21] also known by its acronym PNGA. The PNGA emphasized that inadequate integration of environmental policies threatened the country's sustainable development prospects.[22] It cited two reasons for the inadequacy of existing environmental policies. First, environmental issues cut across several development fields, social, economic and cultural, each the responsibility of different ministries. The Cabinet lacked an effective mechanism for coordinating Cabinet members' or their subordinates' environment-related decisions. On the one hand, created in 1995, MICOA[23] experienced difficulties in supervising activities of other ministries' that affected the environment, especially in the area of natural resource use. On the other hand, lower-level officials in remote areas throughout the country did not have sufficient expertise to assess specific development projects' probable environmental impact. Second, to overcome the environmental threats posed by some development projects required, not apathy, but active public participation. Yet few Mozambicans in government or civil society understood the potential dangers to the environment, or what practical measures might help to avoid them. Nevertheless, the PNGA committed Cabinet, using unspecified mechanisms, but explicitly including public participation, to solving the multiplicity of environmental problems emerging in Mozambique:

> Therefore, the Government will create favorable conditions [for the sustainability of the management of the environment] by relying on the knowledge evidenced in the communities' patterns of use of natural resources, traditional forms of management and communities' lifestyles. In parallel, the Government will also seek to encourage and reinforce the communities' capacity to know and apply general principles and rules on the management of natural resources that guide society as a whole, by delegating to them political and administrative powers as well as by improving cooperation with formal and informal structures.[24]

Recognizing that law[25] can play an instrumental role in the development process, the PNGA declared, "the sustainability of the Country's socio-economic development presupposes the adoption of a clear and adequate legal environmental framework."[26] It pointed out,

> [A] compilation has been made of legislation related to the management of natural resources and the environment which, in general, has identified some gaps, such as, for example, the lack of a general law about the protected areas. However, this work does not enable a detailed evaluation of the existing problems. Therefore, there is no in-depth analysis of all legislation that exists to identify gaps, overlaps and/or the lack of specific regulations, so that it could serve as a basis for a global review on environmental aspects.[27]

The PNGA reported that MICOA drafters[28] had already begun to draft several new laws to foster sustainable national development, and enhance governmental capacity to implement the new legislation's intended solutions. These included an environmental bill for submission to the National Assembly, and new regulations on previously neglected environmental issues like disposal of hazardous substances, and control of air, water and soil qualities.

The PNGA explicitly viewed the proposed environmental bill as a catalyst for further legislative developments in the environmental field:

> In the Country there are several laws and sectoral regulations which, directly or indirectly, deal with the complex environmental question. ... In this context, it is necessary and urgent to adopt a framework environmental law that addresses the environmental aspects as a whole, and serves as an impetus for the formulation and application of specific regulations, such as: the environmental impact assessment regulation, hazardous substances regulation, industrial development regulation.[29]

The PNGA did not specify guidelines as to how the Cabinet should promote legislative solutions, but it did underscore the environmental bill's importance by including it among proposed 'immediate activities'. In sum, the PNGA posed a legislative challenge. It regarded the adoption of an environmental bill as the centerpiece of legislative efforts aimed at solving a complex problem, vaguely expressed as 'management of the environment' in Mozambique. The PNGA did not offer any definition for the expression 'management of the environment'. Implicitly, the PNGA provided three possible criteria for assessing the bill's adequacy. First, the bill should guide Cabinet in building governmental capacity to address environmental problems. Second, it should dignify the role of the community in finding solutions to environmental problems. Third, it should provide a framework to facilitate further legislative reforms.

MICOA's drafters' role in writing the environmental bill

Drafters at the Ministry for the Coordination of Environmental Action (MICOA) undertook to write the environmental draft bill. At an early stage, foreign consultants worked with them on that project.[30] The drafters reviewed the environmental legislation from several countries, including Portugal, Brasil,

Canada, and Sao Tome and Principe, and obtained relevant model laws from the United Nations Environmental Program (UNEP) and the European Union. After drafting their first version of the bill, the drafters raised several questions in what they termed their 'research report,' entitled "Possible Questions on the Environmental Law".[31] Assuming that the foreign laws and model rules expressed universal principles on how governments should manage environmental issues, MICOA's drafters sought to incorporate those principles in their draft. At the same time, they aimed to design provisions likely to ensure that, in the Mozambican context, the bill would prove effectively implemented.[32]

THE 1997 ENVIRONMENTAL LAW'S 'RIGHTS' APPROACH

The Environmental bill's drafters made little effort to examine the nature and causes of the problematic behaviors that, in Mozambique's unique circumstances, seemed to threaten the environment needed to attain sustainable development. Instead they adopted hard core assumptions[33] that underpinned their tendencies both to copy foreign legislation, and to over-rely on doctrine—not country-specific realities—to justify or reject specific provisions proposed for their draft bill.

This section examines the consequences of these tendencies as revealed throughout the debates over the bill's three drafts. It focuses on an assessment of the three drafts under headings suggested by PNGA's (implicit) specification of three criteria for a good legislative solution.[34] These criteria acquire special relevance because they draw attention to some of the underpinnings inherent in institutionalist legislative drafting theory.[35] The section first focuses on the drafters' provisions aimed at shaping the role of governmental agencies in implementing the bill; secondly, delves into the rights-centered approach the drafters used to formulate rules to induce public participation in promoting environmental values; and, third, discusses the drafters' solution to the problem of defining the rules for future legislative developments in the environmental field. It concludes that, in all three respects, the drafters' final bill on its face seemed likely to prove ineffectively implemented.

Coordinating and implementing environmental policies

To overcome the problem of Cabinet's past ineffectiveness in coordinating environmental policies, the drafters proposed two sets of provisions, one addressed to the Cabinet's role, the other on local governments' responsibilities. This section reviews the process by which the drafters evolved both sets of provisions.

In the first and second versions of the bill, the drafters assigned the implementation and supervisory roles over the Cabinet-approved environmental policies to MICOA. Either they listed the substantive duties MICOA ought to discharge, or subsumed that overall responsibility under the provisions of the Presidential Decree Nº 6/95 that created MICOA. In those first versions, they proposed that Cabinet create a National Council for Sustainable Development

(CONDES), a kind of inner-Cabinet unit through which ministers could make joint decisions concerning the management of the environment. Presided over by the Minister for Environmental Coordination, CONDES would include ministers from other portfolios like Agriculture, Fisheries, Mineral Resources, Trade, and Tourism. It would establish channels through which the ministers could undertake joint actions to guarantee sustainable use of environmental components in their respective areas of responsibility: river basins, forests and arable regions, coastal lands, wetlands and other ecologically fragile zones.

In the bill's final version, the drafters changed the implementing provisions in two significant respects. First, the bill no longer referred either to the Ministry for Environmental Coordination (MICOA), or to the portfolio Minister as the Head of the prospective National Council for Sustainable Development (CONDES). Instead, it vested the implementation duty on the Cabinet as a whole, and mandated Cabinet to establish CONDES' composition by decree. Second, the bill eliminated CONDES' responsibility for setting up inter-ministerial channels to promote more effective environmental management. reducing its role to that of Cabinet advisor. Although the drafters endowed CONDES with substantive duties that partially overlapped with those of MICOA under Presidential Decree 6/95,[36] they made no provisions as to how MICOA and CONDES would coordinate their initiatives on those matters.

In the bill's third version, the drafters incorporated a provision under which, at the local government level (ie: urban and rural municipalities), specific 'services' would implement the bill. Written in the passive form, the bill failed to specify which governmental entity—national or local—had the authority to create those services. The existing Local Government Law apparently empowered the Local Councils to introduce them,[37] but the proposed environment bill now appeared to endow the Cabinet, as the ultimate implementing and supervisory body, with the same power.

From the outset, the drafters apparently viewed MICOA as a single governmental agent rather than as a collective body,[38] so they never addressed rules to the several different sets of officials in MICOA.[39] In short, instead of clarifying the implementing procedures, the bill's final version introduced greater ambiguity. By assigning to Cabinet the responsibility for implementing the law,[40] they made more problematic (i) the identification of the specific governmental agent(s) who should implement the bill's provisions, and (ii) left unspecified the criteria and procedures those agents should use to ensure compliance.

The bill's three versions reflected the drafters' difficulties in devising a legislative solution likely to coordinate the activities of the three implementing agencies—Cabinet, CONDES, and Local Councils. In the end, some of the bill's provisions required more than one implementing agency to perform the same substantive duty. Instead of resolving environmental problems, the drafters' final 'solution' seemed likely to contribute to further fragmentation of authority.[41] Since an implementing agency may justify non-performance by claiming that other agencies bear the responsibility, the drafters' final bill seemed likely to aggravate the risk that no agency would assume responsibility for implementing its provisions, leaving unresolved Mozambique's increasingly serious environmental problems.

Whatever arguments the drafters may have considered in their verbal debates, no evidence exists that they provided a written report either to the Cabinet or to the legislature as to the facts they considered, or the logic they employed in designing the bill's implementation provisions. Apparently, they offered neither the Cabinet members nor the legislators any objective grounds on which to assess whether those provisions would likely help overcome the ineffective implementation cited by the PNGA as one of three central problems which the new environmental law should aim to resolve.

Inducing public participation for the promotion of environment friendly behaviors[42]

To promote conscious environment-friendly behaviors, the bill drafters apparently sought to adopt a rights-based approach by formulating a series of provisions that entitled the citizens to three rights: the right to environmental education, the right sue to protect environmental rights, and the right to seek information. The drafters did not, however, clarify whose and what behaviors must change to ensure that citizens would enjoy those rights.

In their first version of the environment bill, the drafters proposed that, subject to any citizen's request, MICOA would implement educational programs to inform the public about their environmental rights and duties, and available techniques and activities for protecting the environment.[43] In the second and third versions, the drafters changed MICOA's role from one of providing environmental education to one of creating the necessary arrangements to promote it.[44] Nowhere in any of the bill's versions did the drafters propose any standards requiring the environmental educational programs to satisfy the stated goals of promoting both public awareness and environment friendly behavior.

For two reasons, the drafters' legislative provisions for encouraging increased environmental education seem insufficient: They overlook the government's weak capacity, and relevant data that reveals past and current policy implementation difficulties.

The drafters apparently assumed[45] that the Mozambican Cabinet or its subordinate entities enjoyed the expertise[46] required to create an environmentally-friendly educational program.[47] On that assumption, they initially aimed to channel the Cabinet's 'behavior' towards administering the available expertise more effectively. Their first draft required the Cabinet to make that expertise directly available to the public through educational programs. The bill's two subsequent versions —presumably written after MICOA's drafters realized that neither the Cabinet nor other agencies had the necessary expertise—required the Cabinet to create the conditions so that competent third parties could offer environmental education programs.

As they worked over the bill, the drafters realized that both governmental action and citizens' participation in promoting environmental policies would ultimately depend, as a pre-requisite, on developing increased environment-friendly competency. Their report[48] stated that the Cabinet and the United Nations Environmental Program (UNEP) had already sponsored competency-enhancing programs tailor-made to specific audiences: judges (including those from the Supreme Court), the general public, governmental agents, and the Law School at Eduardo Mondlane University. Conceivably, the formulation and implementation of these programs yielded valuable empirical data on governmental departments' performance. The drafters, however, seem never to have thought of those programs and their associated implementing behavior as amenable to regulation through the law-making process.[49] They had yet to realize—and bring to bear into the bill-drafting process—the fact that non-legal factors inevitably influence the behaviors of a law's addressee. Institutionalist legislative theory suggests several categories of non-legal factors which might hinder a law's addressee from behaving as prescribed.[50] Had they adequately explored those categories to identify the causes of the responsible agency officials' failure to implement existing environmental rules, the drafters might have included in their final bill provisions likely to alter or eliminate those non-legal causal factors—in particular, the responsible officials' lack of expertise—so that they would more likely introduce the kinds of environmentally-friendly educational programs the new law prescribed.

The bill should have contained provisions to guide the Cabinet in introducing measures to ensure that CONDES and other designated responsible agencies employed officials adequately trained to introduce the new law's environmental-education provisions. However, the drafters did not understand the importance of analyzing the causes of past or on-going environmental education policy initiatives' failures as a logical basis on which to design and justify their bill's detailed provisions. As a result, those provisions did not specify any program to equip the relevant government officials with the necessary capacity to formulate and implement appropriate environmental educational programs. Again, the drafters failed to translate the PNGA's potentially positive policy solutions into legally binding provisions that would contribute to channeling governmental officials' behaviors in ways likely to foster effective public participation in an effective environmental education program.

Fortunately, the story did not end there. In 2002, five years after the 1997 Environment Law's enactment, the Ministry of Education, on an experimental basis, introduced environmental subjects into one primary school's[51] curriculum. Drawing on the lessons from this experimental initiative, the Education Ministry gradually might introduce those subjects in primary schools throughout the country.[52] This policy initiative apparently did not result from a specific provision in the 1997 Environmental Law or a subsequent regulation designed to implement that law. Cabinet may have contributed to that educational initiative, perhaps by instructing a subordinate educational research unit, the

Instituto Nacional de Desenvolvimento da Educação (the Education Development Institute) to introduce environmental subjects into primary education. Even in the absence of a legal norm prescribed by the Environmental Law, if the initiative succeeds in promoting school pupils' environment-friendly behavior, it may contribute to a form of social transformation. Nevertheless, that social transformaton will take place, not as a result of a conscious law-driven Cabinet action, but by chance.[53]

Reliance on chance to promote policy change or social transformation, however, does not conform with a pre-requisite of law-making: That formally-enacted legal norms should serve to promote predictability, a principal tenet of good governance and the Rule of Law.[54]

The right to sue to protect environmental rights

The drafters stipulated a provision that would entitle any individual to sue to protect her rights recognized under the bill.[55] An additional provision prescribed that the 'administrative injunction ['embargo administrativo'] or any other adequate procedural means' may lead to an immediate suspension of the activity that appears to violates the individual complainant's right to 'an ecologically balanced environment.'[56]

The above provisions seemed to reaffirm an individual's constitutional right[57] to enforce her rights in the environmental field.[58] Yet the rule contained in Article 21 (Third Version) stipulates the possibility of alternative procedural means, thus posing a problem of interpretation and implementation. On the one hand, the expression 'administrative injunction' seems to imply that governmental departments[59] could play the primary role in receiving a complaint and eventually decreeing the remedy. On the other hand, the expression 'other adequate procedural means' seems to suggest that the courts would retain jurisdiction. Indeed, Article 20 (Third Version) specifically vested the judicial courts with first jurisdiction to receive complaints on environmental issues.[60]

In sum, in trying to strengthen the protection of citizens' environmental rights by endowing administrative authorities with powers to settle disputes, the drafters left undecided the respective roles of the courts and administrative authorities. In writing provisions about the competent forum to enforce citizens' environmental rights, the drafters did not seek precision.[61] Further, they seemed to ignore the fact that, in today's Mozambique, the judicial system has failed to deliver timely justice.[62]

The right to seek information

The drafters proposed a right for anyone to seek information from the relevant government departments relating to the implementation of either (i) the provisions of the proposed environmental bill, or (ii) any other environment-impacting legislation.[63] In their first version, the drafters adopted rules that defined the kind of government-controlled data that should fall under that right, prescribed the deadline for a governmental department to provide the information, and obliged the applicant to pay the costs for data reproduction. In the subsequent versions, however, the drafters refrained from stipulating any rules that would help to determine the type of information for which a person might ask, from which entity a person should request that information, or the deadline for compliance.

In the bill's first version, the provision on the right to information would allow anyone to access data containing evidence directly or indirectly related to governmental action in the environmental field. That provision probably reflected a background value assumed as universally shared,[64] that disclosure of government-held information constitutes a condition for a democratic state.[65] By incorporating the provision in the bill, the drafters aimed to promote that value in the environmental field. Furthermore, greater public access to governmental information would serve to enhance transparency in the way government officials conduct state business.[66]

By contrast, in the bill's second and third versions, the drafters obfuscated the possibilities for anyone to access government-held records on environmental issues. They stipulated a right for anyone to seek "information related to the management of the environment".[67] Their introduction of the phrase, 'management of the environment'[68], however, left ambiguous the question of what data should count as relevant information. The drafters left unanswered the identity of the government agency which must supply that information. At the same time, they imposed the condition that the supply of information should take place without prejudice to the rights of interested third parties, but failed to establish any criteria as to how a decision-maker (a governmental department or a court) should balance possible competing claims between the applicant and third parties for or against the release of information.

In contemplating a right to access environment-related information, the drafters had reaffirmed an entitlement provided for both in the Constitution[69] and in ordinary legislation.[70] As formulated in the bill's first version, the provision had the merit of specifying the kind of information that governmental entities must provide upon anyone's request. The provision would have allowed the public to access information that governmental departments might otherwise withhold.[71] Yet, in the subsequent versions, the drafters left undefined the responsible governmental departments' role in satisfying the public's quest for environment-related information. Therefore, public access to government-controlled environment-related records could remain severely limited in Mozambique. That possibility proved all too real in the LAVININGO case—and became even more likely after the passage of a new law in 2001.[72]

Conclusion

By stipulating environmental rights for the Mozambican public, the drafters simply (mistakenly) believed that Mozambique's legal system offered an adequate framework for their realization. Apparently, they assumed, implicitly, that Mozambique's current law enforcement practices provided the requisite conditions for a successful implementation of the rights for which the bill provided.[73] The drafters seem never to have considered the possibility of formulating specific criteria and procedures to guide both the rights' beneficiaries and the responsible government agencies in implementing those provisions. In keeping with prevailing values,[74] the drafters accepted as normal the bill's vague, abstract and general declarations of Mozambicans' environmental rights. Far better in a bill to prescribe what social actors must (or must not) do—that is, their specific behaviors—to ensure they protect a particular set of persons' specified access or opportunities; for example, to require educators to prepare and provide environmental information in schools; to require government officials to release specified categories of environment-related documents; etc. Worldwide experience underscores the fact that drafting in terms of 'rights' does not ensure effective implementation of the measures required to realize the rights specified.[75]

THE DRAFTERS' APPROACH TO DEVELOPING AN ENVIRONMENTAL LEGISLATIVE PROGRAM

In the 1997 Environmental Act, the drafters incorporated a two-pronged approach to the development of future legislative environmental programs. First, they stipulated a set of principles that should permeate environmental policies.[76] Presumably, future governmental draft bills, reflecting those principles, would contribute to implementing those environmental policies.[77] In that sense, by adopting several environmental principles, the drafters indirectly provided guidance as to the values that future legislation ought to espouse.

Second, more directly, the drafters included two provisions that required the Cabinet to take further specific legislative initiatives. One provision mandated the Cabinet to adopt regulations to implement the bill.[78] The bill's first and second versions set deadlines by which, in specified cases, the Cabinet should comply,[79] but, unfortunately, the bill's final version did not.

Another provision of the bill directed the Cabinet to take steps designed to adjust existing environmental legislation to the rules contained in the new bill.[80] The bill's first and second versions required the Cabinet to accomplish that law reform within two years after the law's enactment.[81] Again, the bill's final version excluded that deadline.

None of bill's three versions specified which existing legislation required change. The law reform provision apparently simply assumed that, when the new bill came into force, some existing laws would no longer apply in their present form.[82] The provision amounted to an implicit abrogation—totally or partially—of non-specified environmental legislation. By requiring partial repeal of existing laws, the provision implied that, in some respects, a prior law may remain valid side by side with the new bill once enacted into law. Pending the projected law reform, the potential co-existence of both laws may render their implementation difficult.[83] The drafters would have achieved greater precision by specifying the criteria for changing existing laws in the bill, and listing the laws affected in an appendix.[84]

In the bill's final version, the specific provisions on future legislative developments attest to the drafters' drift towards granting the Cabinet unfettered discretion in two respects. First, the drafters' failure to specify criteria for identifying relevant environmental legislation implicitly authorized the Cabinet to undertake reform of virtually any law. In part, the bill's open-ended definition of 'environmental components' included matters as disparate as the air, soil, wildlife "and all the social, economic and health conditions that affect the [local] communities."[85] Local communities lead their lives under a multitude of laws that may impact on one or more of those aspects; under the suggested definition of 'environmental components', any law would potentially qualify as 'environmental legislation'.

Second, as set out in the earlier versions of the bill, the deadline requirement for law reform completion could have served as a reminder that the Assembly of the Republic and the public expected the Cabinet to accomplish some legislative initiatives by a certain deadline. That would have enabled them to hold Cabinet to account. Omission of the deadline requirement permitted Cabinet to delay indefinitely undertaking the necessary law reforms. By withdrawing that requirement, the drafters effectively forestalled one possibility of ensuring Cabinet's democratically responsible behavior.[86] In general, the drafters failed to promote Cabinet's public accountability[87] through the final draft.[88]

The drafters seemed to assume that, subject to changes, the environmental bill's first version incorporated the necessary general principles and norms to promote environmental policies. Rewriting the bill's provisions to render them applicable in Mozambique became the drafters' challenge.[89] In this context, 'adaptation of the bill's provisions' to attain this goal meant involving the drafters in internal debates within MICOA and talking with foreign consultants.[90]

In one respect, the drafters' efforts towards 'adaptation' implied a recognition that, if enacted into law in its original form, the bill might prove inconsistent with prior Mozambican legislation. To identify those potential inconsistencies required legislative research into existing legal norms that specified the substantive areas over which the proposed bill would introduce new prescriptions. Informed by the legislative research findings, the rewriting of the bill would serve to promote an overall consistency in Mozambique's relevant laws. However, the drafters eschewed legal research into Mozambique's relevant laws.[91]

Ultimately, the drafters' final draft missed the opportunity to translate positive policies—old[92] or new[93]– into implementable provisions. Written in convoluted 'legalistic' language, some of the final bill's provisions seemed likely to test the courts' ability to interpret the law's legislative purposes.[94] By relying on the courts as the arbiters of legislative purposes, furthermore, the drafters indirectly contributed to the legislature's abdication from one of its central missions: communication of the law.[95] In sum, the consequences of the drafters' decision to 'adapt' pre-existing environmental principles suggest that—notwithstanding arguments to the contrary[96]— legal transplants may foster less-than efficient results.

EXPLAINING DRAFTERS' FAILURE TO DRAFT AN EFFECTIVELY IMPLEMENTED LAW

Why did Mozambique's drafters write what, both on its face and in practice, seems such a potentially dysfunctional environmental bill? This section adopts a 'process tracing' methodology[97] to discover the underlying causes[98] of their drafting performance. It focuses primarily on two causal factors: the drafters' limited capacity and the authoritarianism of the decision-makers in the ministerial hierarchy. A drafter may serve as an official in a specific ministry's legal department,[99] or come from a broad category of professionals known as 'jurists' or 'legal advisors'.[100] Internal ministerial regulations effectively lump bill drafting activities with others that legal advisors traditionally perform. Under those regulations, legal advisors must hold a law degree.[101] That tends to strengthen a widely-held view that the legal advisors' court-centered skills[102] should also prove useful for legislative drafting.[103]

The drafters' limited capacity

The typical lawyers' legal background, however, ultimately may lead to conflicts with some of the tasks required to design effectively implementable bills.[104] Unaware of that danger, and immersed in the routines that define their overall advisory roles, drafters may find it difficult to explore the possibility of employing new theories, methods, and even techniques that might improve their bill drafting capacity.[105]

Two Mozambican experiences illustrate the way traditionally-trained drafters may ignore—and even, unconsciously, reject—the potential advantages of using legislative theory to translate government policy into the essential detailed provisions of an effectively implemented bill. In both instances, the two senior drafters had participated, in 1996, in a two week legislative drafting workshop in Maputo. There, they actually participated in a group process of using institutionalist legislative drafting theory (along with its associated methodology and techniques) to draft bills designed to help resolve some of the social problems confronting post-civil war Mozambique. To justify their bills' details, they had drafted research reports which demonstrated logically that grounding the bills' detailed provisions on the relevant Mozambican facts would enhance the likelihood that the bills would prove effectively implemented and contribute to attainment of the desired social impact. Yet, despite that hands-on learning experience, neither of these two senior drafters employed that theory as a guide to their subsequent work, one in drafting internal regulations for the Eduardo Mondelane University Law Faculty,[106] the other in reviewing a bill that proposed land reform for all of Mozambique. Those two cases merely serve to underscore the reality—increasingly recognized as the result of experiences in countries throughout the world [107]—that equipping individual drafters, working alone, in the use of legislative theory as a guide remains insufficient. Instead, a program to strengthen a nation's drafting capacity requires institutionalization of an on-going, self-sustainable learning process.[108] That program could engage a country's drafters, working together in teams, in learning to use legislative theory, methodology and techniques in the process of gathering relevant information about their own country's unique relevant circumstances, and drafting, editing and re-editing specific bills to help resolve their own country's social problems.[109]

Senior decision-makers' authoritarianism

Early in the process of preparing the 1997 Environment bill, the drafters met with foreign consultants.[110] Apparently, they internalized the ideas generated by these contacts as the bill's original underlying principles. Interaction with foreign consultants involved an effort aimed at creating an environmental bill partly based on a United Nations Environmental Program (UNEP)'s sponsored model law.[111] At some stage, the drafters genuinely adopted as their own the values on which the bill rested. Confident in their new understanding, the drafters came to see their role as consisting of finding a bill's formulation that suited the Mozambican context.

Yet the drafters' initial formulation of the proposed law did not resonate well with their superiors, the governmental decision-makers. Those decision-makers, for example, seemed to view the provision on the right to information as a threat to their job security.[112] As written, the provision implied that governmental departments would have the legal duty to release government-held records. That might expose the decision-makers' behavior to public scrutiny, a prospect at which they rather frowned.[113] This led to a divergence of perspectives: On the one hand, the drafters implicitly stood by their first version of the bill that incorporated the disclosure principle; they apparently believed the bill would help to promote specific standards for governmental behavior. On the other hand, the senior administrative decision-makers preferred a more ambiguous formulation that would not require specific governmental compliance. From their perspective, the bill needed only to emphasize the symbolic value[114] of expressing the country's adherence to environmental principles commonly shared the world over.

Aware of the administrative decision-makers' objections to the bill's initial formulation of the right to information, the drafters re-wrote the provision to leave undefined the governmental departments' role in disclosing environment-related records. The bill's subsequent versions seemed to testify to a bill-drafting practice that granted the senior decision-makers' unchallenged authority: the adoption of an ends-means methodology that justifies the formulation of a policy goal in accord with the values held by those in power, not grounded on reason informed by experience.[115]

The administrative decision-makers restricted the bill's objectives to creating a symbolic acceptance of environment-friendly policies. The drafters ultimately agreed to confine their role to perfecting the means (the draft bill) of realizing those policies in a legal form. In doing so, they, as well as the administrators, apparently disregarded the widespread evidence in Mozambique and elsewhere that underscored that public access to government information proves essential to effective public participation in a nation's program to protect the environment. Stated bluntly, the bill's slide into ambiguity seems explained by the governmental executives' efforts to retain unfettered power.[116]

Subsequent Cabinet submission of the environment bill to the National Assembly and its members' enactment of that bill into law[117] apparently endorsed this preference for discretion at the top. Under the law, the National Council for Sustainable Development (CONDES) advises the Cabinet on environmental policies *(see* above discussion in section II.B). By a subsequent Cabinet decree,[118] the Cabinet must approve CONDES' internal regulation, and the Prime Minister presides over CONDES.[119] Like the law itself, the decree failed to specify criteria and procedures through which CONDES should perform its substantive duties. In these circumstances, the unfettered power to steer CONDES' activities apparently remained with the Prime Minister.

CONCLUSIONS

The drafters of the 1997 Environmental Law did succeed in introducing general principles with the purported aim of governing environmental policies. Early in the drafting process they drafted provisions in the bill's first version that articulated some underlying democratic values. These included programs to educate the general public as to the importance of protecting the environment, greater public accessibility to governmental records concerning environmental issues, and clear specification of the relationship between Cabinet and agencies responsible for implementing environmental protection measures.

A combination of several institutionalized factors influenced the drafters to formulate increasingly ambiguous provisions, particularly in the bill's third version. These factors included: the drafters' own training and perspectives on the task at hand, and the senior ministry decision-makers' authoritarian influence.[120] As a result, for the most part, the drafters failed to devise clear and precise rules that are likely to ensure implementation of measures to change the intended addressees' behaviors, whether those of the citizens (primary role occupants) or those of governmental departments (with the Cabinet at the helm).

The drafters' predicament might possibly find solution through the adoption of bill-making norms that could serve as a guide in researching and writing a particular bill. The norms should especially stipulate the criteria and procedures through which drafters (and legislators) should justify draft bills in light of inputs obtained from the wider public. Mozambique still lacks them.[121] Bill-drafting rules would help ensure uniformity and predictability in the way governmental departments prepare their bills. They would also serve to deter decision-makers' arbitrariness in shaping the terms of the bill.

Notes

1.. I would like to thank the then-chief legal advisor at the Ministry for the Coordination of Environmental Action (MICOA), Dr. Alda Salomão, as well as her colleague, Dr. André Silva. From them I learned a great deal about how they, as bill drafters, went about writing and rewriting the draft bill that led to the Environmental Law 1997. The mistakes are only mine.
2. *See* LIVANINGO, Letter/Petition Petição, Maputo (Aug. 22, 2003).
3. An Acronym, UTIP stands for Unidade Técnica de Implementação de Projectos, or The Technical Unit for the Implementation of Hydroelectric Projects. Its mission consists of implementing hydroelectric projects on behalf of the Ministry of Natural Resources, and its website is at http://www.utip.org.mz (last accessed on Dec. 20, 2005).
4. *See* LIVANINGO, *supra* note 2 at 2.
5. *See* Art. 19 of law 20/97 (Environmental Law) and Article 7 nº 1 of decree 76/98 (regulation of the environmental impact assessment).
6. *See* LIVANINGO, *supra* note 2 at 7.
7. *See* LIVANINGO, undated leaflet titled Mepanda Uncua Um Mau Negócio (translated: Mepanda Uncua, A Bad Business). It estimated that the dam would displace some 1400 people.
8. *Id.* The proposed project did not have definitive proposals for compensation. Project's compensation proposals had only an 'informal' status, and they did not cover the riparian downstream populations.
9. The dam would only create very few temporary jobs. *See* LIVANINGO, undated leaflet *supra* footnote 7.
10. *Id.* Instead of a dam, alternative sources of energy (sun or wind) would best suit the needs of the local population. Energy from Mpanda Uncua would only serve for export.
11. *See* LIVANINGO, *supra* note 2 at 3 (quoting from a letter dated Jun. 16, 2003 from the UTIP to LIVANINGO.
12. *Id.* (noting that "the [Environmental] Law does not establish the form through which information should be provided").
13. *Id.* (noting that "from the outset, the legislator never wanted to impose an onus on project sponsors, thus leaving it to each one the definition of the best form to give effect to that right on a case by case basis."
14. *See* LIVANINGO Boletim Informativo/Bulletin Ed. nº 6 April/June 2004, 3-4.
15. *Id.*
16. *Id.*
17. Interview with Maurício Sulila, LIVANINGO's Program Officer in Maputo, Mozambique, on Aug. 6, 2004.
18. For the full text of the law, *see Boletim da República Iª Série Nº 40, 3º Suplemento* (Oct. 7, 1997).
19. By definition, the institutions—private companies, powerful individuals, or responsible ministries, or others—which shaped the environmental impact of the nation's development process.
20. *See* Cabinet's Resolution Nº 5/95 of Aug. 3d, 1995, published in the official gazette, Boletim da República Nº 49, Suplemento (Dec. 6, 1995).

21. English translation: National Program for Environmental Management. *See Ministério para a Coordenacão da Accão Ambiental, Programa Nacional de Gestão Ambiental* (Maputo, May 1996) (hereinafter, PNGA).
22. *Id.* at 3.
23. *See* Presidential Decree N° 6/95 of Nov. 16, 1995 in *Boletim da Republica N° 48, Suplemento* (Nov. 29, 1995).
24. *See* PNGA, *supra* note 21, at 67.
25. Here broadly defined to include legislation enacted by the Parliament, Cabinet decrees, implementing regulations introduced by ministries, local ordinances—any rule promulgated by the state at any level.
26. *See* PNGA, *supra* note 21, at 72.
27. *Id.* at 31.
28. They worked at the Ministry for the Coordination of Environmental Action (MICOA), formerly, the National Commission of the Environment (CNA). In the present context, 'drafters' means the lawyers employed by the CNA or the MICOA who participated in writing the bill and eventually carried out whatever research they deemed necessary to justify it. For a broader definition of 'drafters', *see* ROBERT B. SEIDMAN, ET AL., LEGISLATIVE DRAFTING FOR DEMOCRATIC SOCIAL CHANGE: A MANUAL FOR DRAFTERS 5 (Kluwer Law Int'l 2001) (hereinafter, DRAFTERS' MANUAL).
29. *See* PNGA *supra* note 21, at 65.
30. *See* the copy of a fax message, dated Nov. 16, 1997 (hereinafter *fax message)*—copy on file with the MICOA. Subscribed by a consultant, drafter and translator, the message notes that "[There is] a translation of the earlier draft Environmental Bill 1994. *It was the work of a UNEP consultant....*" (Italics added).
31. *See* Possiveis Questões Sobre A Lei Do Ambiente 2 (Sept. 1996)(hereinafter MICOA Drafters' Report 1996)(on file with MICOA). The report provides useful insights into how the drafters approached their task of writing the environmental bill. The report's title suggests that the drafters wrote it after they had completed the actual process of drafting the bill. Although the drafters did not employ a problem-solving methodology, they wrote the report with the aim of addressing possible questions that legislators might raise during debates at the Assembly of the Republic. That report appeared as the only written document in MICOA files in which the drafters sought to justify their draft.
32. The drafters considered acceptable the 'copying of foreign laws or models' as a methodology for drafting the environmental bill. Alan Watson regards legal transplants as a common occurrence. *See* ALAN WATSON, SOURCES OF LAW, LEGAL CHANGE AND AMBIGUITY 27 (1984)(discussing a case that "illustrates the principle that choice of borrowing depends in large measure on the accessibility of the donor source which need not be official").
33. Within the discipline of legislative drafting, most drafters do not seriously challenge those assumptions. In this sense, *see* LARS UDEHN, THE LIMITS OF PUBLIC CHOICE A SOCIOLOGICAL CRITIQUE OF THE ECONOMIC THEORY OF POLITICS 6 (1996)(quoting Imre Lakatos, *Falsification and* the *Methodology of Scientific Research Programmes,* in CRITICISM AND THE GROWTH OF KNOWLEDGE 133(Imre Lakatos and Alan Musgrave, eds., 1970). Yet, hard core assumptions may become the subject of scientific inquiry. In this sense, *see* HAROLD KINCAID,

PHILOSOPHICAL FOUNDATIONS OF THE SOCIAL SCIENCES 228 (1996) (noting that "Lakatos's views are generally an improvement over positivism, but they suffer from at least two problems. First, hard cores *are* tested" (italics in the original)). In fact, following a common practice in bill drafting in Mozambique, the drafters in this case did not test their assumptions.

34. *See* above, this Chapter, text at n.24.
35. *See* DRAFTERS' MANUAL, ch. 4, at 22-23, and ch. 7. Yet, the above aspects deserve attention because, as stated, the PNGA implicitly holds them as potentially crucial for the proposed bill's success.
36. For example, Article 3 (1) (d) of Presidential Decree 6/95 required MICOA "to impart an interdisciplinary approach into the entities that plan and implement the exploitation of natural resources." Compare that requirement with the one imposed on CONDES under Article 5 (f) of the Third Version: "to formulate recommendations to the natural resources-Ministers [e.g.: agriculture, fisheries, industry] on matters of relevance to their respective portfolios." Another example is Article 4 (f) of the Presidential Decree 6/95, which empowers MICOA "to recommend to the Cabinet the creation of environmental incentives". Similarly, Article 5 (d) of the Third Version of the bill assigns to CONDES the power "to prepare proposals for the creation of incentives, financial or otherwise, to stimulate the economic agents to adopt environment friendly practices in the daily use of the country's natural resources."
37. *See* the Law on Local Government (Law 2/97) published in the Official Journal *Boletim da República, Serie Nº 7, 2º Suplemento* (18.02.97). Article7, nº2 (b) states that "[the Local Government]'s administrative autonomy comprises the following powers: (b) to create, organize and oversee services that it requires to pursue its mission." Further, as part of this mission, Local Governments have decision-making powers over environmental issues (Articles 46 and 78).
38. Or, as a 'complex organization.' In this sense, *see* ANN SEIDMAN AND ROBERT B. SEIDMAN, STATE AND LAW IN THE DEVELOPMENT PROCESS: PROBLEM-SOLVING AND INSTITUTIONAL CHANGE IN THE THIRD WORLD 130-131 (1994) (hereinafter, SEIDMAN AND SEIDMAN (1994)).
39. However, the first and second versions of the bill had formulated rules seeking to address the role played by the Minister for Environmental Coordination.
40. Conceivably, a more complex organization than the portfolio Ministry (MICOA).
41. *See* GERALD GARVEY, PUBLIC ADMINISTRATION, THE PROFESSION AND THE PRACTICE A CASE STUDY APPROACH 3 (1997).
42. Or, the problem of inducing public participation in environment friendly initiatives, such as: the 'management of the environment.'
43. First Version, Art. 20 (1).
44. Second Version, Art. 22 and Third Version, Art. 19.
45. The drafters' initial assumption ran contrary to the earlier policy finding that had shown that Mozambique lacked the necessary expertise. *See* PNGA, *supra* note 20, at 30.
46. In the present context, 'environmental competency'— or environmental expertise—means the mastery of the necessary knowledge and skills with which deci-

sion-makers and the public could either take environmental friendly decisions or follow environment friendly behaviors.

47. That presumption might hold true in the more "developed" countries where earlier drafts of environmental bills first took shape.
48. MICOA drafters' Report (1996), *supra* note 31, at 3.
49. Building on the lessons learned from governmental performance that empirical data had yielded, the drafters could have included provisions to mandate future governmental action in the field.
50. For a discussion of these factors, *see* SEIDMAN AND SEIDMAN (1994), at 123-125; and ch. 2 of this volume, esp. pp. 35-37.
51. Located in Moamba, a district in the southern province of Maputo.
52. *See* the SUNDAY WEEKLY DOMINGO (Maputo), Jun. 30, 2002.
53. In this sense, *see* JOHN W. KINGDON, AGENDAS, ALTERNATIVES AND PUBLIC POLICIES 212-213 (1984)(noting that "an open policy window is an opportunity for advocates to push their pet solutions or to push attention to their special problems. Indeed, advocates in and around government keep their proposals and their problems at hand, waiting for these opportunities to occur. They have pet solutions, for instance, and wait for problems to float by to which they can attach their solutions, or for developments in the political stream that they can use to their advantage").
54. In this sense, *see* SEIDMAN AND SEIDMAN (1994), at 42. *See also* DANIEL A. MAZMANIAN AND PAUL A. SABATIER, IMPLEMENTATION AND PUBLIC POLICY 25 (1983).
55. *See* Third Version, Art. 20 (1) and Art. 20(2).
56. *See* Third Version, Art. 21.
57. *See* Article 82 of the Mozambican Constitution (1990), which declares: "The citizen has the right to resort to the courts against the acts that violate her rights recognized by the Constitution and the law."
58. Article 72 of the Constitution had already recognized Mozambicans' right "to live in a balanced environment."
59. Or, 'administrative entities.' Notice that under Article 413 (1) of the Code of Civil Procedure (1967), state (central government) or local government officials may order the suspension of the construction of buildings initiated by a private person "in violation of a law or a regulation." Further, on May 6, 1992, the National Assembly adopted Law N° *5/92. See Boletim* da *República Iª. Série N° 19* (May 6, 1992). The Law gives jurisdiction to the Administrative Court over decisions taken by administrative authorities on matters such as the award of licences for the exploitation of areas pertaining to public domains. Article 10 (1), (2); and Article 25 (g). Conceivably, exploitation of these areas may adversely impact on the citizens' right to an ecologically balanced environment. Should they seek protection of their right from the Administrative Court, or should they rely on the judicial courts?
60. Nothing in those provisions suggests that judicial courts would only have appellate jurisdiction over environmental cases.
61. The bill should have aimed at prescribing *precise* behavioral patterns, the observance of which would likely lead to the protection of environmental rights. In writing a bill, 'precision' should become a guiding principle. *See* Jack Stark, *Teaching Statu-*

tory Law, 44 J. LEGAL EDUCATION 579, 583 (1994)(noting that "because statutes are written to effect policy decisions, their main virtue is accuracy in the sense of precisely effecting the desired policy").

62. *See* BOAVENTURA DE SOUSA SANTOS AND JOÃO CARLOS TRINDADE, CONFLITO E TRANSFORMAÇÃO SOCIAL UMA PAISAGEM DAS JUSTIÇAS EM MOÇAMBIQUE 76-87 (2000).
63. *See* First Version, Art. 19 (1).
64. As noted earlier on, the drafters saw their mission as consisting of writing a bill that would work in the Mozambican context as well as reflect universally held principles.
65. *See, e.g.*, BERNARD SCHWARTZ, ADMINISTRATIVE LAW 147 (3d ed., 1991)(noting that, in America, under the Freedom of Information Act, disclosure constitutes the general rule); KENNETH F. WARREN, ADMINISTRATIVE LAW IN THE POLITICAL SYSTEM (3d ed., 1996)(asking with some irony whether the administrators "could not see that a viable democratic system cannot function if the people are unable to obtain the information necessary to intelligently scrutinize governmental operations?")
66. *See, e.g.*, Lori Udall, *The World Bank and Public Accountability: Has Anything Changed?,* in THE STRUGGLE FOR ACCOUNTABILITY 393 (Jonathan A. Fox & L. David Brown, *eds.*, 1998)
67. *See* Second Version, Art. 21 (1); Third Version, Art. 18.
68. They defined 'management of the environment' as meaning 'the sustainable rational use and reuse of the environmental components.' *See* the provision on definitions: Article 3 (First Version), Article 2 (Second Version), and Article 1 (Third Version). As formulated, the concept does not help identify the addressees whose behavior should change for the fulfillment of any right. More importantly, as incorporated in the provision on the right to information, the concept indirectly exonerates governmental agencies from any specific duty to act. Literally, anyone—whether acting on behalf of governmental agencies, or not—can generate and store information that has some relationship with the environment.
69. *See* Articles 74 (1), (2), (4) of the Mozambican Constitution (1990).
70. Through Resolution 5/91 of Dec. 12, 1991, Mozambique's Assembly of the Republic had ratified the United Nations International Covenant on Civil and Political Rights. *See Boletim da República* Ia *Série Nº 50, Suplemento* (December 12, 1991). Article 19 (2) of the Covenant gives everyone the right "to seek, receive and impart information". It implies that individuals may actively take initiatives to obtain information in whatever form (written, electronic, etc). It also imposes on the States the obligation to adopt legislative measures aimed at satisfying the public demand for information. The State's obligation derives from Article 2 (2) of the Covenant which stipulates that a State Party "undertakes to take the necessary steps...to adopt such legislative or other measures as may be necessary to give effect to the rights recognized in the present Covenant." *See also* MANFRED NOWAK, U.N. COVENANT ON CIVIL AND POLITICAL RIGHTS COMMENTARY 343-344 (1993)(noting that "although such a subjective right to be informed is still largely unrecognized in case law, the rapid development of the modern information and communication society is leading in many States to progressive statutory duties to provide information, particularly on the part of the public administration").

71. The Cabinet had adopted Decree N° 36/89 (Nov. 27, 1989) on *The Norms Applicable to the Functioning of the State Services. See Boletim da República Iª Série N° 47, 3° Suplemento* (Nov. 27, 1989). The Decree gave State officials the discretion to rank 'official correspondence' according to a continuum of classified categories of documents, namely: State Secret, Secret, Confidential, Restricted, and Normal (Articles 11 (1) and (3)). Nowhere did the Decree define the matters that should fall under one or another of those categories. Subsequently, the cabinet adopted Decree N° 30/2001 on *The Norms Applicable to the Functioning of Public Administration Services* (Oct. 15, 2001). *See Boletim da Republica Iª Série N° 41, Suplemento* (Oct. 15,2001). Though repealing the 1989 decree, the 2001 decree restated the State officials' discretionary powers in classifying "official correspondence." Art. 85.
72. A subsequent law actually narrowed the right to seek information from governmental departments. *See* Law N° 9/2001 (Jul. 7, 2001) on the Rules of Procedure Applicable to Administrative Disputes ("Processo Administrativo Contencioso"). *See also* Boletim da República Iª . Série N° 27, Suplemento, Jul. 7, 2001]. Under that Law, a citizen may petition the Administrative Court to enforce her right to access records held by governmental departments. However, in petitioning the Court, the citizen must show evidence that she intends to entertain further proceedings—judicial or administrative (Articles 93 (1) and (3)). Also, her right of information does not apply to matters deemed confidential (Art. 93 (2)). Therefore, as a general principle, governmental departments do not have the obligation to disclose information about their records to the public. *See also*, World Bank Report N° 23815-MOZ Project Appraisal Document for a Public Sector Reform Project 7 (May 6, 2002) (noting that "there is no freedom of access to information in place that would provide for citizens to be better informed").
73. The drafters believed that the bill would only require additional regulations for implementation. For that purpose, they vested the Cabinet with regulatory powers. *See* Art. 35 (1) (First Version), Art. 38 (2) (Second Version), and Art. 32 (Third Version).
74. The 'abstractness' and 'generic character' of the rules probably reflected the prevailing values that a legal norm should satisfy.
75. *See* DRAFTERS' MANUAL, at 243.
76. Examples of principles adopted in the bill included: conservation of the natural environment, citizens' participation, sustainable development. *See* First Version, Art. 4; Second Version, Art. 4; Third Version, Art. 4.
77. Subject to the realization that a law constitutes a translation of policy into an implementable action. *See* Gavin Drewry, *Political Institutions: Legal Perspectives*, in A NEW HANDBOOK OF POLITICAL SCIENCE 191, 192 (Robert E. Goodin & Hans-Dieter Klingemann, eds., 1998)(noting that "Laws are the medium through which policy is translated into action. Laws are an important resource for public policy-making", (quoting R. Rose, *Law as a Resource for Public Policy*, 39 PARLIAMENTARY AFFAIRS 297 (1996); SEIDMAN AND SEIDMAN (1994).
78. *See* First Version Art. 35 (1); Second Version Art. 38 (2); and Third Version Art. 32. Implicitly, this provision raises the issue of the extent to which the Assembly of the Republic may delegate law making powers to the Cabinet. Under the Constitution, the Assembly has the supreme law making power (Article 133 (1) states that "The Assembly of the Republic is the highest legislative organ in the Republic of

Mozambique"). On the other hand, the same Constitution endows the Cabinet with the capacity to issue decrees (Article 157 (1) states that "The normative acts of the Council of Ministers take on the form of decrees").

An overlap seems apparent as to the substantive domains over which the Assembly and the Cabinet have constitutional powers to enact legal norms. For example, the Assembly may adopt "norms to regulate the activities of the State and the economic and social life through laws and deliberations of a generic character" (Article 133 nº 2). Likewise, the Cabinet may "promote and regulate economic activities as well as those of social sectors" (Article 153nº 1 e)), "direct and coordinate the activities of Ministries and those of other organs subordinated to the Council of Ministers" (Article 153 nº 2 b)). Mozambican legal scholars have yet to address the issue of possible conflicts that may arise from that overlap as well as the degree to which the Assembly may delegate its own law making powers to the Cabinet.

Elsewhere, one author has argued that a legislature cannot help but delegate law making powers. *See* KENNETH F. WARREN, ADMINISTRATIVE LAW IN THE POLITICAL SYSTEM 98 (3d ed. 1996)(arguing that "because legislators cannot possibly be expected to draft legislation and attach meaningful standards to every phase (unanticipated and critical policy questions will always be left for administrators to resolve), less emphasis should be placed on seeking standards"). *But see* BERNARD SCHWARTZ, ADMINISTRATIVE LAW 46 (3d ed. 1991)(noting that "if there is no standard in the statute to limit delegations of power, the administrative agency is being given a blank check to make law in the delegated area of authority".); WILLIAM F. FOX, UNDERSTANDING ADMINISTRATIVE LAW 51 (3d ed. 1997)(noting that "a lack of precise standards emanating from Congress permits the exercise of virtually unfettered discretion by non-elected agency officials"); MAKING DEVELOPMENT WORK—LEGISLATIVE REFORM FOR INSTITUTIONAL TRANSFORMATION AND GOOD GOVERNANCE (Ann Seidman, et al., eds., 1999), ch. 5, Boxes 5-10.

79. One deadline would apply to Cabinet approval of an environmental impact assessment regulation (6 months since the entry into force of the Environmental Law; *see* Art. 35 (2) (First Version), and Art. 38 (2) (Second Version)). Another deadline would apply for the approval of other environmental regulations (2 years in the First Version (Art. 35 (1)), or 3 years in the Second Version (Art. 38 (1)).

80. *See* First Version, Art. 34 (1); Second Version, Art. 37 (1); Third Version, Art. 31.

81. *See* First Version, Art. 34 (2), and Second Version, Art. 37 (2). As with the provision for issuing regulations, the Third Version did not stipulate any time for governmental performance.

82. Indeed, absent any other draft provision on the abrogation of past relevant laws, the Cabinet would not have the mission of reforming existing environmental legislation if the latter conformed to the rules contained in the new bill.

83. For example, all versions of the draft bill proclaimed two principles: "conservation of nature" and "citizens' participation in the management of the environment." *See* First Version, Articles 4 (b), (c) and (d)—conservation of nature, Article 4 (f)—citizens' participation; Second Version: Articles 4 (2), (3) and (4)—conservation of nature, Article 4 (6)—citizens' participation; Third Version: Articles 4 (1) and (2)—conservation of nature, Article 4(4)—citizens' participation). None established any ranking between those principles, leaving unclear how to treat an existing law that conformed with one but not the other.

To illustrate the difficulty: An earlier legislation might contain a provision that promotes the conservation principle, but not citizens' participation. For example, to foster a stable reconstitution of wild animal populations, one provision of a law might forbid hunting in specific periods of the year. Yet, another provision of the same law might allow governmental agencies to issue hunting permits through a decision- making process that excludes citizen inputs. Pending the intended law reform, an implementing agency might face the challenge of how to uphold one principle or the other, or both. For possible doctrinal answers, *see* WILLIAM D. POPKIN, MATERIALS ON LEGISLATION POLITICAL LANGUAGE AND . THE POLITICAL PROCESS 667-717 (1993). Clearly, the drafters could have avoided the uncertainty of doctrinal answers by crafting more clearly defined provisions in the Environmental Law.

84. At the time of drafting the bill, some legislative research, although not fully completed, had already identified some of the relevant environmental laws. *See* PNGA, *supra* note 21, at 31-34. These might have provided the intended reform's starting point.
85. *See* Art. 2 of the bill's Second version and Art. 1 of the bill's Third version. The first version had provided a narrower definition restricted to 'natural environmental components' (Art. 3) which included matters such as air, wildlife, but did not refer to a community's socio-economic conditions.
86. *See* KENNETH F. WARREN, ADMINISTRATIVE LAW IN THE POLITICAL SYSTEM 153 (3d. ed. 1996) Discussing public administrators' public accountability, the author suggests that "democratically responsible behavior by public agency employees is any legally and procedurally proper action that leads to the efficient accomplishment of publicly sanctioned and desired goals" (id.).

    In Mozambique, the Constitution imposes on the Cabinet the duty to guarantee 'the administration of the country.' *See* Art. 152 (1) of the Mozambican Constitution (1990). Viewed from this perspective, the Cabinet holds office as the highest administrative agency in Mozambique. Therefore, through its behavior, the Cabinet should also take the lead in observing the dictates that apply to competent and accountable public administrators.
87. *See* Seidman, et al., *supra* note 78, at 7 (defining accountability as meaning that "decision-makers justify their decisions publicly, subjecting their decisions to review by recognized higher authority, and ultimately by the electorate").

    By another omission in the final version of the bill, the drafters withdrew the provision—contained in prior versions—that would have required the Cabinet to present yearly reports about the environment to the Assembly of the Republic. *See* Art. 6 (3) of the First and Second Versions.
88. The Constitution imposes on the Cabinet an overall duty to report to the Assembly of the Republic about "the realization of internal and external policies and about the Cabinet's activities under the law." *See* Constitution of Mozambique (1990), Art. 151. That vague constitutional provision represents but a weak source of legitimacy for the Assembly of the Republic to hold the Cabinet to account.
89. *See* MICOA Drafters' Report 1996, *supra* note 31, at 2.
90. Interview with Dr. Alda Salomão in Maputo (Oct. 31, 2002).
91. There is only one exception: the drafters did probe into the norms governing the role of MICOA. That process led them to confer on MICOA the power to implement the bill in the Second Version. Although they had compiled and even

interpreted past enviornment-related legislation, they failed to think through the implications for their draft bill.

92. In 1991, having adhered to the United Nations Covenant on Civil and Political Rights, the Cabinet had embraced an open-ended policy of enhancing the Mozambican public's access to information in whatever form—written, electronic, etc. The Covenant presupposed that legislative measures would provide for adequate policy implementation. *See* Article 2 (2) of the Covenant. In listing the types of government-held records that should become accessible to the public, the environmental bill's first version aimed to translate that broad Covenant-touted information policy into the environmental field. It would have given phrase, ' information related to the management of the environment,' more precise meaning.

93. The environment bill's first version would have had the merit of promoting innovative policies expressed in terms of broad (inchoate) values, namely: transparency and accountability. As formulated in the first version, the right to information provision would have helped to remove the veil of secrecy that surrounds instances of governmental behavior in the environmental field. Under it, the public could have availed itself of records needed to scrutinize governmental behavior, creating a condition for governmental implementing agencies' transparency and accountability.

    Couched in rational argument, inchoate values may permeate the formulation of governmental policies. *See, e.g.*, INTERMINISTERIAL COMMISSION FOR PUBLIC SECTOR REFORM, GLOBAL STRATEGY FOR PUBLIC SECTOR REFORM 2001-2011 11 (Oct. 2001)(good governance); WORLD BANK REPORT N° 23815-MOZ: PROJECT APPRAISAL DOCUMENT FOR A PUBLIC SECTOR REFORM PROJECT 6-7 (May 6, 2002) (accountability). In that way, value-inspired governmental policies might find their way into a draft bill's provisions. The critical issue remains, however: How to ensure those provisions' effective implementation in a country's unique circumstances—an issue the environment bill's drafters ducked by dropping the provision altogether from the final version.

    For an outline of 'accountability' and 'transparency' as inchoate values, *see* Seidman, et al., *supra* note 78, at 40 and 7.

94. Yet, the drafters had failed to offer guidance on how the courts should interpret the bill's provisions.

95. See N. J. Jamieson, *Towards a Systematic Statute Law*, 3 OTAGO L. REV. 543, 544 (1976) (noting that the failure in drafting comprehensive legislation is "to reverse the invariable rule of liability in communication whereby responsibility goes with the active instead of the passive, the bestowing instead of the receiving, aspects of the process by which ideas are shared").

96. *See* UGO MATTEI, COMPARATIVE LAW AND ECONOMICS 133 (1998)(arguing that"if a transplant happens in a competitive scenario, it is likely that... the transplanted rule or doctrine is more efficient than other possible alternatives").

97. *See* Alexander L. George and Timothy J. McKeown, *Case Studies and Theories of Organizational Decision Making*, in 2 ADVANCES IN INFORMATION PROCESSING IN ORGANIZATIONS 35 (Lee S. Sproull, et al., eds. 1985)(noting that "this procedure ['process-tracing'] is intended to investigate and explain the decision process by which various initial conditions are translated into outcomes... As we understand process-tracing, it involves both an attempt to reconstruct actors' definitions of the situation and an attempt develop a theory of action. The framework

within which actors' perceptions are described is given by the researcher, not by the actors. However, because that framework often is revised after observations of behavior (in fact, the original framework itself may be based on previous observations of behavior), the externally imposed theoretical framework is certainly shaped by actors' self-definitions, even if it is not designed specifically to capture such self-definitions").

98. In this context, a 'cause' or a 'causal factor' means a "transformative *potential* of phenomena". In this sense, *see* RAY PAWSON AND NICK TILLEY, REALISTIC EVALUATION 34 (1997)(discussing the successionist and the generative conceptualizations of causation in both the natural and the social sciences).

99. Ministers have discretion to create and abolish ministerial legal departments. For example, until the adoption of Ministerial Decree N° 133/2000on September 27, 2000, the Ministry for the Coordination of Environmental Action did not have a legal department. Another example: In 1997, claiming that the education sector faced new challenges, the then -Minister of Education issued a Ministerial Decree to restructure the Ministry and exclude the legal department. *See* Ministerial Decree N° 104/97 of November 5, 1997, in *Boletim da República Iª Série N° 45* (Nov. 5, 1997). Subsequently, a new incumbent issued a new Ministerial Decree which reinstated the legal department. *See* Ministerial Decree N° 59/2000 (Art. 13), in *Boletim da República Iª Série N° 26* (Jun. 28, 2000).

100. *See, e.g.,* Ministerial Decree N° 117/87, Annex II, *in Boletim da República Iª Série N°41* (Oct. 14, 1987).

101. *Id.*

102. In Mozambique, legal training emphasizes the imparting of legal skills, especially the interpretation and the application of legal norms, that may prove more helpful for a career in the judicial system. *See* Taibo Mucobora, *Formação Juridica Superior em Mocambique,* paper presented at the Workshop On Professional Training In The Justice Sector, Maputo, May 30 to Jun. 2, 2000 (noting that "the traditional law course syllabus obeys a concern biased towards private law and for court activities"). Mucobora was Dean of the Law School at Eduardo Mondlane University.

103. *See* Edward L. Rubin, *Law and Legislation in the Administrative State,* 89 COLUM. L. REV. 369, 369 (noting that "the principal reason why we lack a theory of modern legislation is that legal scholars have focused so heavily on the judiciary.... When legal scholars turn to statutes, they tend to devote their efforts to the problem of judicial interpretation").

104. For a debate over alternative bill drafting theories, see the series of articles published in Seidman, et al., *supra* note 78.

105. Not only in drafting, but in any profession, routinized behaviors may undermine rationality and pervert efforts to introduce change. *See* Robert E. Lane, *What Rational Choice Explain,* in THE RATIONAL CHOICE CONTROVERSY 107, 109 (Jeffrey Friedman, ed., 1996)(noting that "repetitive decision making leads to overconfidence, impairing rationality" (quoting Hillel J. Einhorn & Robin M. Hogarth, *Decision Making Under Ambiguity,* in RATIONAL CHOICE: THE CONTRAST BETWEEN ECONOMICS AND PSYCHOLOGY (Robin M. Hogarth and Melvin W. Reder, eds., 1987)).

106. *See* Luis B. Nahe, *Proposta de Regulamento da Faculdade de Direito 2002 (Draft Regulation of the Law Faculty of Eduardo Mondlane University 2002).* The draft served as the basis for the adoption of the current Regulation of the Law Faculty available

at http://www.uem.mz/faculdade/direito/documentos.htm (last accessed in July 2005); Jennifer Garvey, *Relatório Projecto de Revisão da Lei de Terras 21 de Janeiro de 1997* (*Report on the Reform Draft Land Law, January 21 1997*).

107. *See* report of evaluation of similar attempts to equip drafters with an institutionalist legislative drafting theory to strengthen their capacity to draft effective legislation to foster good governance and development, *see* Sara Johnson-Steffey, Boston University School of Law Program for Legislative Drafting for Democratic Social Change-Final Evaluation Summary (June 8, 2004)(on file at the Heller School, Brandeis University).

108. In this sense, the need for 'coordinating ideas' as to how to design a program to change a nation's legal culture seems crucial. *See* MALCOLM M. FEELEY AND EDWARD L. RUBIN, JUDICIAL POLICY MAKING AND THE MODERN STATE 233 et. seq. (1998) Feeley's and Rubin's analysis of the possibilities of 'coordinating ideas' to improve judicial policy making may offer a potentially valuable approach to institutionalising an effective legislative learning process not only in Mozambique, but elsewhere .

109. The International Consortium for Law and Development (ICLAD) aims to assist country nationals' efforts to institutionalize that kind of a program. *See* the organization's official website http://www.ICLAD-law.org.

110. *See supra* note 30.

111. In an interview, my contact source confirmed the MICOA drafters' adhesion to the UNEP-sponsored bill's underlying values and policies. The drafters may have (implicitly) justified their initial acceptance of the principles they transplanted into their bill by *analogical reasoning: As a country, Mozambique shares common values with other countries, such as Portugal, Sao Tome e Principe, etc. These countries have adopted Environmental Laws that presumably reflect those values. Therefore, Mozambique could validly adopt similar laws.*

Yet, the drafters'reasoning process apparently relied on a limited range of country cases from which they derived the supposedly analogical features. Those features may not prove relevant as the basis for a sound policy decision to extend the legal solution introduced in the available country cases to Mozambique. *See* GARY KING, ET AL., DESIGNING SOCIAL INQUIRY 213, note 3 (1994)(cautioning against the danger posed by the 'availability heuristic': "a psychological fallacy of reasoning that occurs when decision-makers (here, the drafters) under uncertainty choose analogies based on recency or availability, hence systematically biasing judgments," *id.* (quoting JUDGEMENT UNDER UNCERTAINTY: HEURISTICS AND BIASES (Kahneman, Slovic, & Tversky, eds., 1982.). *See also* Seidman et al, *supra* note 78, ch. 4 (urging drafters "to understand not only foreign law's black letter text, but how it actually worked in its home-country's unique context").

Cass R. Sunstein suggests some criteria that, used in analogical reasoning-arguments, might help extend a judicial solution from one case to another within the same country jurisdiction: principled consistency, focus on particulars, incompletely theorized judgments, and principles operating at a low- or middle-level of abstraction. CASS R. SUNSTEIN, LEGAL REASONING AND POLITICAL CONFLICT 67-69 (1996).

112. Interview with the contact source (a drafter) at the Ministry for Environmental Coordination (MICOA), Oct. 31, 2002.

113. Elsewhere in the world, administrative decision-makers have also experienced fears arising from expanded public access to government-held information. *See, e.g.*, KENNETH F. WARREN, ADMINISTRATIVE LAW IN THE POLITICAL SYSTEM 187 (3d ed., 1996).

114. A symbolic law seeks to promote symbolically the interests of a particular stakeholder without necessarily looking for change in problematic social behaviors. *See* Robert B. Seidman, *Justifying Legislation: A Pragmatic, Institutionalist Approach to the Memorandum of Law, Legislative Theory, and Practical Reason*, 29 HARVARD J. LEGISLATION 14 (1992).

115. *Id.* at 31.

116. *See* Seidman et al., *supra* note 78, at 6 (noting that "Ministers generally prefer unlimited discretion—for 'discretion,' read 'power.' The Rule of Law and good governance alike abhor it.... Precise drafting constitutes a front line trench in the war to improve governance and protect the Rule of Law").

117. *See Boletim da República Iª Série Nº 40, 3º Suplemento* (Oct. 7, 1997).

118. Decree Nº 40/2000 of Oct. 17, 2000 *in Boletim da República Iª Série Nº 41* (October 17, 2000).

119. Art. 1 (1) (a).

120. The bill drafters' shift in position lends credence to the thesis that legislative staff can hardly sway obstinate decision-makers. In this sense, *see* ABNER J. MIKVA AND ERIC LANE, LEGISLATIVE PROCESS 109 (1995)(noting that "even in the [congressional] committee, where an entrepreneurial staff can exercise the most clout, the members themselves must resolve the major controversies on issues of enough concern to generate public attention. *The staff may have considerable leverage over marginal issues, but it does not extend to the major concerns of constituents. The arm twisting and peer-group pressure necessary to enact any piece of controversial legislation remains the prerogative of the members—much as some staff would like to think otherwise.* Consequently, leaving the details of legislation to the staff is not harmful but rational, sane, and effective, for then the members are free to 'wheel and deal' on the big issues." (emphasis added).

121. As my contact sources revealed to me in Mozambique, at the Cabinet level, no specific legal rules exist to guide governmental departments to prepare draft bills. Each Ministry follows its own practice.

Some *ad hoc* norms exist, such as those contained in the Internal Regulation of the National Assembly. They may serve well the post-bill making phase. Also, some separate initiatives at the National Assembly and at a project then funded by the State University of New York (SUNY) have tried to suggest some general rules on bill drafting.

Chapter 5

Policy-Making and Development in South Africa

by Neva Seidman Makgetla

By the early 2000s, South African government leaders commonly argued that they had established a host of good policies that had not been adequately implemented. In effect, they meant that the policies instituted since 1994 had worthy objectives, but lacked effective implementation strategies.[1] This view essentially redefined policy to mean government aims, rather than programmes to achieve those aims. Such a definition diverges sharply from the normal understanding, which sees policy as to the measures to achieve goals, not the goals themselves.

We here explore the policymaking process with a view to explaining these weaknesses.[2] Analysis suggests that most policies were drafted largely by paid consultants, generally from foreign aid agencies or private companies. Most consultants did not base their recommendations on appropriate or thorough research. They effectively excluded or largely ignored inputs from key stakeholders, especially organized labour and poor communities. Finally, virtually no policies included regular review or response processes to identify and overcome defects in the original design.

Some but by no means all of these weaknesses were corrected in Parliament and the National Economic, Development and Labour Council (NEDLAC), a national forum for consulting stakeholders on economic policy. But government departments frequently circumvented both institutions by issuing policies as regulations or administrative directives.

The first section of this paper briefly reviews policy outcomes, outlining the key challenges facing South Africa a decade after liberation. The second section uses an institutionalist process model to analyse the policy-making process. The last section presents three case studies of policy development in South Africa - the Growth, Employment and Redistribution (GEAR) strategy, the annual national budget, and the Integrated Manufacturing Strategy.

South Africa

THE CHALLENGES

After 1994, the South African state made great progress in consolidating democracy and improving services to the poor. Nonetheless, largely thanks to extraordinarily high unemployment and fairly slow economic growth, progress toward prosperity and equity remained disappointing, especially compared to expectations at the time of liberation.

We here evaluate developments since liberation in three areas: the democratisation of the state, the provision of basic infrastructure and social services to poor communities, and economic inclusion and growth.[3]

Considerable progress was made in establishing democratic and participatory institutions. These included, amongst a host of others, Parliament as well as NEDLAC; elected local governments required by law to consult widely on policy; and participatory structures to govern schools and hospitals. In addition, South Africa adopted laws to ensure administrative justice and access to information.

The formal establishment of democratic institutions did not, however, automatically empower the historically disenfranchized – in South Africa, poor black communities and constituencies.[4] The poor often lacked the organisation and resources to engage effectively with the new institutions.[5] Before 1994,

South Africa had a host of mass-based organisations united in their rejection of apartheid. Thereafter, as the impetus of the struggle dissipated, many of these organisations failed. Only the unions and churches remained relatively strong.

The weakness in popular organization emerged clearly from Parliamentary hearings and comments on legislation on economic issues. Most received inputs almost exclusively from (white) businesspeople. As a rule, only inputs from the union federation Congress of South African Trade Unions (COSATU) and occasionally the South African Council of Churches (SACC) broke the monotony.

Besides having to consolidate democracy, the new government had to extend basic services and infrastructure to the poor. Under apartheid, the state designed public services to serve rich white communities while neglecting, underfunding and understaffing black areas. As a result, compared to other middle-income countries, South Africa lagged behind in access to basic government services.

Table 1: South Africa's rank amongst reporting countries[a]

	SA rank	number of countries reporting
GDP	49	163
Indicators of access to services and poverty		
Access to improved sanitation	74	148
Access to water	76	152
Children under weight, aged under 5	67	144
Children under height, aged under 5	83	139

Note: a. Data refers to various years between 2000 and 2004. *Source:* UNDP, Human Development Report 2004, available at http://www.undp.org (last accessed in May 2005). Calculated from relevant statistical tables.

As Table 2 shows, the government made considerable progress in extending infrastructure, especially with the gradual relaxation of fiscal policy after 2000. The main social services showed similar improvements.[6] In addition, the government provided social grants to the elderly and to poor children, ensuring income transfers on a scale that was probably unique amongst developing countries. These transfers substantially reduced poverty levels, accounting for some two thirds of the income of the poorest 20% of the population in 2000.[7]

Table 2: Access to infrastructure, 1996 to 2003

	Percentage of households with access to service			Average annual increase in share of households with access	
Basic service	1996	2000	2003	1996-2000	2000-03
Electricity for lighting	64%	71%	79%	2.1%	3.6%
Electricity for cooking	51%	51%	59%	0.0%	5.0%
Piped water	82%	83%	86%	0.3%	1.2%
Flush toilet	52%	54%	57%	0.6%	1.6%

***Source*:** Calculated from, Statistics South Africa. October Household Survey 1996 and Labourforce Survey, September 2000 and 2003. Tshwane. Databases on CD-ROM.

Government increased user charges for most of its services, including education, even as it improved physical access.[8] As a result, by the mid-2000s some poor households were again shut off. Telecommunications had the worst record. The state-owned telecommunications utility closed down, mostly for non-payment, some 80% of the three million lines rolled out between 1997 and 2003.

To address this situation, from 2000 the government introduced a policy framework that called on local governments to provide a limited amount of free electricity and water for poor households. Unfortunately, implementation was fairly haphazard. Different municipalities applied divergent standards, while many poor communities lacked capacity to implement the policy at all.[9] Household surveys found virtually no change in the share of very poor households paying for water before and after the establishment of the policy. Moreover, rapid rural-urban migration meant that although millions of households gained access to piped water, the share of very poor households without it remained virtually unchanged.

Table 3: Access to and payment for piped water, 1996 and 2003

	1996		2003	
monthly income	**% with piped water on site**	**of whom: paying for water**	**% with piped water on site**	**of whom: paying for water**
Up to 1000	63%	74%	62%	78%
R1001 to R2500	64%	72%	70%	84%
R2501 to R3500	61%	69%	70%	83%

Source: Calculated from Statistics South Africa, October Household Survey 1996 and Labourforce Survey, September 2003. Tshwane. Databases on CD-ROM.

Compared to democratization and the extension of infrastructure, the South African government made little progress in establishing a more inclusive and equitable economy. On the one hand, unemployment soared from the already high level left by apartheid. Income inequality, as measured by the Gini coefficient, worsened after 1994.[10] On the other, economic growth remained slow by world standards, although faster than in the late 1980s and early 1990s.

As the following table indicates, South Africa's economic performance did not match up to other middle-income countries for most of the period after independence.

Table 4: Growth, investment and unemployment compared to other countries

	GDP growth 1990-2001	GDP per capita[1] 2001	Investment as % of GDP 2001	Unemployment rate 1998-2001[2]
South Africa	2.1%	10,910	15%	23%
Middle-income countries	3.4%	5,390	24%	5%
of which:				
Malaysia	6.5%	7,910	29%	3%
Chile	6.3%	8,840	21%	10%
South Korea	5.7%	15,060	27%	4%
Egypt	4.5%	3,560	15%	8%
Brazil	2.8%	7,070	21%	10%

Notes: 1. The GDP per capita is here calculated in terms of purchasing power parity, which seeks to measure actual output without taking exchange rate fluctuations into account. 2. The unemployment rate is given for one year between 1998 and 2001. *Source:* The World Bank, World Development Indicators 2003 (2003).

Growth from 1994 to 2004 averaged just under 4%, while investment stagnated well below levels required for more rapid development. After a downturn in the late 1990s, growth in the 2000s remained around 3,5%, largely as a result of a slightly more relaxed fiscal policy combined with high commodity prices. From 2003, however, it was associated with a substantial increase in the balance-of-trade deficit and slow growth in gold mining and manufacturing. Employment grew primarily in retail trade and construction, reflecting the roots of growth in cheap imports and government investment. The long-term sustainability of the expansion and the resulting jobs thus remained somewhat dubious.[11]

Table 5: GDP growth and investment rate, 1994-2004

Year	% growth in GDP at market prices	Investment as % of GDP
1994-1996	3.6%	14.8%
1997-1999	1.8%	16.0%
2000-2004	3.4%	15.8%

Source: GDP data calculated from Statistics South Africa, data on GDP, available at http://www.statssa.gov.za (last accessed in May 2005). Investment rate calculated from SARB, long-term data series on national accounts, available at http://www.resbank.co.za (last accessed in May 2005).

The following graph shows the rise in unemployment between 1994 and 2002. In 2003 and 2004, the unemployment rate levelled out at just under 30%. At the same time, incomes remained low, with nearly 40% of workers earning under R1000 a month through the independence decade, while the purchasing power of R1000 dropped by over half. (R(rand) is the South African currencty.)

Figure 1: South African unemployment and incomes, 1995, 2001 and 2004

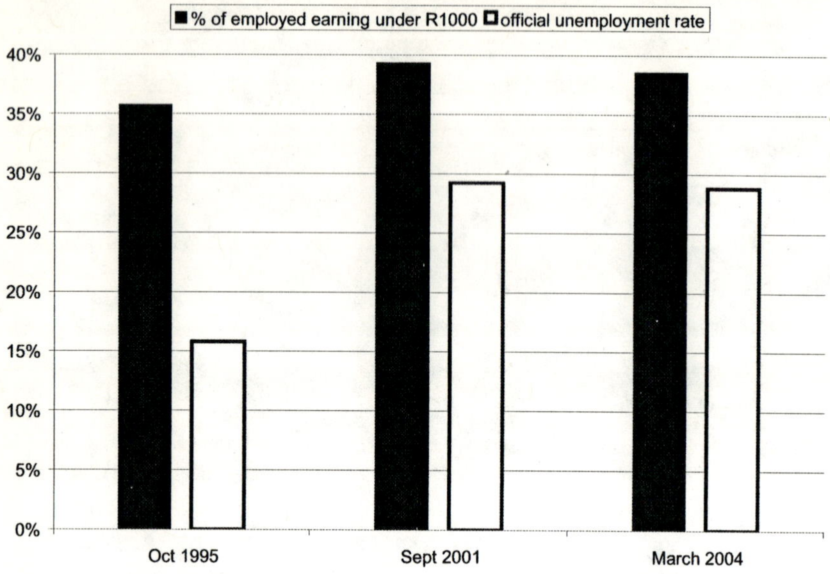

Note: The official definition of unemployment, used here, classes workers who want paid jobs but are too discouraged to seek it as "economically inactive," rather than as unemployed. *Source*: Figures calculated from *Statistics South Africa, South Africa in Transition (2001) for 1995*; and from *Statistics South Africa, Labour Force Survey, Sept. 2001 and Mar. 2004*, both available at http://www.statssa.gov.za

Two factors led to the rapid increase in the unemployment rate. First, in the late 1990s, the share of the population seeking paid employment climbed 4% a year, far faster than the overall labor force.[12] Second, job creation lagged behind the rate of population growth.[13] The relatively slow expansion in employment reflected

- Low economic growth concentrated on capital-intensive heavy industry, especially minerals, heavy chemicals and auto, and
- Continued differences in access to productive assets and economic services.

In these circumstances, it is not surprising that inequalities related to class, race and gender persisted and possibly even deepened. Despite the emergence of a small but vibrant black elite in the state and the private sector, most Africans continued as poorly paid workers, or scraped out existence as hawkers or subsistence farmers in the former homeland areas.

Table 7: South African economic status and incomes by race and gender, 2003[1]

	African women		African men			
% of adults:	Former homeland[2]	Other areas	Former homeland[2]	Other areas	Coloureds/ Asians	Whites
Not economically active	51%	33%	43%	26%	35%	36%
Unemployed	30%	34%	27%	29%	18%	5%
Employed	19%	33%	30%	45%	47%	59%
- Formal sector	7%	18%	18%	36%	41%	55%
- Informal sector	8%	6%	11%	9%	3%	4%
- Domestic work	4%	9%	0%	1%	2%	0%
% of employed earning under R1000/month[3]	53%	81%	30%	60%	11%	2%
% of working-age adults	20%	21%	16%	20%	12%	10%

Notes: 1. The former homeland areas are here represented by the rural areas of KwaZulu Natal, Mpumalanga, North West, Limpopo and the Eastern Cape. This area also includes some commercial farming areas. Virtually no Coloureds, Asians or Whites live in the former homeland areas. Gender is not shown for these groups due to lack of space, but the gender differences are in any case much lower than for Africans. 'Not economically active' means neither earning an income nor trying to. 2. As noted, the data refer to an area largely but not perfectly contiguous with the former homeland areas. 3. In US dollar terms, R1000 fluctuated between $76 and $166 between 2002 and 2004, depending on the exchange rate. *Source: Statistics South Africa, Labourforce Survey* (Sept. 2003). Tshwane. Database on CD-ROM.

In short, while the South African state made considerable progress in overcoming the legacy of apartheid, results did not match up to the (inordinately optimistic) expectations held by much of the population before 1994. Shortcomings emerged primarily in the inability to overcome the interlinked challenges of high unemployment and massive inequalities in incomes and assets. The question here is how the policymaking process contributed to this outcome.

POLICYMAKING PROCESSES AND OUTCOMES

In the early 2000s, various authors analyzed policy-development processes as one factor behind the government's relatively limited success in overcoming the economic inequalities left by apartheid. We here briefly explore this discourse, and then consider the research agenda that flows from the institutionalist model described on page 113. The following section uses this agenda to analyse some representative policy-making processes in South Africa.

In its study of the first ten years of democracy, the Presidency contended that uneven outcomes reflected the fact that government did not control the economy directly. In contrast, it argued, the state directly managed the roll out of services and democratic institutions, and therefore showed greater success in these areas.[14]

This approach suggests that effective policy interventions must entail government control over decisionmakers. In fact, as the ROCCIPI research agenda emphazises,[15] most development policies depend on reshaping the environment for private individuals and organisations. This is especially true when dealing with market economies and family matters, where the state almost never has direct control over key actors. Development strategies succeeded precisely in situations where states have managed to guide the private sector consistently and rigorously toward activities that could create broad-based employment and growth.[16] The central question, then, becomes why the South African state did not achieve its aims in this regard.

Two recent studies[17] agree that policy weaknesses after 1994 largely reflected the inadequate involvement of working and poor people in policy development. These key constituencies could not, then, ensure that government focused consistently and realistically on their concerns. The studies' authors, Mhone and Edigheji argue further that the adoption in 1996 of the GEAR, an unpopular, conservative economic strategy, both required and deepened the exclusion from policy processes of representatives of the majority.

The institutionalist model of policymaking adopted here suggests ways to analyze this shortcoming more consistently and concretely. In particular, it indicates where and how policy-development processes systematically built in both inflexibility and a bias against the poor.

The following diagram illustrates the institutionalist approach. It indicates that to understand the policy-development process, we need to analyze

1. *The sources of information used.* For instance, unions will emphasise different facts and experiences than employers.
2. *The criteria used to analyse information and define policy aims.* A focus on economic growth alone will likely generate different measures from a concentration on sustainable employment creation and equity.
3. *Who actually drafts the policy.* Even with clear criteria and information, the policymakers' biases will have a substantial influence on the shape of government strategies.
4. Whether the policy includes *monitoring and response systems*, to ensure that stakeholders can report problems encountered in implementation and that officials reform measures appropriately.

Figure 2: A model of policy development

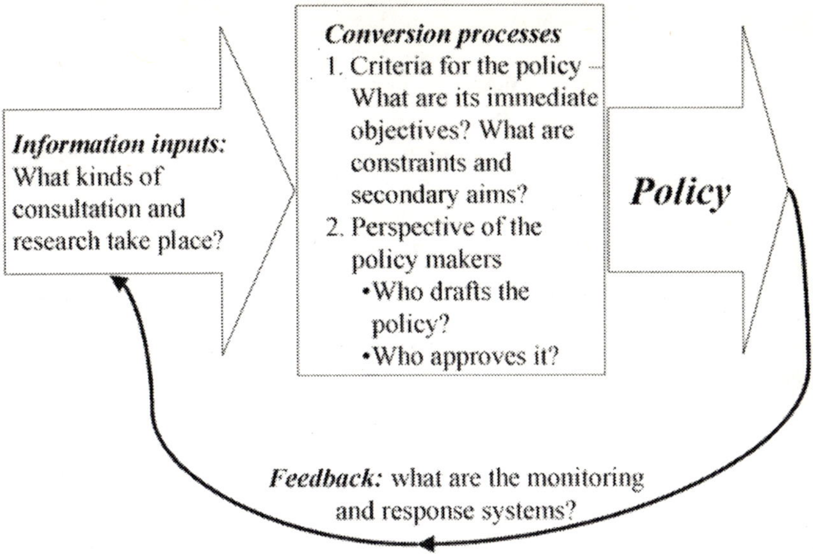

Source: Adapted from *Ann Seidman, Robert S. Seidman & Nalin Abeysekere, Legislative Drafting for Democratic Social Change: A Manual for Drafters 131* (Kluwer Law Int'l, 2001).

While the South African government did not establish standard procedures for policy development, the model highlights some general weaknesses.

To start with, drafting was generally carried out by private consultants and foreign advisors under the supervision of bureaucrats – what Khosa terms 'design teams.'[18] As a rule, as demonstrated in the case studies below, these teams did not prioritize employment creation or economic equity. Most targeted either short-term poverty relief or improvements in competitiveness and economic growth.

Political leaders could have maintained more consistent transformatory priorities. But their role was generally limited to demanding a policy and then revising the design team's proposals. Furthermore, strict compartmentalization in government made it difficult for a Minister to engage rigorously with policies deriving from outside her or his own department.

The dominance of design teams was reinforced by the failure to involve democratic institutions in key policy processes. The executive submitted only a tiny share of its policies for approval by the ruling party, the African National Congress (ANC). Often, too, it circumvented Parliament by relying on policy decrees and regulations, rather than passing legislation. Increasingly, however, when the executive did send legislation to Parliament, it accepted substantial amendments.

Second, in terms of inputs, most policy processes lacked both systematic research and widespread consultation. Government did not adopt a coherent approach or set standards for policy research. Each design team was free to choose whatever methodology it wanted. With few exceptions, at best they described the basic problem and then considered solutions deriving from international experience. At worst, they simply rejected out of hand research that supported opposing views.[19] Few design teams explored systematically either the factors giving rise to the problem in South Africa itself, or the likely social and economic impact of proposed measures.

Consultation at NEDLAC could have ensured broader sources of information as well as perspectives from the dominant stakeholders. NEDLAC provided a forum for policy engagement by representatives of organized business, organized labor and the state, with participation of community groups on issues related to social development.[20]

The NEDLAC Act required that government table at NEDLAC all policies with major implications for socio-economic conditions. But only the Departments of Labour and Trade and Industry felt bound by these provisions. Other departments submitted policy proposals only on a highly selective basis, so that many important issues never came up for discussion at NEDLAC at all.

In any case, even when departments tabled policy proposals at NEDLAC, officials often made no real effort to accommodate the views of organized business or labour. All too often, they saw themselves as defending "their" policies, making occasional concessions to outside demands, rather than seeing consultation as a way to improve their proposals.

Third, very few policies included systematic review or feedback mechanisms. At most, they would incorporate a formal commitment to an overall evaluation after two or three years. Often, the review never took place. In any case, a once-off review cannot substitute for systems to ensure on-going oversight and monitoring as the basis for rapid response to failures.

Procedures for developing policies were neither standardized nor uniform in South Africa, so the extent of these weaknesses varied substantially between specific cases. The following section illustrates them by considering three very different instances.

CASE STUDIES OF POLICY DEVELOPMENT IN SOUTH AFRICA

In each of the following cases, we first describe the policy and its outcomes or, in more recent instances, likely results. We then analyse the policy-making process through the categories of the institutionalist flow model described above.

GEAR

In 1996, the government published GEAR, which since then has dominated economic policy debates in South Africa. In the words of the U.S. State Department,

> The Government of South Africa demonstrated its commitment to open markets, privatization, and a favorable investment climate with its release of the crucial Growth, Employment and Redistribution (GEAR) strategy - the neoliberal economic strategy to cover 1996-2000.[21]

GEAR's conservative tendency emerged in commitments to cut the government deficit and taxes relative to GDP, reduce tariffs, control wage increases and accelerate privatization. At the same time, the government said it would prioritize anti-poverty spending programmes and accelerate training for workers.[22] To expand employment creation, GEAR provided some tax incentives for investment in labour-intensive activities.[23]

GEAR promized to speed up growth, investment and employment creation, with specific targets set through 2000. It failed on all three counts, as the following table shows. Only the cuts in government borrowing and inflation exceeded GEAR expectations. In stark contrast, economic expansion, investment, government spending and above all job creation remained far below GEAR's predictions.

The U.S. State Department concluded that GEAR

> ... had mixed success. It brought greater financial discipline and macroeconomic stability but has failed to deliver in key areas. Formal employment continued to decline, and despite the ongoing efforts of black empowerment and signs of a fledgling black middle class and social mobility, the country's wealth remains very unequally distributed along racial lines.[24]

In large part, GEAR's disappointing outcomes reflected the failure of its strong supply-side assumption that cuts in government borrowing relative to GDP would encourage private savings and investment. As a result, the economy would grow, and government spending would rise in real terms despite the limits on borrowing and taxation. Instead, as government cut its deficit in the late 1990s, company savings and investment plummeted. Net company savings dropped from 6% of the GDP in 1997 to 3% in 2000, despite the fall in government dissavings from 5% to 2%.

The implementation of GEAR also proved problematic. Government measured its implementation of GEAR almost exclusively in terms of the fiscal targets, especially the level of taxes and government borrowing relative to the GDP. The treasury incorporated these parameters consistently into its annual budgets. In contrast, government did not report systematically on more qualitative aims, including those around anti-poverty programmes and labour-intensive growth.

As a result of this strategy, government expenditure fell about 1% a year in real terms in the late 1990s. When governments reduce their spending, they almost always find it easier to cut investment projects than personnel and services. In this case, government investment fell from 7.9% of the budget in 1997

Table 8: GEAR targets and actual performance of the economy, 1996-2003

	GEAR projections			Actuals			
	1996	2000	Average	1996	2000	Average	Actual, 2003
Model characteristics							
Fiscal deficit (% of GDP)	5%	3%	4%	-5%	-3%	-3%	-3%
Real bank rate	7%	3%	4%	14%	8%	12%	11%
Real government investment growth	3%	17%	7%	14%	-6%	-2%	9%
Real parastatal investment growth	3%	10%	8%	11%	-20%	-1%	17%
Real private sector investment growth	9%	17%	12%	8%	6%	1%	1%
Real non-gold export growth	9%	10%	8%	12%	10%	5%	-2%
Outcomes							
GDP growth	4%	6%	4%	4%	4%	3%	2%
Inflation (CPI)	8%	8%	8%	6%	7%	6%	0.3%
Employment growth (non-agricultural formal)	1%	4%	3%	0%	4%	1%	6%
New jobs per year ('000s)	126	409	270	20	256	83	650
Real export growth, manufacturing	10%	13%	11%	8%	22%	9%	-7%
Gross private savings (% of GDP)	21%	22%	21%	21%	18%	19%	17%
Government dissavings (% of GDP)	3%	1%	2%	5%	2%	3%	1%
Resource envelope (1995 billions)	161	179	167	161	162	160	193
Change in resource envelope	n.a.	6.1%	2.1%	n.a.	3.5%	0.1%	6.5%

Source: GEAR projections: National Treasury, *Growth, Employment and Redistribution: A Macroeconomic Strategy*, p. 7 and, for resource envelope, Appendix 9 (unnumbered pages). Pretoria, 1997, available at http://www.treasury.gov.za (last accessed in Dec. 2004). Actual results: Fiscal deficit: Budget Review 2000, Table 3.3, p. 46; Budget Review 2001, Table 3.3, p. 45; MTBPS 2004, Table 1.2, p. 10; real bank rate – predominant nominal interest rate from SARB, *Quarterly Bulletin*, June 1999, p. S-28; December 2002, p. S-28, December 2004, p. 2-28, deflated using CPI; investment figures – SARB long-term data series on national accounts, downloaded from http://www.resbank.gov.za in December 2004; real non-gold exports calculated using volume indices for exports from SARB, *Quarterly Bulletin*, December 2002, p. S-87 and December 2004, p S-89; GDP growth from long-term data series on national accounts, downloaded from http://www.resbank.gov.za in December 2004; CPI from StatsSA, long-term data series on inflation, downloaded from http://www.statssa.gov.za in November 2004; employment growth from Business Trust, *Employment and Unemployment In South Africa: A Brief Description*, Johannesburg, 2004, Table 4, p. 27, and Statistics South Africa, *Labourforce Survey*, March 2004, downloaded from http://www.statssa.gov.za in January 2005; manufacturing exports from TIPS EasyData, nominal values for manufacturing exports, deflated using CPI, downloaded from http://www.tips.org.za in June 2004; figuring for savings from SARB long-term data series on national accounts, downloaded from http://www.resbank.gov.za in December 2004; figures for resource envelope are nominal total expenditure from National Treasury, *Budget Review 2002*, Table 1, p. 190 and *Budget Review 2004*, Table 1, deflated using CPI for March recalculated with 1995 = 100. Downloaded from http://www.treasury.gov.za in December 2004.

to 6.1% in 2000. By 2003, government investment was lower as a percentage of GDP than it had ever been since 1946, when the data series began.

From its adoption, GEAR was profoundly unpopular with the ANC's main constituencies.[25] Analysing the policy processes that generated it help explain both its internal weaknesses and why it was adopted in the face of substantial opposition both inside and outside the state. We here consider the composition of the drafting team; the criteria established for the policy; the inputs utilized; and the feedback mechanisms.

1. The ***drafters*** of GEAR comprized a design team combining consultants from leading (historically white) universities and a state-owned development bank (the Development Bank of Southern Africa), government officials and two World Bank advisors. With one exception, the team consisted of white men.[26] Most had been opponents of the apartheid state before 1994, but none had worked full-time for the democratic movement or the ANC. None were elected or directly accountable to the ANC's constituencies.

2. In terms of ***criteria***, GEAR was finalized by the National Treasury as an urgent response to the Mexican capital crisis in 1995. The treasury started work on the strategy at least a year earlier, but had been unable to overcome opposition within the state itself. During the crisis, however, GEAR's proponents argued that government had to reassure foreign investors by urgently adopting a conservative macro-economic policy. Otherwise it could suffer capital flight. This kind of situation had just hit Mexico and was threatening in Asia, leading to extraordinary increases in interest rates and currency depreciation.[27]

The main criteria for GEAR thus became whether it reassured foreign investors by meeting their demands, which focused on macroeconomic stability, rather than job creation, equity or short-term growth. It did little to respond directly to the claims of the ANC's historic constituency – black workers, professionals and small business, the unemployed and rural poor. Instead, it essentially argued that government should first satisfy business, which would increase investment, ultimately causing a trickle-down effect to benefit society as a whole.

In this, GEAR's basic strategy contrasted sharply with the Reconstruction and Development Policy (RDP), the ANC's manifesto from the early 1990s, before it came to power. The RDP had generally emphasized substantial growth in government services to black communities as the basis for economic growth and employment creation.

3. GEAR relied essentially on three types of ***inputs***: macro-economic models from both state and private institutions, proposals from national government departments, and comments from Cabinet members. It was developed in secrecy, and consequently did not incorporate inputs outside these rather narrow channels.

To justify the fiscal targets, in particular, the GEAR's authors used only one type of evidence: They ran their proposals through four macroeconomic models. Yet all these models essentially assumed what had to be proved - that is, that government borrowing in South Africa crowded out private investment. Their basic simulations built in the untested presumption that increased government borrowing relative to GDP would lead to higher interest rates and thus lower investment.

In fact, econometric analysis demonstrates that private investment in South Africa historically lagged public investment. Moreover, the crowding out hypothesis assumed that government borrowing would directly influence interest rates and therefore private investment. But the Reserve Bank essentially set basic interest rates in line with monetary policy.

The design team also invited inputs on specialized areas from some departments, notably Trade and Industry and Labor. But these inputs were held within narrow limits. The design team prevented senior officials from the Department of Labor from seeing the full document, giving them only the chapter on the labor market.

The draft of GEAR was submitted to the Minister of Finance and subsequently approved by Cabinet. The Minister delayed the submission to Cabinet by a few weeks in order to incorporate a stronger commitment to equity and employment creation. He did not, however, require substantial changes in the fiscal targets.

After Cabinet approval, the treasury published GEAR as national policy. This approach effectively by-passed the institutions designed to ensure broader debate and buy in on key policies. GEAR formed no part of the ANC's elections manifesto; it was not tabled for discussion at NEDLAC or subjected to Parliamentary hearings or debate. It was presented to the ANC's national executive only after it had been adopted by Cabinet. At that point, Cabinet portrayed the document as essentially non-negotiable.

4. GEAR included no ***review*** mechanisms. Since the aim was to reassure investors, supporters argued that the state could not afford any hint that it might modify its policies. As a result, the policy lacked a mechanism for managing unintended consequences. In particular, when growth did not take off as predicted, the deficit and tax targets required cuts in government spending – contrary to supporters' predictions of continuing, although slower, increases. The lack of a review mechanism meant that that the fiscal targets could not be reconsidered despite this unexpected and contractionary impact.

In short, the policy-making process that produced GEAR showed substantial flaws. In technical terms, it depended not on in-depth research, but on macro-economic simulations that relied as much on theoretical assumptions as on evidence about the South African economy. In addition, the drafting process largely excluded representatives of the ANC's constituencies.

GEAR's impact went beyond economic policy. It undermined the unity of the democratic movement and increased scepticism about government policies in the labour movement, the churches, the universities and other sections of civil society. In 2004, the Presidency's ten-year review explicitly noted the need to build stronger partnerships with these stakeholders as well as with business.[28]

From this standpoint, the Growth and Development Summit (GDS), held in 2003 through NEDLAC, represented a significant turn away from GEAR. The GDS provided space for engagement between government, organized business, organized labour and community representatives.

In contrast to GEAR's emphasis on economic growth as a panacea, the GDS agreements focused heavily on the need to direct growth to create employment, ensure greater equity and increase productive investment. They incorporated commitments to expand public employment, support black economic empowerment, build a co-operative movement, reform the financial sector to serve poor households and small enterprise, and direct procurement toward local producers. A critical agreement provided a framework for tripartite development of industrial strategies geared to sustainable job creation.

The GDS agreements resulted from essentially corporatist negotiations. They did not lead directly or automatically to government policy decisions, and were often neither clearly drafted nor specific. Implementation has remained slow and often only partial.

Despite these shortcomings, the GDS represented an important first step toward more inclusive policy making and implementation. Perhaps most important, it obtained the commitment of big business and other powerful stakeholders to developmental efforts, rather than a focus on short-term interests. The critical challenge then became to sustain engagement and action on that basis.

The national budget

South Africa's national budget – which Parliament approved annually as law – allocated government funds between national departments and provinces. In effect, it provided a national financial plan, which government increasingly sought to link to defined outputs. In the early 2000s, the initiation of the Policy Co-ordination and Advisory Service (PCAS) in the Presidency and Cabinet clusters on critical issues began to provide an alternative, more substantive co-ordination mechanism. Still, the budget remained by far the best established and most powerful national planning process.

The budget had special significance in South Africa. Under apartheid, the state consciously directed its spending to relatively prosperous white and, to a lesser extent, Coloured and Indian communities. From the time it took power in 1994, the democratic government sought to restructure spending to ensure greater equity. That meant, above all, raising funding for social grants, services and infrastructure in black communities, as well as supporting the restructuring of the economy toward job-creating growth.

Government's success in this project remained mixed. All in all, it did much more to improve social spending than to restructure the economy.

Overall fiscal policy limited the impact of the budget. In the late 1990s, GEAR cut overall spending. This probably had a contractionary impact on the economy and certainly limited government's ability to fight poverty, maintain public investments, and drive redistributive programmes such as land reform and support for small enterprise. From 2000, government spending increased again, providing substantially more scope to improve both service provision and economic services. Still, as noted above, increases in user fees continued to limit benefits to the poor.

Within the limits of a fairly tight fiscal policy, government shifted expenditure toward poor households and raised the share of social spending. As the following table shows, the share of police, health, education and other social services rose steadily, while the shares of defence and economic services declined.

Figure 3: Government spending by major functions, 1983 to 2002

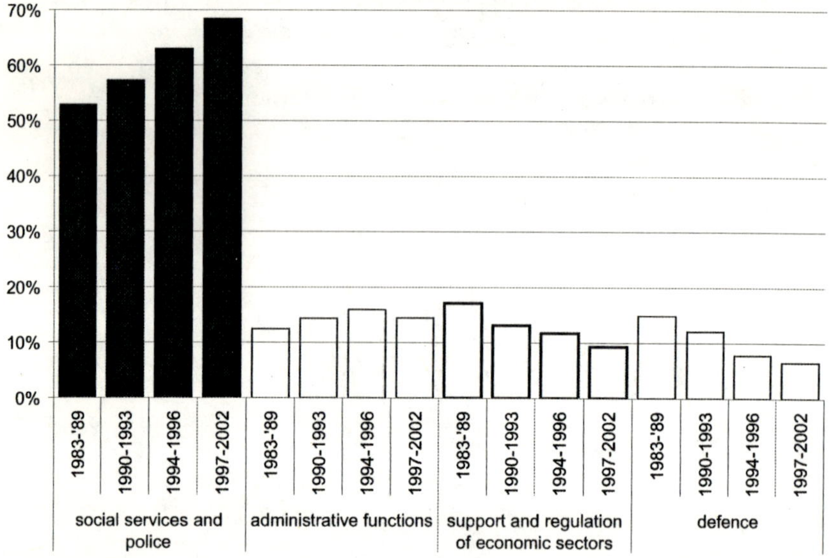

Source: Calculated from, SARB, long-term data series on public expenditure, available at http://www.resbank.gov.za (last accessed in Dec. 2004).

Schneider argues that the basic nature of the state appears in the structure of the budget.[29] Thus, the classical administrative state would focus its spending on the bureaucracy and security, while the developmental state would emphasize economic services. In contrast, welfare states would put the bulk of their expenditure into social protection. Following this argument, budget policies in South Africa suggested a welfarist rather than a transformatory approach.[30]

Again, we can understand this outcome in terms of the nature of the policy-development process. From this standpoint, the highly institutionalized annual cycle of the budget made it unique.

The Constitution required complex interactions between the national and provincial governments around the budget. In essence, the national government set the overall fiscal policy, since provincial administrations had only very limited capacity for raising their own revenues and borrowing. The national treasury then allocated funds between national departments and the provinces. The Constitution gave responsibility for most security and economic functions and for policies on social services to the national state. Four fifths of provincial allocations went on health, education and welfare.

The analysis of policy development here focuses on the national budget process, which was essentially replicated at the provincial level.

The budget ***drafters*** largely resided in the Treasury. As with other government departments, after 1994 the Treasury staff shifted gradually from predominantly white and Afrikaner men to a more representative (and usually much younger) group of officials, most of whom had supported the democratic movement. By the mid-2000s, the Treasury had developed considerable capacity to guide spending within government functions in line with national aims.

In these circumstances, the Treasury's mandate effectively set the main ***criteria*** for the budget. Its over-riding objective was to ensure that expenditure remained within the limits set by fiscal policy. While its strategy grew steadily more expansionary in the early 2000s, it still preferred to risk slower economic growth and social development rather than higher debt and taxation.

Within the constraints set by fiscal targets, the Treasury sought fairly consistently to direct expenditure to the poor. It also aimed to increase government investment while restraining personnel costs. It did not, however, have the mandate or capacity to drive a policy to restructure the economy, and this area remained largely neglected.

These priorities largely shaped the overall structure of government spending. The $5 billion arms deal signed in the late 1990s formed the main exception – and was also one of the rare cases where Cabinet did not support a treasury position.

The hegemony of the Treasury's viewpoint led to two important contradictions in budgetary policies:

First, the Treasury's emphasis on restraining costs repeatedly tempted Treasury into excessive optimism about the ability of the private sector to roll out services for the poor. Yet the private sector cannot provide services where households cannot pay for them unless the state supplies a subsidy. In consequence, given mass poverty, the savings for the state from private delivery often proved limited, while high user fees shut out many expected beneficiaries.

Second, the Treasury argued that efficiency required a continual decline in personnel costs. This position ignored the apartheid history of understaffing in black communities. In the event, efforts to downsize employment while raising investment often undermined services. Moreover, wage restraint led to a swelling outflow of skilled people from the major public service professions – health, education and policing in particular. By the mid-2000s, the government had begun to speak of a major skills shortage in the public sector.[31]

In terms of ***inputs***, the budget drafters relied principally on other departments and Cabinet. The budget remained secret until published in February for the financial year starting in March, and Parliament could debate but not amend it. This limited interaction made it harder to ensure the allocation of resources in line with the needs of the ANC constituency.

The process of drafting the budget started with the development of overall resource envelopes by the treasury at national and provincial level. Departments then provided inputs on how they would use the funds provided. In theory, this enabled them to allocate funds in line with new policies and needs. In practice, weaknesses in departmental financial planning led to considerable inertia, making it difficult to phase out unwanted programmes or initiate new ones.

In most departments, the budget never became a strategic exercise to support transformation, but instead extrapolated existing trends. Financial managers, and not the departmental leadership as a whole, developed draft budgets. Yet, at least until the 2000s, in most national departments the top financial staff had joined the public service long before 1994. The slow pace of change in financial staff arose in large part because Director Generals were generally very anxious to avoid audit queries, and nervous that new officials could not manage government's complex procurement and accounting rules. Ministers were supposed to ensure political guidance, but many did not feel competent to engage with the detailed technicalities of the budget.[32]

To encourage more strategic budgeting, from 1998 the national treasury published three-year budgets in the Medium-Term Expenditure Framework. Departments often responded, however, by simply projecting existing spending trends, rather than using the medium-term perspective to phase in more appropriate programmes. The template for the medium-term budgets, which included almost all the detail of annual budgets, made them less useful for strategic planning.

Departments had to defend their initial budget proposals to the Budget Council. Under the system inherited from apartheid, this function was managed by public-service officials headed by the Director General of State Expenditure. In contrast, the Budget Council – established in the late 1990s to ensure stronger political leadership – brought together provincial and national finance ministers. Still, the Budget Council remained limited to the national and provincial treasuries, without involving other stakeholders or departments.

In theory, final Cabinet approval provided the broader strategic oversight required for effective budgets. In fact, Cabinet rarely initiated substantial changes in Treasury proposals. It formally approved initial allocations as well as final estimates. Typically, however, by the time it considered the budget, the level of detail made it difficult to engage. Moreover, fiscal policy proves daunting for most people, even Ministers.

There was virtually no scope for detailed inputs from outside the executive. In the British tradition, the budget was strictly secret until announced in February for the government financial year starting in March. The treasury frequently requested inputs, but in the absence of a published draft, those inputs necessarily remained *ad hoc*. At NEDLAC, constituencies tried to have a discussion on fiscal principles such as taxation and the structure of expenditure, but the lack of documentation prevented systematic engagement.

From 2001, leading civil society organizations – COSATU, the South African Council of Churches and the South African NGO Coalition – produced an annual review of the budget called the People's Budget. But the national treasury only engaged directly with them in 2005. Instead, to demonstrate a commitment to openness, the Minister's budget speech regularly mentioned comments received through the treasury website from the public at large – or, more precisely, from the tiny, mostly well-off minority with access to the Internet.

Every year, Parliament passed the budget as law. Under legislation dating back long before 1994, however, it could not amend the budget, but only vote it up or down. Since rejection of the budget would constitute a vote of no confidence, this requirement effectively ruled out amendments. The 1996 Constitution required a change to the law to permit Parliamentary amendments, but as of 2005 the government had not made the necessary amendments. The treasury argued that a more open fiscal process would lead at best to speculation, and at worst to political deadlock and demands for unsustainably high expenditure.

In short, public and Parliamentary inputs into fiscal policy remained largely unstructured. They took place through the press, general engagements at NEDLAC and Parliamentary debates, rather than in forums that permitted an effective discussion of the details of the budget. Treasury could then pick and choose amongst comments in shaping the budget for the following year.

The budget included a host of formal ***review*** mechanisms, ranging from the national treasury's annual and exhaustive Budget Review – published with the annual budget – to annual audits. But these mechanisms measured the budget only against treasury's objectives of controlling government spending and shifting expenditure toward the poor. They did not analyse whether expenditure patterns supported economic development and job creation. Nor did they evaluate underlying treasury policies such as user fees and public-private partnerships.

The Treasury explicitly tried to substitute increased transparency and improved communication about the budget for stronger Parliamentary control and public engagement. Its main measures included annual updates of the medium-term budget policy to cover the upcoming three-year period and publication of more details on programmes included in the budget.

In sum, the effective control of the national treasury department over the budget process helped explain both successes and failures in directing resources to meet national goals. Treasury succeeded in imposing a restrictive fiscal policy under GEAR, although it permitted substantially greater growth thereafter. Within the limitations set by its fiscal policy, it worked consistently to encourage departments to use resources for anti-poverty programmes. But it did not have an equally clear vision for the economic services, which tended to fall behind. In addition, the new anti-poverty programmes did not translate into a stimulus for economic development, in part because of under-resourcing and in part because they were not oriented consistently to expand economic engagement and employment creation.

Finally, Treasury officials persistently ignored the fact that most South Africans simply could not afford to pay for basic services. The consequent insistence on privatization and user fees wherever possible reduced the benefits of many anti-poverty programs.

The Integrated Manufacturing Strategy

Before 1994, the democratic movement argued strongly for a 'developmental state' that would restructure the economy to ensure employment creation and equity. This commitment remained part of the government's language. Even the generally free-market GEAR argued, in a subordinate section, for a structural shift toward more labour-intensive industries.

Yet the main policy on industrialisation, the Integrated Manufacturing Strategy (IMS), was published as a draft only in 2002, and had not been finalized by mid-2005.[33] It remained largely irrelevant to key development initiatives, including the GDS and efforts both inside and outside the state to develop sectoral strategies. This situation arose in part because the policy-development process did not provide an adequate forum for resolving deep-seated disagreements amongst stakeholders.

To understand the differences between the IMS and the structural approach historically adopted by the democratic movement, we first locate it in the broader debate between competitiveness and structural development strategies. We then summarize the IMS and its outcomes. The final section outlines the policy-development process around the strategy.

Both competitiveness and structural strategies differ from extreme free-market versions of the 'Washington Consensus' by recognising that the state plays a crucial role in development. But they differ fundamentally about the nature of that role.

Competitiveness strategies essentially argue that the state must protect property rights and provide public goods, especially infrastructure, skills development and basic social services. They go beyond free-market orthodoxy only in the degree of state involvement in these areas. But they agree with the free-market tenet that the state should not, except in extreme cases, explicitly target the structure of ownership or production. That should be left to private actors reacting to market conditions. In this view, the state's role is to make the market work effectively and efficiently, then let private choices determine production and ownership.[34]

Supporters of structural strategies agree that the state must act to ensure greater overall efficiency. They argue, however, that even with improved infrastructure, skills and services, market forces may not spontaneously overcome the narrow production structures and incomplete value chains typical of developing countries. In line with earlier dependency theories, they argue that the critical challenge is to diversify into new industries and to strengthen the linkages between commodity production, manufacturing and services. By extension, the state should identify and support necessary changes in the structures of production and ownership. For this approach, the developmental states of Eastern Asia provide the main model.[35]

In South Africa, the line between competitive and structuralist approaches reflected debates about the relative importance and causes of unemployment and slow growth.

- Competitiveness approaches essentially argued that pervasive inefficiency and consequently slow growth arose because the apartheid state intervened in markets. In particular, they blamed the long history of high protection to support import-substitution industrialization, inefficient state control of basic infrastructure and, in the 1980s, massive strategic investments in petrochemicals and arms.
- In contrast, the structuralist approach argued that economic policies must focus on South Africa's mass poverty and unemployment. These challenges arose from a combination of continued dependence on minerals, which can no longer create substantial employment, and the historic denial of productive assets and skills to the majority of the population. The state should thus seek to diversify the economy while improving basic economic and social services for poor communities.[36]

Overall, the IMS aligns with a competitiveness approach. It is internally contradictory, however, with substantial gaps between its aims, analysis and strategies. Although it acknowledges the central importance of dealing with unemployment and inequality, its proposals emphasize instead the need to enhance efficiency. It suggests virtually no measures to address joblessness.

The IMS was rooted in the observation that while the opening of the economy after 1994 led to increased exports, overall growth, unemployment and inequality remained little affected. By extension, the core challenge was to define ways the state could shape integration with the world economy to achieve greater benefits.

The IMS analysis started with the argument that the democratic government had to open the economy in order to overcome the distortions imposed by concentrated ownership and the history of protectionism. In the 1990s, it said, cuts in tariffs and other measures to reduce obstacles to international trade and capital flows succeeded in raising productivity and encouraging economic diversification.

From these initial arguments, the IMS concluded that the state should focus on factors that prevented broader benefits from globalisation. As the main blockages, it pointed to:

- Shortcomings in infrastructure, particularly transport and communications, as well as high input prices generally;
- Continued dependence on historic comparative advantage, especially reliance on cheap resources and labour plus privileged market access, which are not viable in a globalizing world;
- Job shedding in manufacturing as a result of relatively rapid growth in capital-intensive sectors and rapid improvements in productivity;
- Slow progress by small and micro enterprise and black economic empowerment, although the IMS did not explain this problem;
- Inadequate partnerships between the state and key stakeholders.

This analysis pointed to measures to deal with broad inefficiencies. But it provided little guidance for programs to address unemployment and inequality.

The confusion on this critical issue emerged in contradictory summations of the proposed growth path. Thus, as various points, the IMS suggested,

> ...the trajectory envisioned for the economy as a whole by government [is] beneficiation of natural resources, knowledge intensity, and export orientation....[37]

> The long-term trajectory of the growth path is secured through building integrated value matrices that include regional platforms for production-expanding opportunities, increasing value addition and knowledge-intensity, and building equity and wider participation in the economy....[38]

> At the core of the accelerated trajectory is knowledge intensity, which means utilising and developing the knowledge and skills of our people in order to integrate information and communication technologies, technology, innovation and knowledge-intensive services into the functioning of the economy as a whole....[39]

The proposed trajectories all had knowledge intensity in common, and little else. Nowhere did the IMS explain how rising knowledge intensity would support employment and equity. In the event, it often means bringing in technologies that further displace labor. Moreover, persistent inequalities in skills and access to technical education severely limited the ability of black communities to benefit from high-tech opportunities.

The IMS located itself as an elaboration on the government's earlier Microeconomic Reform Strategy,[40] which was also essentially a competitiveness approach. The Microeconomic Reform Strategy emphasized skills development, innovation, finance for small enterprise and black economic empowerment, improved infrastructure and input costs, and sector strategies aimed primarily at increasing exports. The DTI's role in this context was to champion industrialization in general, develop sector-specific strategies, and provide support for manufacturing enterprises across the economy.

The IMS was notably short of practical proposals. As the basis for sectoral work, it advocated analysis of value matrices – that is, the chain of production from raw materials to final output, plus related services and distribution. In terms of the competitiveness/structural dichotomy, however, it gave divergent priorities. Although it suggested at one point that analyzes should identify job-creating activities within the value matrix,[41] it generally emphasized cost-cutting as a near-exclusive goal.[42]

More specifically, the IMS's proposals for specific sectors – clothing, agro processing, minerals beneficiation, tourism, auto, crafts, pharmaceuticals and biotechnologies and information and communication technologies – focussed narrowly on increases in high-tech exports. These efforts were not likely to generate jobs or provide opportunities for smaller enterprise on a large scale.

The IMS ended with sections on the importance of partnership, especially with business and labour through NEDLAC, and monitoring against prioritized objectives. These included "Gross Domestic Product (GDP), employment, investment, exports, small business development, Black Economic Empowerment (BEE), women's empowerment, future competitiveness and the geographic spread of social and productive investment."[43] This varied list of aims could not help officials decide between trade offs, for instance between job creation and competitiveness.

The results of the IMS were mixed.

Little evidence emerged of more integrated, knowledge-intensive or faster growth in manufacturing or manufacturing exports. In the early 2000s, the value of the rand dominated trends in manufacturing. When the rand dropped precipitously in late 2001, industrial exports increased; when it rose, they declined substantially. The lack of a clear policy on the rand pointed to the failure of the IMS to define a trajectory for industrial policy.

The DTI itself apparently saw the development of sector strategies as central to the IMS.[44] But the dualist approach rooted in the IMS persisted.

NEDLAC sponsored tripartite sector processes focused explicitly on job-creating growth. Most made only very slow progress, in large part because organized business and labor had limited policy capacity, while government officials did not drive the process or ensure a focus on employment. Even when sector strategies led to worthwhile agreements, government departments often ignored them. The two exceptions were the agreements on the financial sector and discussions on the chemicals industry, where business put in greater effort to develop and implement innovative proposals.

Meanwhile, the DTI forged ahead with the development of strategies geared narrowly to increasing exports, without engaging business or labour until the strategies were finalized. This approach caused confusion and delays at best, and at worst unrealistic proposals and more uneasy relations with the hoped-for partners.

The process of developing the IMS reflected a logjam over policy, which helped explain the failure to finalize it. On the one hand, both business and labor rejected the IMS as overly focused on formal manufacturing, and therefore unable to restructure the economy as needed. On the other hand, DTI officials maintained a narrow focus on competitiveness. They were able to continue to work on sector strategies even in the absence of consensus on industrial policy – although it seemed unlikely that these strategies would prove effective in the absence of support from either business or labour.

In terms of the policy process, the **drafters** of the IMS remained strictly within the DTI. A large number of internal drafts circulated, with different authors essentially re-starting the process periodically. The first published draft, written by an economist recruited to the department mainly for that purpose, focused narrowly on proposals to develop formal manufacturing through a focus on enhancing knowledge-based production (which remained very poorly defined).

This draft became the basis for getting broader **inputs**. It was discussed at NEDLAC and in Parliament. The main criticism that arose in both forums was the failure to emphasize job creation and equality, and the lack of direction for restructuring the economy to achieve those aims. The inclusion of these broader inputs remained mixed at best. New drafters at the DTI essentially added employment creation and equity as explicit priorities. They did not, however, fundamentally rethink the analysis of the economy or the actual proposals. The result was an ambiguous and contradictory document.

The IMS did support improvements in **monitoring**. The process demonstrated the difficulty of altering basic priorities, however. Evaluation of employment clearly remained an afterthought, while the department does not include any indicators for investment.

Of a total of 56 key achievements listed in the DTI's 2003/4 annual report, only one related directly to employment creation. The DTI made no published attempt to monitor overall trends in employment and equity, or to link these trends to its own efforts. Moreover, the indicators monitored generally reflect departmental outputs, such as supporting export pavilions and building a new campus, rather than broader economic outcomes.

In sum, the process of developing the IMS pointed to the importance of broader inputs in ensuring more appropriate policies. At the same time, it underscored the need for systems to ensure that officials genuinely engaged with outside inputs. Otherwise, they may just pay lip service to other views while continuing to pursue their own aims.

At the same time, the IMS pointed to a profound contradiction in the role of the state in driving development. To be effective, the state must give leadership, both enforcing policy priorities that consistently reflect national needs and providing the technical capacity to propose sustainable measures. But it must also test proposals against stakeholders' practical experience and maintain enough support to avoid unnecessary resistance.

From this standpoint, the failure of the IMS largely arose because the government did not give unambiguous mandates to DTI officials both

- To ensure a clear emphasis on addressing the central economic problems of unemployment and poverty, and
- In that context, to work with organized stakeholders to ensure sustainable solutions, rather than relying solely on their own expertise.

CONCLUSION

Discussion of governance in South Africa has generally remained at the level of state and class. Analysis of policy development processes using an institutional model that focuses on the aims, the drafters, inputs and feedback processes provides a more concrete view, generating more practical proposals.

From this standpoint, the inability of economic policy in South Africa to ensure consistent growth in the first decade of independence arose largely from the failure of the state to re-orient the national economic departments to focus on equity and employment creation. Instead, these departments tended to emphasise growth within the existing structures of production and ownership. They largely ignored inputs from stakeholders, even when compelled to engage at NEDLAC or in Parliament. This approach to policy development failed to stimulate much more rapid growth or to ameliorate mass poverty.

By the mid-2000s, this approach was increasingly contested within government, notably through the work of the Presidency. Much greater efforts were being made to define structural changes needed to bring about more equitable development. Moreover, the government made a commitment to work more closely with the main stakeholders to achieve these aims. These efforts were reinforced by the existence of NEDLAC and Parliament, which provided an institutional platform to obtain boarder inputs into the policy process.

The effort to establish a more effective development strategy remained contested both within the state and outside it. Success seemed likely to depend, above all, on the ability to ensure more inclusive, accountable and systematic policy processes geared explicitly to meeting the needs of the majority of South Africans.[45]

Notes

1. *See* Policy Co-ordination and Advisory Services (PCAS), Toward a Ten-Year Review 11 (Pretoria, South Africa); M. Khosa, Toward Effective Delivery: Synthesis Report on the Project Entitled "Closing the Gap Between Policy and Implementation in South Africa" 48 (Johannesburg, South Africa: Centre for Policy Studies 2003).
2. Unless otherwise noted, observations derive largely from the author's personal experience of the policy process, first as a government official from 1995 to 2000, and then as a member of the Policy Unit of the union federation COSATU.
3. These categories align with those suggested by the government's Toward a Ten-Year Review, *supra* note 1.

4. *See* GOVERNANCE IN THE NEW SOUTH AFRICA: THE CHALLENGES OF GLOBALISATION (G. Mhone & Omano Edigheji, eds., Univ. of Cape Town Press, 2003).
5. KHOSA, *supra* note 1, at 47.
6. *See generally* R. Autry & N. Makgetla, *Socio-Economic Rights and the Distribution of Government Services*, in SOUTH AFRICAN HUMAN RIGHTS COMMISSION, TEN YEAR REVIEW OF SOCIO-ECONOMIC RIGHTS (forthcoming 2006, manuscript on file with the authors).
7. I. Woolard, *Impact of Government Programmes Using Administrative Data Sets: Social Assistance Grants*, PROJECT 6.2 OF THE TEN YEAR REVIEW RESEARCH PROGRAMME 11 (Presidential Communications and Advisory Service, Pretoria, South Africa 2003).
8. *See* Autry & Makgetla, *supra* note 6; DONALD MCDONALD & JOHN PAPE, EDS., COST RECOVERY AND THE CRISIS OF SERVICE DELIVERY IN SOUTH AFRICA (Zed Press, 2002).
9. *See* PEOPLE'S BUDGET CAMPAIGN, PEOPLE'S BUDGET 2005-2006: PROPOSALS BY PEOPLE'S BUDGET CAMPAIGN (2004), available at http://www.naledi.org.za (last accessed in Sept. 2005).
10. *See* C. Simkins, *What Happened to the Distribution of Income in South Africa Between 1995 and 2001?* (Department of Economics Working Paper, University of the Witwatersrand 2004), available at http://www.sarpn.org.za (last accessed in Sept. 2005); C. Ardintgon, *et al.*, *The Sensitivity of Estimates of Post-Apartheid Changes in South African Poverty and Inequality to Key Data Imputations* (Centre for Social Science Research Working Paper No. 106, University of Cape Town 2005), available at http://www.sarpn.org.za (last accessed in Sept. 2005).
11. The balance of trade deficit rose from a R8 billion surplus in 2002 to a R44 billion deficit in 2004. 2004. Employment rose by about 5% in 2003/4, but dropped by 2% in the first quarter of 2005.
12. Possible reasons include the increased expectations of African, especially women, who were formerly pushed into the former homelands; rising education levels; and substantial retrenchments in parts of the formal sector, which would push other family members to seek paid work. *See* PCAS, *supra* note 1, at 36.
13. The data on job creation are inaccurate and contested. Government has argued that employment creation has been fairly robust. *See* PCAS, *supra* note 1, at 36. But that approach ignores fundamental problems with the data on employment. In particular, Statistics South Africa has increasingly included new categories as informal workers, notably subsistence farmers and hawkers. It is therefore virtually impossible to determine whether the reported growth in informal work reflects a real increase in economic opportunities or merely the reclassification of existing occupations from economically inactive to employed. Once the definitions stabilised from 2000, the share of informal employment declined. In contrast, data on formal employment seem reasonably accurate, although they probably understate job losses in mining. Overall, formal employment rose around 1% a year between 1998 and 2003, while the population grew at about 2% a year. For a more substantial discussion, *see* N. Makgetla, *Unpacking the Unemployment Data* (paper presented to COSATU CEC in 2003, Johannesburg, South Africa).
14. *See* PCAS, *supra* note 1, at 75.

15. *See* Ann Seidman, Robert S. Seidman & Nalin Abeysekere, Legislative Drafting for Democratic Social Change: A Manual for Drafters 93 (Kluwer Law Int'l 2000) Ch. 4; Ch. 2 this volume, pp. 35-37.
16. *See* Eun Mee Kim, Big Business, Strong State: Collusion and Conflict in South Korean Development, 1960-1990 32 (SUNY Press, 1998); The Developmental State 287 (Meredith Woo-Cumings, ed., Cornell Univ. Press 1999); Neva Makgetla, *A Developmental State for South Africa?* (Discussion document for COSATU Central Committee, Aug. 2005), available at http://www.cosatu.org.za (last accessed in Nov. 2005).
17. Mhone & Edigheji, eds., *supra* note 4; Khosa, *supra* note 1.
18. Khosa, *supra* note 1, at 49.
19. For instance, in 2002/3, the environmental minister refused to accept research showing that a ban on thin plastic bags would cost thousands of jobs and require the junking of millions of rand of equipment. Yet his department had helped design and manage the research project through NEDLAC. Similarly, in the early 2000s modelling by foreign consultants designing the policy for restructuring electricity generation initially found that privatisation would lead to higher, not lower, tariffs. At a meeting to present the findings, the senior partners in the consultancy were clearly taken aback by this outcome. Perhaps less surprisingly, the consultants' model went through at least two drafts, with the final version reversing the initial results.
20. NEDLAC is structured into four chambers – trade and industry; public finance and monetary policy; labour market; and social development – with community representation only in the last. It is administered by management and executive committees with representatives of all four constituencies, and holds an annual summit to look at strategic issues.
21. *See* State Department Bureau of African Affairs, Background Note: South Africa (2004), available at http://www.state.gov (last accessed in Jan. 2005).
22. National Treasury, Growth, Employment and Redistribution 2 (1996), available at http://www.treasury.gov.za (last accessed Sept. 2005)
23. *Id.* at 17.
24. State Department Bureau of African Affairs, *supra* note 21.
25. *See* Mhone & Edigheji, eds., *supra* note 4.
26. The only exception, the late and much missed Professor Guy Mhone, a respected and accomplished Malawian economist, was then working for the Department of Labour and only participated from a fairly late stage.
27. This analysis is based on the author's experience while working in the Presidency and the Department of Labour while the GEAR was drafted.
28. PCAS, *supra* note 1, at 103.
29. Benjamin Schneider, *The Desarrollista State in Brazil and Mexico*, in Woo-Cumings, ed., *supra* note 16, at 287-8.
30. People's Budget Campaign, People's Budget 2006-2007: Proposals by People's Budget Campaign 9 *et seq.*, available at http://www.naledi.org.za (last accessed in Sept. 2005).
31. *See* Thabo Mbeki, *Media Briefing on Cabinet Lekgotla* (Jul. 24, 2005), available at http://www.gov.za (last accessed on Jul. 24, 2005).

32. For instance, in 1997 in an engagement with a Minister, it became clear that he did not even understand that the printed budget estimates were expressed in thousands of rands.
33. DTI, A Guide to the Microeconomic Reform Strategy, available at http://www.dti.gov.za (last accessed in Mar. 2005).
34. This approach is well articulated in the latest World Development Report (World Bank 2004), which supports strong measures to improve the overall investment climate, as opposed to "targeted interventions," about which it is very cautious.
35. *See e.g.* Woo-Cumings, eds., *supra* note 16; Kim, *supra* note 16.
36. *See e.g.* UNDP, Human Development Indicators 2004 (2004); COSATU, Discussion Document on Industrial Strategy (2005), available at http://www.cosatu.org.za (last accessed in Aug. 2005); Neva Makgetla, *The Post-Apartheid Economy*, 100 *Rev. African Political Economy* 31 (2004); ANC, The Freedom Charter, available at http://www.anc.org.za (last accessed in Jan. 2005).
37. DTI, *supra* note 33 at 30.
38. *Id.* at 32.
39. *Id.* at 3.
40. *Id.*
41. *Id.* at 38.
42. *Id.* at 39.
43. *Id.* at 54.
44. M. Mpahlwa, *The DTI Budget Vote, Vote 32, by Minister of Trade and Industry, National Assembly* (Jun. 14, 2004), available at http://www.gov.za (last accessed in Aug. 2004).
45. In 2005, the Presidency began a process to introduce Regulatory Impact Assessments (RIAs). Proposals at the time of writing suggested that these processes would require that departments (1) clearly state the problem to be solved by a policy, (2) define the impact on government priorities, especially growth, investment, employment creation and equity, and (3) consult consistently with stakeholders in the process of analysing the likely effects. This type of systematisation of the policy process was bound to face resistance from officials anxious to retain power over the policy process as well as from sections of business, including the consultants upon whom departments relied for technical advice. Still, if introduced, it would certainly help align government policies and ensure more sustainable outcomes.

PART III

ONE POSSIBLE APPROACH

Chapter 6

Justifying A Bill to Establish A Law and National Integrated Development Commission in Zambia: A Research Report

By Lucian Ng'andwe

Lucian Ng'andwe's chapter comprises the research report which he drafted to justify a proposed law to establish a Law and National Integrated Development Commission in Zambia. The law would empower the Commission to conduct research and design bills to transform the socio-economic institutions that, after half a century of independent government, still perpetuate external dependence, unemployment, and deepening poverty for most Zambians. Ng'andwe's report illustrates how, using legislative theory's problem-solving methodology as a guide, drafters can organize available evidence as a logical foundation for conceptualizing the details of effectively implemented legislation to facilitate efforts to transform dysfunctional institutions.

Working with Zambian colleagues[1], Ng'andwe drafted the bill to establish the Commission primarily to encourage on-going discussion of the possibilities (and limits) of using law to transform the institutions that shape major economic sectors' impact on the development process of a country like Zambia. In the summer of 2004, he 'workshopped' the bill and the accompanying research report in Zambia,[2] discussing it with government, parliamentary and university personnel. and leaders of civil society organizations.

As always in a democratic law-making process, Ng'andwe's research report and bill remain drafts, subject to revision in light of new facts provided by further research and discussions with Zambian stakeholders. In effect, it serves to open an on-going dialogue concerning the possibility of establishing a Commission as a new institution for introducing effectively implemented legislation to transform the institutions that, since independence, thwarted Zambian efforts to fulfill all Zambians' basic needs. —***Editors' note***

INTRODUCTION

Despite the existence of significant mineral and agricultural wealth in a land area larger than England, Zambia's population of 10.7 million[3] lives in an externally dependent economy characterized by growing unemployment[4] (an estimated 40 percent of the formal labor force) and increased poverty (two-thirds of the population lives below the poverty line).

Part III: One Possible Approach: A Law and Development Commission

In the last three decades of the 20th Century, as real world prices of Zambia's main export, copper, declined, growing unemployment and falling real incomes have made Zambia one of the world's poorest countries:

> From the middle of the 1970s onwards, Zambia registered a declining economic performance and most social indicators continued to fall. For example, between 1974 and 1988, the country's external receipts from metal declined by 23 per cent. The economy continued to suffer from high inflation, huge budget deficits, and a distorted price structure. By 1992, the annual inflation growth rate reached a record 190 per cent. The situation deteriorated to such an extent that in 1985, the World Bank re-classified Zambia from a low-middle income to a low-income country. By the early 1990s, Zambia had reached a level where the UN General Assembly included it on the list of least developed countries.[5]

Proclaiming their desire to exercise state power through law to improve the majority of Zambians' quality of life, the first two post-independence governments followed essentially contradictory development strategies, first nationalizing, then privatizing the mines on which Zambia's economy remains dependent. Neither of the strategies effectively halted growing unemployment and increasing poverty.

> Despite some recent positive trends in the area of stabilization, Zambia's economic decline remains among the worst in Sub-Saharan Africa. The decline in per capita GDP has been accompanied by real wages decline; rising unemployment; and a noticeable reduction in transfers from the state to the average household. The prevalence of high poverty levels, thus, constitutes one of the main problems in Zambia today. The majority of the people in Zambia suffer from weak purchasing power, homelessness, and insufficient access to basic social services and necessities such as education, health, food and clean water. The Zambian government has defined poverty as lack of access to income, employment opportunities, normal internal entitlements by the citizens to such things as freely determined consumption of goods and services, shelter and other basic needs of life that include education. The conditions under which unsupported children and women; the disabled; women-headed households; lactating mothers; widows, and the unemployed currently live, put together, constitute a proxy for poverty in Zambia today.[6]

The extent and severity of poverty in Zambia has emerged as that country's most serious social problem. To facilitate the use of state power through law to transform the relevant economic institutions that perpetuate that problem, this research report proposes a bill to establish a Law and National Integrated Development Commission. Once established, that Commission would conduct research, draft laws and submit them to the relevant Ministers and Parliamentary Committees for debate and possible enactment. The bills drafted would aim to facilitate the transformation of the key institutions in each major sector of the economy: mining, agriculture and fisheries, trade, industry, finance, and social and economic infrastructure.

The bill specifies criteria and procedures likely to ensure that the Commission will design legislation likely to lead to a restructured and adaptive economy characterized by growth, employment and equity, for all the inhabitants and communities in all provinces. The requirements for realizing this goal include:

- an integrated manufacturing economy, using the nation's rich mineral and agricultural resources, capable of attaining high levels of value added;
- an efficient, strong and responsive state structure capable of facilitating implementation of measures designed to achieve a balanced, integrated national economy;
- a geographic spread of social and productive investment to foster increasingly productive employment opportunities; and
- the nation-wide social infrastructure essential to creating a skilled, informed and adaptable citizenry.[7]

Fitting the social problem[8] addressed by the bill into the larger context

In the economy of Zambia, the production and export of copper has had an 'extraordinary dominance' (Bostock and Harvey, 1972). Zambia became an extreme case of over-dependence on the production and export of a single product, copper. Its social and economic structure remained characterized by a narrow urban community, mainly located on the 'Copper Belt,' shaped over more than a century by the requirements of the copper industry and the growth of its associated labor force.[9]

First, despite its dependence on copper exports, Zambia, itself, could not significantly influence world copper prices. For the most part, Zambian development remained at the mercy of fluctuating global market prices primarily dominated by the relative decline of industrialized countries' demand for copper.

Second, over the years, Zambia's efforts to expand copper production and exports to earn foreign exchange aggravated environmental problems caused by the long and dangerous processes of smelting copper ore. These heavily polluted the air and water sources. The people living and working in the mines' immediate vicinity—the mine workers and their families—remained most vulnerable to these negative environmental consequences.

Except for a brief period in the immediate post-independence era, foreign-owned companies dominated ownership and control of Zambia's copper industry. They imported technology, finance, equipment and skilled managers, while exporting the mines' output together with much of the profits they produced. Pre-independence political control focused on a limited, distorted form of development by building up the narrow corridor along the line of rail[10] to meet the needs of those engaged in the profitable associated mining, trade and financial business.

The main social impact of the mines on the remaining primarily rural areas resulted from the colonial governments' imposition of a cash poll tax. As its primary aim, that tax forced able young men to leave their farms to work for wages on the mines, contributing, over the years, to the mass migration of the labor which their families might otherwise have used to develop the rural area's other resources. Biases —racial, urban/rural, wage sector, and regional—all reflecting the colonizers' stereotypes that favored the white settlers and the copper mining industry—grew into deeply, firmly-established components of Zambian economic and social institutions. Colonial rule had denied the majority of Zambians the education required to understand and use law to transform the inherited institutions that distorted Zambia's economy. At the time of independence, only a few hundred Zambians had a secondary education. Less than a hundred had graduated from university. Zambia also inherited a weak administrative system and a social infrastructure sharply skewed to serve the (primarily expatriate) elite.[11]

When Zambia won independence in 1964, changing the institutions that perpetuated the nation's heavy dependence on copper production and export would require fundamentally restructuring a wide range of socio-economic institutions throughout the country. In a brief post-independence period, when high world copper prices provided the necessary revenues, the Kaunda government did finance more schools, hospitals and roads. Neither of Zambia's post-independence governments, however, made major efforts to use state power through law to improve the nation's governance system, or to design new laws to fundamentally transform the nation's inherited economic institutions.[12] As a consequence, when real world copper prices began to fall in the 1970s, the majority of Zambians' living standards declined. By the end of the century, agricultural employment—predominantly subsistence production—accounted for 85 percent of the total national labor force of 3.4 million people. Industry employed six percent, and services nine percent of all workers. Formal employment opportunities and informal sector returns continued to decline as the economy continued to shrink. Almost half of those who sought jobs could not find wage employment.[13]

Within three decades after attaining independence, Zambia's economic fortunes had dramatically changed. Zambia had become one of the poorest and the most indebted countries in Sub-Saharan Africa; 69 per cent of rural Zambians lived in absolute poverty (as against 27 per cent of the urban dwellers); 85 per cent of Zambians earned less than US$1 per day (the second highest percentage worldwide); 98 per cent of Zambians earned less than US$2 per day; and 47 per cent of Zambians did not live to reach their 40th birthday[14] (the 4th highest percentage worldwide).[15]

This research report proposes a new Law and National Integrated Development Commission to facilitate the formulation and enactment of legislation that will engage the Zambian government together with all elements of civil society (especially the poor and vulnerable most affected by the present misuse of the nation's resources) in transforming the inherited institutions that perpetuate and aggravate unemployment and poverty for most Zambians. To transform those institutions which define Zambia's economy, its society, its system of governance, and its state of development, government must use law[16] and legal order[17] to overcome poverty, vulnerability and poor governance.

A brief review of Zambia's political-economic and social history from 1970 to 1991 reveals important experiences which conditioned and influenced the majority of Zambians' behaviors, attitudes and actions in their efforts to improve their quality of life. The next sub-section, describes the institutional factors that, as the new millennium opened, perpetuated and aggravated Zambia's socio-economic underdevelopment.

A brief history

At independence, Zambia inherited a dualistic economy heavily dependent on the mining sector for employment, foreign exchange earnings and government revenue. During the first decade of independence, Zambia seemingly enjoyed one of the highest rates of growth in Sub-Saharan Africa. The new government policy focused on expanding the mining sector, for the most part neglecting traditional sectors including agriculture, which still employed most Zambians. Prices for its major export, copper, remained high and financed the government's efforts to build relatively advanced import-substitution industries.[18]

This brief history reviews two phases of Zambia's post-independence development strategies: first, nationalization, and then privatization of industries.

Nationalization of Industries: 1964-1991

In the first post-independence decade, the United National Independence Party government, led by President Kenneth Kaunda, sought to use law to introduce sweeping economic reforms. These included widespread nationalization of local and international private companies in several sectors of the economy: mining, manufacturing, transport and trade. The government declared as its motive the necessity of transferring economic power from foreign and sectional interests to Zambians, and the promotion of rapid economic development through increased state involvement and investment in the various sectors.[19] By the mid-1970s, a hierarchy of state holding companies, at the summit of which lay the Zambia Industrial and Mining Corporation (ZIMCO), held most of the nation's major enterprises.[20] Wholly owned by the government, ZIMCO controlled 80 per cent of the economy and had subholding companies in nearly all sectors of the economy.

At the same time, to ensure significant state control over the distribution and administration of land, the government altered the inherited land tenure laws to replace freehold tenure in favor of leasehold, in theory vesting all land in the Presidency. The government also introduced social reforms with a view to providing free education and health for all. It created what began as a swiftly expanding network of government schools and higher learning institutions, as well as hospitals and health centers. Discouraging private and exclusive health, educational and other social facilities, the government proposed rapidly to develop a social welfare system aimed at supporting all members of the Zambian society.[21]

In other words, through state-ownership in the 'modern' urban sector, the new Zambian government sought to spur a swift expansion of investment, infrastructure and employment. For almost a decade, taking advantage of the the high prices of copper and significant financial reserves available at independence, the new government seemed to have sufficient resources to sustain these developments.[22] It introduced relatively few measures to accelerate production in the predominantly peasant agricultural sector.[23]

The State Owned Enterprises (SOEs), referred to as 'parastatals,' rapidly grew to occupy a central position in the nation's industrial, commercial, transport, agricultural, service, and financial sectors, including banks and insurance. Operating in sheltered markets, a number received government subsidies and grants. Controlled partially or wholly by the government, these state enterprises produced over half of Zambia's annual gross domestic product (GDP). Between 1973 and 1979, they employed one-third of the formal sector workers.[24]

Over the next decade and a half, however, falling world copper prices slashed government's shares of profits and tax revenues. Experiencing low profitability, underinvestment and rising indebtedness, the Zambian parastatals confronted growing difficulties. These included:

- a run-down service sector, industry and state shops;
- scarcity of consumer goods, many of shoddy quality, and sold at controlled prices;
- declining productivity and low capacity utilization;
- an over-staffed road-, air-, and water-transportation sector, apparently headed for total collapse (government ultimately liquidated many companies in this sector);
- the layoff of thousands of workers;
- chronic shortages of foreign exchange (controlled by cumbersome procedures that aggravated the scarcity of consumer goods;
- seemingly widespread corruption, nepotism, incompetence and inefficiency.[25]

Subjected to government bureaucracy, the State Owned Enterprises seemed characterized by lack of quality control management, inefficient leadership, and political interference in their day-to-day operations. Government officials often appeared to appoint and remove chief executives arbitrarily, without prior consultation with the boards of directors. This rotation, seemingly influenced by individuals' loyalty to the ruling party, partly reflected the shortage of competent managers, inefficiency, and efforts to prevent chief executives from building personal empires. No law granted those dismissed a right to appeal or to try to exculpate himself or herself.[26]

No law specified the qualifications required for appointment to boards of directors. Some politicians appointed had neither competence nor knowledge about parastatal operations. Some allegedly rejected professionally-devised strategic and business plans because an enterprise's chief executive lacked political support.[27]

In hopes of winning re-election, some senior politicians exercised pressure to ensure location of new industries in their home areas to provide new jobs for their constituents. In the 1980s, for example, a senior UNIP politician persuaded the government to site a steel project at Mumbeji, in North-Western Province. Only after spending hundreds of millions of Kwacha (the Zambian currency) on building essential infrastructure did government conclude that the project would prove economically unfeasible.[28]

Another weakness arose from the civil service procedures' incompatibility with commercial operations. Reportedly, some of the civil servants responsible for working with the SOEs remained poorly trained and motivated, lacking in initiative and slow in decision-making. Even when they did not possess skills suited to promoting business-like behavior, some intervened in day-to-day parastatal decision-making.

By the end of the 1980s, the Zambian government, having fallen deeply in debt, had come under increasing pressure from the IMF, World Bank and donors to pursue an orthodox structural adjustment program, with privatization as a key component. Although President Kaunda's UNIP government accepted the principle of privatization in 1990, its initial plans for implementation remained quite limited.

The situation changed after the elections of November 1991 when the majority of voters voted into office the Movement for Multi-Party Democracy (MMD), headed by Fredrick Chiluba. Almost immediately, the MMD launched a comprehensive privatization program which transferred a majority of state enterprises to the private sector.[29]

Privatization of State Owned Enterprises: 1991 to date

The MMD government under President Fredrick Chiluba embarked on an ambitious and aggressive program which, its proponents claimed, would liberalize, restructure, and reactivate the economy "by focusing on the engine of growth being through private initiative and private sector development."[30]

While Zambia's privatization program received praise from many quarters, perhaps the 1998 World Bank study of Privatization in Africa provided the most influential assessment. Authored by Oliver Campbell White and Anita Bhatia, that study evaluated the privatization programs pursued in ten Sub-Saharan countries.[31] On the basis of eight measures of the countries' programs' design, implementation and results, the authors concluded that Zambia's program proved the 'most successful.' They suggested Zambia offered examples of the 'best practices' that other countries should imitate.[32]

In Zambia, however, the sale of the parastatals[33] generated widespread debate. Before the dissolution of ZIMCO, its spokespersons publicly complained that the Zambia Privatization Agency (ZPA) had grossly undervalued the companies it privatized. The business community and the public widely echoed this view. On its part, ZPA accused ZIMCO of interfering in its work and mismanagement by allowing the pilfering of equipment, stripping off of assets and a general run-down in many of the companies for which it had remained responsible.[34]

In some instances, trade unions and the workers openly resisted privatization of the firms for which they worked. In one instance, workers sought a High Court injunction to stop ZPA from selling Cleanwell Dry Cleaners because of alleged rampant corruption and malpractice in the way the ZPA handled the sale of this company. They argued that the Agency manipulated the process to thwart the workers' own efforts to buy and manage the company. The Court agreed to apply an injunction. Later ZPA allowed a management buyout.[35]

The Chiluba government claimed the sale of the giant mining conglomerate, ZCCM, would prove crucial to the success of the program and to the resuscitation of the Zambian economy. Government and business sources, as well as the ZPA, maintained the large-scale foreign investment that Zambia needed depended on the successful privatization of ZCCM. Valentine Chitalu, then Chief Executive of ZPA, declared: "This... would have an impact on the lives of each and every Zambian, so we better do it right."[36]

The privatization program continued to receive wide criticism in Zambia because of its policy, its manner of implementation, and the negative consequences arising from it. Privatization led to a loss of key and strategic industries to foreign control and management. Many Zambians argued that, as privatization proceeded, the country became a dumping ground for cheaply produced goods, mainly from South Africa and Zimbabwe. Often subsidized by multinationals and other foreign companies, the import of these goods allegedly contributed to the collapse of Zambia's efforts to build its own local manufacturing base.[37]

Some critics, especially in the labor movement, maintained that the earnings of Zambian employees of state-owned industries had contributed to an economic multiplier effect. As privatization led to massive layoffs and rapidly growing unemployment, this multiplier effect ceased.[38] By November, 1994, Ministry of Labor and Social Security statistics showed that job losses had risen to over 92,000. By 1996, after the dissolution of Zambia Airways and United Bus Company of Zambia and retrenchments by a number of other companies, that number had risen to over 150,000.[39] As the numbers of redundancies and unemployment levels rose, domestic support for privatizations became increasingly limited and unenthusiastic.[40]

As the new millennium opened, new debates emerged as to the probable impact of privatizing the remaining state-owned-enterprises, like the Zambia

National Commercial Bank, Zambia Electricity Supply Corporation and Zambia Telecommunication Corporation. Critics argued that privatization would replace efforts to achieve equitable distribution of these services by profit maximization motives. Logistical and infrastructure constraints prevented private enterprise from earning adequate profits by extending critical services, like transport and banking facilities, to remote rural areas. Already, cutbacks had reduced those areas' inhabitants' access to these kinds of essential services. The prices of goods that still reached them remained so high that, typically, they attracted more admirers than buyers. Increasingly, social and economic activities would remain concentrated in the urban areas.[41]

To a significant degree, Zambia's post-independence development patterns reflected the way inherited institutions perpetuated external dependence on the export of copper in the face of overcrowded global markets, accompanied by continued un- or underdevelopment of the nation's human as well as agricultural and other mineral resources. The import-dependent industry and social welfare programs introduced by state intervention after independence had only marginally changed the copper-based export enclave carved out during the colonial era. Their initial seeming success relied heavily on copper earnings for essential foreign exchange to finance required inputs, as well as the government revenues to maintain the nation's social infrastructure. In contrast, the privatization program seemed, inevitably to leave essential production and investment decisions at the mercy of the elite-controlled institutions that shaped Zambia's lopsided, externally dependent markets.[42]

Would further privatization aggravate growing unemployment in the so-called 'modern' urban sectors, and inequities throughout the nation? Would the benefits of limited copper output go primarily to the wealthy few associated with remaining privately-owned mines and associated trading and financial enterprises, and line-of-rail agricultural estates? Would growing numbers of impoverished urban unemployed and traditional peasants—isolated in the nation's vast, remote, and relatively under-populated rural areas—find themselves increasingly forced to struggle for survival for bare subsistence? The Zambian people and their government confronted a challenge: How could they exercise state power through law to develop their nation's potentially valuable resources to fulfill all Zambians' basic needs?

Focus of this research report

This research report aims to demonstrate that law potentially comprises a 'lever' which the Zambian government might use to foster increasingly productive employment opportunities and an improved quality of life for all Zambians. Using legislative theory's problem-solving methodology as a guide, the report lays a basis in facts and logic for designing detailed provisions for a Law and National Integrated Development Commission. Following legislative theory's problem-solving methodology's four steps, each section of this report provides the essential evidence to demonstrate that, logically, the proposed enabling act's detailed provisions likely will ensure that the Commission will strengthen the Zambian government's capacity to produce effective transformatory law.

Since law can only try to change the behaviors that comprise a social problem, the report's second section describes whose and what behaviors comprise government's failure to draft, enact and implement essential transformatory laws. These consist of the Cabinet, including the Presidential staff, who formulated overall policy without considering how to use law to ensure its effective implementation; ministry personnel, including ministers, civil servants (especially those in agencies responsible for economic planning) and legislative drafters who did not formulate adequate change-oriented legislation to submit to the legislature; and legislators and their staff who neither originated nor adequately assessed the bills they received in terms of their potential for transforming the inherited institutions that geared Zambia's economy to copper exports while leaving underdeveloped its other potentially rich human and natural resources.

Analyzing the causes of each set of relevant social actors' (role occupants' and implementing agency officials') problematic behaviors, section three begins the search for facts to show that the explanations hypothesized prove consistent with the available evidence. Building logically on that foundation, the report's fourth section describes the detailed provisions of a bill to establish a Law and National Integrated Development Commission. It demonstrates that those details likely will help to alter or eliminate the causes of the problematic behaviors identified in section three, and induce more appropriate law-making behaviors in each sector of Zambia's economy to foster nationally-integrated, people-oriented development.

THE SOCIAL PROBLEM THE BILL AIMS TO HELP RESOLVE

This section briefly describes the post-independence law-making processes that—appearing increasingly arbitrary and sometimes corrupt—condemned most Zambians to struggle for bare survival. For at least four decades, Zambia's national law-making institutions failed to draft laws to transform Zambia's inherited dysfunctional economic institutions and ensure increasingly productive employment opportunities and rising living standards for all Zambians. That constitutes the social problem the proposed Commission aims to help resolve.

Legislative theory emphasizes that law can only change dysfunctional institutions by altering the behaviors which comprise them. This section describes the relevant law-makers' behaviors which proved inadequate to transform Zambia's inherited institutions to facilitate balanced, integrated national develoment: The executive branch (ministers, civil servants, drafters primarily responsible for introducing, drafting and implementing laws to regulate the economy); and the legislative branch (Members of Parliament and their Parliamentary staff) responsible for enacting the necessary laws, overseeing their implementation and maintaining two-way communications with their constituents as to laws' social impact.

The surface appearance of the law-making problem

For almost four decades after independence, Zambian law-makers paid little attention to the legislative details required to fundamentally change the institutions that, in every sector of the national economy, perpetuated dependence on copper exports. Mostly, they perceived copper mines as the main 'engine' of development, and left the settler-owned line-of-rail estates along the Copper Belt's railroad line—mostly still foreign owned and employing low-paid Zambians as workers—to produce most of the nation's marketed agricultural produce.

Peasant agriculture, for nearly a century undermined by colonial taxes and other measures designed to force young men to abandon farms to work on the mines, never really recovered. Built during early post-independence prosperity the new urban infrastructure enabled the younger generations, educated in newly-built schools, to abandon agriculture for employment and the anticipated excitement of urban life. Trade and finance, still dominated by big (often foreign-owned) companies, used the financial surpluses generated in Zambia, not to facilitate development of agricultural and other resources in Zambia's vast remote areas, but in existing mining and line-of-rail enterprises—or shipped their profits abroad.

Whose and what behaviors contributed to Zambia's deepening poverty and unemployment?

Zambia's social problems occurred neither by accident, nor because of mystical forces, whether supernatural or the market's 'invisible hand.'[43] They arose as a result of the behaviors of particular sets of actors ('role occupants'[44]), in this case, the law-makers who proved unable to translate government's stated socio-economic policies into effectively-implemented law.

In Zambia as elsewhere, law comprises government's primary tool for transforming inherited dysfunctional economic institutions. Law only 'works,' however, by prescribing and ensuring implementation of changes in the repetitive patterns of behaviors that comprise those institutions: The mining companies, comprised of mine managers and the remaining mine workers; the 'line-of-rail estates'[45] run by settler farmers (now including migrant white South African and Zimbabwean farm owners); the Zambians who do the physical labor; the owners of the financial and trading firms and their employees; the millions of small-scale farmers struggling primarily simply to subsist in remote provinces. Zambia's new governments could only change those institutions by changing the laws that structured these inherited relationships; and providing the skills, technologies, and financial means which all Zambians need to participate in increasingly productive activity in a more integrated national economy.

The proposed Commission would substitute new law-making behaviors (institutions) for those that contributed to Zambia's two post-independence governments' failure to use law to transform the economic institutions that perpetuated Zambia's unemployment and poverty. This research report provides descriptive hypotheses, backed by facts,[46] as to the relevant primary role occupants and implementing agency officials: The ministry officials, legislative drafters, legislators and officials who prepared, enacted, or sought to implement legislation and subordinate regulations.

By the end of the 20th Century, Zambia's law-makers had introduced no new legislation to effectively alter the way, in every sector, inherited colonial institutions hinged Zambia's economic development to exports of copper to an increasingly overcrowded world market. Instead, the post-independence ministries proposed and the legislators enacted new laws that granted government agencies broad discretion in deciding what detailed measures to undertake to achieve government's often vaguely-stated development objectives: first nationalization of industries, and then privatization. In implementing these laws' relatively vague prescriptions, government civil servants tended to make their decisions behind closed doors. They seldom published detailed reasons or evidence to help the public understand their decisions' likely social consequences.

Over nearly half a century, government officials made remarkably few efforts to use law to transform economic institutions. When politicians made demands on them to carry out proposals for economic development (for instance, to nationalize or privatize the mines), with few exceptions, they proposed to implement these programs through existing agencies and legal structures. When Zambia nationalized the mines, for example, Government merely adopted the British law that Zambia 'received' during the colonial period: Government purchased 51 percent of the shares of the existing copper-mining companies, retaining the foreign (the South African Anglo-American Group) partner's personnel as managers. The law-makers did not change the laws governing the relationship between management and shareholders; so far as either the legislators or the general public went, the managers continued to make their detailed decisions anonymously and secretly.[47]

As elsewhere, to propose new legislation to remedy a perceived imperfection in an existing law, a Zambian official wrote a memorandum[48] to the Parliamentary Counsel, or provided a 'layman's draft' of the provisions they thought the bill should contain. These memoranda or layman's drafts showed no uniform quality. Usually, they described the proposed bills' general contours, leaving the drafters to fill in the substantive details. When requested by a Minister to draft new laws, Zambian drafters, like those elsewhere, mainly copied another country's law (frequently Britain's); compromised between competing interest groups' claims;criminalized unwanted behavior; or drafted very general provisions that granted administrative officials broad discretion in working out the details.[49] The entire drafting process took place in secrecy, almost entirely within the civil service establishment. Drafters and other officials submitted the draft bills to Cabinet and Parliament accompanied by 'memoranda of law'—typically, little more than a one-paragraph statement of the bill's objectives, and a simplified explanation of each section in 'non-legal' language.

In sum, Zambia's new government officials generally did not effectively use law to transform the institutions that hinged the Zambian economic development to the fortunes of an increasingly overcrowded world copper market. The primary social actors responsible for this failure included the Ministers and their staff who did not perceive this as the central problem, and proposed policies that centered on the assumption that the copper mines remained the vital key to economic success; the ministry drafters who adopted 'entropic' methods ill-suited to producing transformatory legislation; legislators who generally, unquestioningly, voted for bills proposed by their parties; and ministry officials who, given broad discretion in implementing new laws, made decisions that often appeared arbitrary, and sometimes corrupt. Each set of the role occupants' problematic behaviors requires some explanations of the underlying causes. The next sector provides these explanations.

EXPLANATIONS

This third section suggests explanatory hypotheses as to the causes of each set of relevant 'role occupants''problematic behaviors. These hypotheses serve to guide the process of gathering and analyzing the available facts as to Zambian circumstances, as well as other countries' experiences,[50] as to the probable causes of each set of role occupants' problematic behaviors.[51] Once proven consistent with the available evidence relating to Zambian circumstances, these explanatory hypotheses lay a basis in facts for logically designing legislative measures likely to alter or eliminate the causes identified by those warranted hypotheses. In other words, once warranted by the available facts, the hypotheses provide a sound basis for formulating the detailed provisions of an enabling act to establish the proposed Commission as a new and more appropriate law-making institution.

This section suggests explanatory hypotheses for the problematic behaviors of each set[52] of the relevant role occupants in the Zambian law-making process: The ministry officials, legislators and drafters. The end-notes identify sources of the relevant facts that demonstrate those hypotheses seem consistent with the available evidence.[53]

The Law[54]

The several sets of actors identified in this report behaved within a framework of laws remarkable for its vagueness. The Zambian Constitution contained some limits on the legislative power, but prescribed no procedures to control the law-drafting process. A Cabinet Memorandum detailed those procedures, but required of a bill's proponents no detailed, structured justification for a bill. It required the drafter to accompany the bill with a 'memorandum of law', but did not specify the memorandum's content.[55]

Following British practice, Zambia's Civil Service Regulations required a civil servant in charge of a proposed bill to consult 'interested parties'. Other than those whom the senior civil servants considered an appropriate 'interested party', the colonial-imposed Government Secrets Act made it a crime to reveal to an unauthorized person anything learned in the course of government employment.

In Zambia, as elsewhere, laws abounded prescribing that relevant ministers implement specific bills. Save for prescriptions addressed to the Ministry of Finance and Economic Planning, however, no Ministry had a formal legal duty to develop new, transformatory laws in the sector of the economy for which the Ministry had responsibility.

With respect of the copper industry, Zambian Company Law, inherited from the British, required that, when making decisions concerning company actions, directors—including directors of state owned corporations—should take into account only the shareholders' interests—not those of the workers or the general public.

Officials in the ministries concerned with economic development

Officials responsible for preparing and putting forward long-term plans for economic development included Ministers and ministerial officials. Making their decisions secretly and anonymously, these officials never tried to generate transformatory or change-oriented legislative programs to submit to the legislature. A review of institutionalist legislative theory's ROCCIPI categories (explained in this book's second chapter) suggests several possible interacting causes of these problematic behaviors.

Objective factors

Designated officials in the government of the day had the Opportunity to recommend decisions—first to impose state-ownership, then to privatize the mines and other industries. However, they did not have the Capacity[56]—the training and skills—required to formulate and implement appropriate detailed rules (whether in the form of legislation or administrative regulations), or to assess their decisions' social impact. The existing law granted ministers the power to make policy in general terms, giving ministry officials broad discretion as to details. As a rule, civil servants had to carry out policy within the existing legal framework; typically, that mandate excluded efforts to transform that framework.

Ministry officials almost never acquired theoretical or practical tools for translating policies into effectively implemented legislation. Instead, following British tradition, they typically formulated broad policies, leaving the details to drafters. Drafters too often focused on techniques without regard to substance and copied laws from elsewhere regardless of evidence as to their suitability to Zambia's specific circumstances.

Too often, the Process[57] by which ministry officials, including the drafters, made their decisions—the rule-making institutions—excluded all but parties selected by the civil servants as 'interested'—typically the owners and managers of business, not the representatives of the workers, the unemployed, or peasants in remote rural areas.

The ministry decision-making processes remained secret, with no requirements that officials state reasons or provide facts for their decisions. They seldom incorporated adequate provisions for monitoring and supervising officials; no specifications existed as to who might participate in providing inputs and feedback (typical procedures excluded the poor and vulnerable). Making their decisions in secret, officials did not justify them to any save their hierarchical superiors, and to those 'interested' persons whose inputs they invited. That left the officials primarily dependent on existing powerful institutional interests for whatever inputs and feedback—facts and logic—they considered.

Subjective factors

The objective realities outlined above essentially permitted ministry officials to make their law-making decisions in light of their own subjective Interests and Ideologies[58]—and these did not always coincide with the public interest. Professional advancement required conformance with government's rules. Broad grants of discretion exercised in secret, furthermore, fostered deal-making in the officials', not the public's interest.[59]

The (inherited) governing ideology required ministry personnel to serve government of the day. They could not take initiative outside established policies. More particularly, the colonial organizational ethics perceived civil servants as administering a 'night watchman state,' concerned with law and order and collecting taxes.[60] That perception advised officials that their task consisted of implementing existing law and, perhaps, where they found difficulties in the law, suggesting incremental changes—but not proposing institutional changes. By the 1980s, the international financial institutions' myth that government withdrawal and restoration of 'market forces' would foster optimal resource development tended to reinforce that ideology.

Legislative drafters

Zambian legislative drafters' problematic behaviors involved using entropic methods, usually behind closed doors, and justifying a bill only with flimsy 'memoranda of law'.[61]

Objective circumstances

Zambian law, inherited from their colonial forbears, gave Zambia's drafters the Opportunity to draft bills' substantive details. They lacked Capacity, however, to design those details in ways reliably likely to induce the bills' prescribed behaviors. Trained as lawyers in the British tradition, (some of those trained before or immediately after independence may have learned to draft in the English or Canadian Parliamentary Counsel's Chambers.[62]), they did know the techniques required to chain words together. They had never considered, let alone studied, law's potential as an instrument of social change. Lacking any theory or methodology for designing legislation, they could not design bills likely to induce changed new behaviors required for institutional transformation.

The institutionalized drafting Process within which Zambian drafters worked required them neither to design nor to justify their bill in terms of facts and logic. None of the drafting methods they employed required analyzing available empirical evidence as to the nature of existing institutional behaviors or their causes—an essential foundation of reasoned law-making decisions.

Subjective factors

Their traditional British training convinced the drafters that they had no responsibility for their bill's 'policy' or substance, but only for those bills' linguistic form.[63] They ignored the reality that a bill's words inevitably influence its substance. Yet drafters who, in the very act of drafting, make decisions about a bill's policy while denying it, inevitably engage in unreasoned—and therefore arbitrary—law-making.

Legislators

In line with British tradition, new Zambian legislators seldom originated legislation. Usually with little or no debate or explicit reasoned choice based on available evidence, the majority simply voted to enact Government bills into law.

Objective causal factors

The Rules gave legislators responsibility for enacting legislation, supervising its implementation and maintaining two-way communications with their constituents. Those rules provided no details as to how legislators should assess bills, giving them discretion to follow political dictates without regard to reason or evidence. In particular, no rules required them to consider legislation likely to foster institutional change.

Few, if any of Zambia's Members of Parliament had the Capacity to read and fully comprehend the implications of a law's detailed provisions.[64] Nothing required drafters to accompany bills by reports that provided a background of logically organized evidence as a basis for assessing those details in terms of the public interest. Very few legislators had knowledge about the subject-matter of the bills relating to economic development—for example, the mining industry's role in perpetuating Zambia's external dependence. Legislators had neither theoretical nor practical tools for assessing whether proposed legislation would introduce needed institutional transformation.

In terms of the Parliament's decision-making Process, no rules required the legislators or their committees to use reason grounded on an examination of available evidence. Legislators mainly made their decisions through a process of bargaining between interest groups in the course of which each presented their own claims and demands. The resulting bargains typically remained dominated by those with the greatest power—political, social or financial, or, not infrequently, a combination of all three.

Subjective factors

Most legislators' personal Interests tended to encourage them, at least in part to ensure their re-nomination, to vote for government bills without questioning their likely social impact. The election list system made it difficult to challenge government; ultimately, legislators depended for renomination on the party and government leaders. Sometimes, MPs responded to pressures imposed by those with power. Some changed their votes for benefits promised by powerful interest groups for themselves, their families, relatives or friends.

'Humanism,' the ideology of Zambia's ruling political party after independence, remained too vague to guide legislators in assessing proposed transformatory legislation's details.[65] After the 1991 elections, the new governing party replaced Humanism by a free market ideology that called for privatizing all state enterprises, regardless of evidence as to the probable social impact.[66] Different legislators' ideologies varied, but, without legislation that clearly specified criteria and procedures, most responded to beliefs widely-disseminated by dominant power groups: Perhaps a belief that to achieve development requires attracting foreign investors within existing markets; or cynical attitudes such as 'everyone else does it; why not me' that seemed to justify acceptance of corrupt favors offered by powerful lobbies.

Line (implementation) ministry officials

Line officials often draft, promulgate and implement subordinate regulations. Parliamentary acts frequently empower them to draft and implement detailed administrative rules required to carry out legislation's aims. In Zambia, as elsewhere, not infrequently, line ministry officials simply never got around to drafting mandated subordinate rules. Occasionally, they drafted subordinate regulations that appeared arbitrary, and even seemed to contradict the parliamentary act's main thrust.[67]

Objective factors

The broad discretion typically granted by the original Parliamentary acts gave line ministry officials the Opportunity to draft a wide range of differing rules—or simply to do nothing at all. Their Capacity, however, remained limited. Typically, they had received the same or less training in legislative drafting techniques as had their colleagues who drafted the original enabling laws. They also had little or no idea about how to gather or organize the relevant available facts to formulate, far less to justify, their rules' details in terms of reason and experience. The Process by which they decided on the rules' substantive details usually took place behind their ministry doors. Usually, they received inputs only from the powerful individuals or interest groups whom they chose to consult.

Subjective factors

Drilled in the British civil service tradition of serving the government of the day, few ministry officials had any idea of how to formulate and implement the details of subordinate rules to foster institutional transformation. Pressured by powerful outside interests, some—especially, apparently, in the Chiluba era of privatization of public assets—succumbed to the opportunity to advance, not the public interest, but their own.

Summary and conclusion of explanations

The hypotheses in this report's third section identify specific causes of the relevant sets of behaviors that seem to have hindered Zambia's first post-independence law-makers from using law to transform the institutions that fostered Zambia's external dependence, unemployment and poverty. These underscore the law-makers'—both ministry officials' and legislators' —lack of capacity to gather and organize available evidence as basis for drafting and assessing proposed legislation likely to work. They also point to the lack of transparency, accountability, and participation in existing law-making processes. Once warranted by available evidence, the explanatory hypotheses lay a basis in facts for designing the detailed provisions logically likely to alter or eliminate the existing law-makers' problematic behaviors, and induce new behaviors more likely to help resolve the targeted social problem. Building logically on the explanations advanced, this report's fourth and final section proposes detailed provisions for an Act to establish an effective Law and Integrated National Development Commission.

DETAILED PROVISIONS FOR A DRAFT ACT TO ESTABLISH A ZAMBIAN LAW AND NATIONAL INTEGRATED DEVELOPMENT COMMISSION

To overcome Zambian law-makers' failure to formulate, enact and implement effective transformatory legislation, this report proposes detailed provisions for an Act to establish a Law and National Integrated Development Commission. Using legislative theory's problem solving methodology as a guide, this fourth section demonstrates that the details of the proposed law authorizing establishment of that Commission logically will likely overcome the causes of law-makers' existing arbitrary behaviors. Its detailed provisions require the Commission, in designing and justifying transformatory laws, to rely not on whim but on reason informed by experience.

This fourth section shows that the proposed Act's detailed provisions seem likely to ensure that a well-trained Commission staff, working in the context of clearly defined criteria and procedures, will prepare and submit carefully crafted draft legislation to the Zambian Cabinet and Parliament. The Commission will accompany each bill by a well-constructed research report that provides the relevant facts, logically organized, to justify its detailed provisions. Once enacted, the Act should initiate a rational process for using law to transform the dysfunctional institutions in each sector of Zambia's economy to ensure they contribute effectively to creating productive employment and improving all Zambians' quality of life.

This fourth section outlines the proposed Act's provisions as to how the Commission and its sector subcommittees will function: Who will appoint their members; those members' qualifications for appointment; their powers and duties; the criteria for their decisions, and the processes by which they make those decisions in ways likely to prove transparent, accountable, and—as far as possible—participatory; and the mechanisms for settling disputes, imposing sanctions, and monitoring and evaluating the resulting laws' social impact.

Necessary elements of an enabling act for a Law and National Integrated Development Commission in Zambia

Section three of this report's analysis underscored the necessity for incorporating in the proposed Act a clear statement of the Commission's purpose: To conduct necessary research and draft legislation likely to prove effectively implemented to transform the inherited economic institutions that perpetuate Zambian external dependence, unemployment and poverty. That statement should serve to limit the Commission's discretion in achieving those tasks by specifying the criteria and procedures its officials' must use. The Commission should

1. work with universities, research institutes, concerned civil society groups and stakeholders to conduct research on the way in which, in each of Zambia's major economic sectors, existing socio-economic institutions perpetuate the misallocation of resources;
2. based on that research, draft carefully-designed legislative proposals (bills) likely to facilitate the essential transformation of those inherited institutions to reallocate resources to provide increasingly productive employment and an improved quality of life for all Zambians;
3. accompany the submission of each bill by a detailed research report that provides the relevant facts, logically organized, to justify that draft law's detailed provisions by demonstrating that they will prove effectively implemented and produce the desired social consequences;
4. submit each draft bill and report to the relevant ministries, Cabinet and Parliamentary committees, as well as to the media and interested stakeholders, to facilitate review and introduction of additional facts and reasons that might lead to useful revisions;
5. submit the completed bill and report to Parliament, as the nation's highest law-making body, for a final review and ultimate enactment.

The following subsections describe the design of the proposed Act's major provisions.

The proposed Law and National Integrated Development Commission

Appointment of qualified Commission members

Part III: One Possible Approach: A Law and Development Commission

The Act will authorize the President, with the approval of a majority of the Parliament, to appoint well-qualified members of the Law and National Integrated Development Commission. These must include adequate representation of relevant ministries responsible for regulating institutions in major sectors of the economy: banking and finance; industry and commerce; agriculture (including fishing and forestry); economic and social infrastructure (including public works and transport) and trade. The members will also include legislators and their staff, especially of Parliamentary Committees responsible for introducing legislation to facilitate relevant institutional changes.

Other members shall include elements of civil society drawn from the major sectors relating to which the Commission will conduct research and draft legislation. These may include trade unions; business institutions; universities and other institutions engaged in relevant research; and other Zambian-based non-government organizations (NGOs).

The Commission will appoint qualified sectoral sub-commission or committee members to conduct and supervise relevant research and to translate policy into effectively implemented transformatory legislation for specified sectors of the economy. The Commission will have the responsibility to contract or otherwise make arrangements for research relevant to preparing transformatory legislation. It will also review draft legislation and accompanying research reports to ensure they fit into an overall national program for transforming institutions to restructure the Zambian economy.

The Commission's specific powers and duties

The Act will include a clear statement of the Commission's powers and duties to help ensure that it has the financial resources and institutional support necessary to remain relatively independent. Within the limits imposed by terms of reference specified in the Act, the Commission will have powers:

i) of the purse that means, power to make decisions concerning the allocation of their own budget;
ii) to decide the areas of research and who should undertake them, including specifying the inputs and feedback from poor and vulnerable as well as human rights and environmental interest;
iii) to subpoena[68] officials and civilian respondents to ensure their cooperation.

Criteria governing the Committee decision-making process

The Commission's decision-making processes must prove accountable,[69] transparent,[70] and participatory,[71] grounded on available evidence and rational debate. To ensure this, the Commission will have a duty of accompanying each legislative proposal with a research report that provides the evidence, logically organized, to demonstrate that it will prove effectively implemented and produce the desired social impact.

The alternative solutions considered

Several sources suggest ideas for alternative legislative solutions: Other governments' experiences in trying to use law to transform analogous dysfunctional institutions (analyzing their mistakes may prove especially helpful); the relevant literature on ways to improve governance while facilitating democratic social transformation; the Zambian drafters' own ideas, formulated in the process of examining the evidence of Zambia's own experience.

Other countries' relatively recent experiences in using law to foster balanced, integrated industrial growth do not seem very helpful. South Korea's industrial strategy between 1953 and 1986,[72] for example, did seem to have fostered a rapid transformation of a largely agricultural to a relatively highly-industrialized economy. South Korea experienced several advantages, however, which Zambia and other African countries seem unlikely to enjoy.[73] South Africa's post liberation experience—although it began with the highest level of industrial development in SubSaharan Africa—reveals serious institutional constraints, but suggests possibilities for engaging stakeholders in more participatory decision-making processes.[74]

At the end of the day, Zambian law-makers, including its drafters, must fashion a solution designed to alter the problematic behaviors that persist in Zambia's specific circumstances. The proposed Commission must design detailed legislation which, in Zambia's unique circumstances, seems most likely to foster effective institutional transformation. That underscores the necessity for empowering the proposed Commission to overcome problems posed in the past by the ministry officials', drafters' and legislators' inadequate capacity and the too-frequently non-transparent, non-accountable, and non-participatory law-making processes by which they formulated, enacted and implemented new legislation.

Description of the bill's detailed provisions as the preferred alternative

This sub-section contains a detailed description of the proposed Act's provisions relating to the Law and National Integrated Development Commission as an implementing agency. (see Appendix to this chapter, pp. 160-168 for the draft bill.)

i) The Act authorizes the Commission to establish subcommittees

a. to conduct research and draft legislation for specified Zambian socio-economic sectors to foster more balanced, integrated sectoral and national development.
b. A subcommittee will accompany its bill by a detailed research report to demonstrate that the bill's detailed provisions, grounded on facts and logic, will likely effectively lead to a more appropriate allocation of resources.

ii) The Act specifies substantive criteria by which the Commission (and its designated sub-committees) will conduct the necessary research as a basis for drafting a bill and an accompanying research report, These criteria aim to ensure:

a) basic services to all to alleviate poverty and to eliminate regional disparities within and between provinces;
b) the optimal employment of each given sector's human and physical resources, contributing to the production of consumer necessities, as well as appropriate tools and equipment, while expanding productive employment opportunities and fulfilling all Zambians' basic needs;
c) the realization of each sector's potential economic linkages with other economic sectors, insofar as possible providing each sector's required inputs, and a potential market for each sector's outputs;
d) the provision of necessary training for each sector's labor force, including technical skills as well as those needed for improved management, marketing and finance;
e) adequate credit facilities, at subsidized rates of interest, to facilitate efforts to start small and medium-sized projects;
f) the protection of small-scale start-up projects from external competition;
g) cooperation with neighboring Southern African states in developing larger-scale projects to foster expanding region-wide specialization and exchange directed to utilization of advanced technologies to increase productivity in the use of regional agricultural, mineral, and human resources.

iii) The Act will require the Commission and its designated sub-committees to employ transparent and accountable rule-making procedures that facilitate public participation based on the use of reason informed by experience. To achieve those aims, the procedures should include:

a) accompanying every bill by a research report that, tracking the problem-solving methodology, informs the legislature and the public of the logic and facts that underpin the bill's detailed provisions;
b) provisions to ensure notice to, and facilitate comment by, stakeholders;
c) the publication of bills and the reports at public hearings where all the affected stakeholders—especially the poorest and most vulnerable[75]—can contribute information relevant to nature and causes of the behaviors that comprise the social problem addressed by the rule; and suggestions for using community resources to help alter those behaviors;
d) annual Commission reports to the legislators and the public to strengthen the nation's elected representatives' capacity to assess whether the Commission in fact conducts its law-making duties in the public interest.

iv) Building capacity: The draft Act provides for training Commission members and ministerial officials in the uses of law as an instrument for transforming institutions. It empowers the Commission, as it deems necessary, to employ qualified and well-trained experts[76] to conduct the relevant research to conceptualize and draft detailed transformatory bills for each sector.

v) Submission of the bills and research reports to the relevant ministries: The Commission will submit each bill to relevant ministries and Parliamentary Committees, accompanied by an adequate report that provides facts and logic to demonstrate that it will prove effectively implemented and produce the desired social consequences.

How the proposed Commission likely will address the causes of the identified problematic behaviors

This subsection demonstrates how the establishment of a Law and National Integrated Development Commission logically seems likely to overcome the causes of Zambian law-makers' problematic behaviors—their failure to formulate and implement effective legislation to transform the inherited economic institutions that perpetuated unemployment and poverty in Zambia.

First, the explanations for ministry officials' (including drafters') failure indicate that their training and ideology tends to support drafting and implementing legislation designed, not to change, but to maintain inherited institutional structures. In addition, drafters generally believed that they only needed to learn techniques without concern for bills' substantive impact. To overcome these underlying causes, the enabling act will specifically establish a new agency (the Law and National Integrated Development Commission), with a staff trained to conduct research and draft essential transformatory legislation. The enabling Act will ensure the appointment of appropriately qualified Commission members and a sufficient number of staff members well-trained in legislative theory, methodology, techniques, and social science research methods.

A second set of explanations suggest that, with little knowledge of how to assess, let alone initiate bills, the Members of Parliament too often engaged in a discourse of power, not reason informed and experience. By providing research reports that provide the factual and logical bases for proposed laws, the Commission will ensure legislators can examine the available evidence and make reasoned decisions as to proposed bills' probable role in achieving a more self-reliant, prosperous economy.[77]

Statement of the preferred solution's probable social impact

This subsection should assess the available facts to demonstrate that the socio-economic benefits of implementing the enabling act's detailed provisions, including its anticipated impact on the Zambian economy and the lives of its nationals, outweigh the probable social and economic costs. In particular, these estimates should include the law's probable social impact on Zambia's poor majority, and on valued but poorly represented interests, especially the rule of law and the prevention of rampant corruption which negatively affects the economy of Zambia.[78] By including an estimate of a bill's probable socio-economic costs and benefits, the research report helps legislators and the public to decide whether and when to support its enactment.

a. The economic costs include out-of-pocket costs to the Zambian Treasury for setting up the Commission, and financing its subcommittees' research and drafting work. Depending on the size of the Commission, including the numbers of employees and the bill-drafting projects it undertook each year, the Ministry of Finance could estimate these costs. As a percentage of total government expenditures, they should prove small, perhaps one or two percent. The Commission might keep the research costs down by encouraging:

i. university personnel to offer students course credit for gathering relevant information from villagers in their home areas, workers employed in specified enterprises, unemployed in urban shanty towns, or interviews with enterprise administrators and managers;[79] and

ii. leaders of civil society groups—churches, cooperatives, unions, community organizations—to equip their members with the knowledge and skills they would need to gather and weigh the relevant information.[80]

b. The establishment of the Commission may, over time, include more, but more difficult to quantify, economic and social benefits: The bills drafted, once enacted, could stimulate government private, and civil society initiatives to give more attention to how to employ Zambia's human and physical resources to improve the nation's social and economic infrastructure, and to introduce new productive and income-generating activities. In turn, these could provide new opportunities for employment to improve the quality of all Zambians' lives.

MONITORING AND EVALUATION

The proposed enabling Act incorporates specific provisions for on-going monitoring and evaluating of the Commission's research and law-making activities. These include specific mechanisms for involving representatives of all the stakeholders, especially poor and vulnerable groups, in assessing the law's implementation and its social impact. For this purpose, the enabling Act stipulates that the Commission must report annually to the Parliament on the details of the research and drafting projects it has undertaken. For each drafting project undertaken that year, these annual reports must include:

*Information on the processes employed to gather the relevant evidence, specifying which groups provided inputs to the decisions made (especially noting the presence or absence of inputs from the poor and vulnerable);

*the costs of the information-gathering processes employed by each drafting project;

*the main issues raised in debates over the bills' and reports' details;

*the Parliament's final decision as to whether or not to enact the bill produced, and the reasons for that decision;

*the steps taken to monitor and evaluate each new law enacted; and,

* an appendix that, for each law enacted, includes the responsible implementing agency's assessment of that law's implementation and social impact.

CONCLUSION

This draft research report illustrates how legislative theory's problem-solving methodology guides the collection and organization of available evidence to justify enactment of an Act to establish a Law and National Integrated Development Commission in Zambia.

Almost half a century after the end of colonial rule, Zambia and its people still suffer from the distorted use of the country's human and vast natural resources. The inherited colonial legal order still shapes the economic and social institutions—the repetitive patterns of behavior of government officials and other role occupants— that lock Zambia's political economy to the export of copper to global markets. Zambia's post-independence governments continued to pursue the old strategy of expanding copper exports, keeping the economy dependent on colonially-imposed 'comparative advantages' which consisted of low cost of minerals and agricultural products, and labor-intensive manufactures—all produced by low wage labor.

This report aimed to justify the detailed provisions of an Act to establish a new law-making institution, the Law and National Integrated Development Commission. A prerequisite for improving the quality of life for all Zambians, the Commission could help strengthen the law-making process and facilitate every Zambian's participation in the intertwined processes of achieving good governance and development. Recognizing the importance of productive work and self-reliance in achieving human and economic development goals, the report highlights employment and income generation as essential to enable all Zambians to earn a decent livelihood. It underscores the importance of effective participation of all groups of civil society, not only business and public administrators, as partners in the process of managing Zambia's resources to accelerate the pace of all Zambians' attainment of economic well-being. Democratic participation and cooperation based on reason informed by experience offer a sound foundation for building a better economy and future.

By drafting new laws to fit Zambia's specific realities, each justified by a research report structured by legislative theory's problem-solving methodology, the proposed Law and National Integrated Development Commission will foster experiment and innovation in Zambia's development enterprise. At the same time, the Act's specification of the detailed criteria and procedures the Commission must employ should help to make arbitrary legislative decisions less likely.

This report has demonstrated the likelihood that the Commission can meaningfully address the Zambian government's past over -dependence on the production and export of copper, which has left almost half of all Zambians unemployed. Elimination of the social problems identified in this report requires effective law likely to transform the economic institutions that perpetuate Zambia's poverty and dependence. This research report proposes a new law-making Commission as a fruitful way to begin that transformation.

APPENDIX

The translation of a proposed legislative solution into a bill's detailed provisions proves a critical step in determining whether and how the responsible agency—here the Commission —effectively implements the new law, and its probable social impact. Form links inextricably with substance to enable readers to make that essential assessment. This Appendix provides the text of the draft bill.

THE LAW AND NATIONAL INTEGRATED DEVELOPMENT COMMISSION ACT (ZAMBIA)

CHAPTER I: GENERAL PROVISIONS

1. Short title

This Act may be cited as "The Law and Development Commission Act".

2. Objectives

(1) In this Act:

a. 'Commission' means the Law and National Integrated Development Commission mentioned in Section 3;

b. 'institution' means a repetitive pattern of social behaviors.

(2) A person construing this Act shall do so to make it probable that the Commission drafts, and submits to the relevant Minister and to the Speaker of the Parliament, proposed bills that, if adopted as law or as subsidiary legislation, tend towards achieving the following objectives:

a. A national integrated economy that—

   i. increases employment, productivity, and freedom from economic dependence, and improves the quality of life for the majority of Zambians and the quality of governance in Zambia, and

   ii. includes new, socially cost-effective, interactive institutions in finance, trade, industry, mining, agriculture, and in the infrastructure for the Zambian economy;

   and

b. the creation and improvement of institutions that tend towards a national integrated economy in terms of subparagraph (a), and the transformation or abolition of institutions that create conditions favorable to unemployment, poverty, external dependence and poor governance in Zambia;

(3) In addition to the objectives mentioned in subsection (2), a person construing this Act shall do so to make it probable that:

a. If adopted as law or as subsidiary legislation, a proposed bill that the Commission submits to a relevant Minister or Director of an agency actually induces the behaviors it prescribes;

b. Commission practice conforms to rules for Commission decision-making, made pursuant to section 4, that prescribe maximum feasible transparency, accountability, and stakeholder and public participation; and

c. the Commission accompanies a bill with a research report, made pursuant to section 6, that justifies the bill in terms of empirical evidence based on sound research, and of rational calculation.

CHAPTER TWO: ESTABLISHMENT OF THE COMMISSION

3. Establishment of the Commission

(1) This Act creates the Commission as a body corporate.

(2) The Commission consists of members appointed, and holding tenure, pursuant to Schedule A of this Act.

CHAPTER THREE: POWERS AND DUTIES OF THE COMMISSION

4. Powers and duties of the Commission: the Annual Plan of Work

(1) In this Act, 'Plan of Work' means the Plan of Work mentioned in Subsection (2).

(2) Subject to subsection (3), after considering submissions from members of the public, from Government and from its own staff, the Commission shall prepare the Plan of Work.

(3) Not less than 30 days before the time set by the Commission for deciding on the Plan of Work, the Commission shall give the widest feasible public notice inviting suggestions for inclusion in the Plan of Work, including suggestions for specific drafting projects.

(4) The Commission shall annually, and not less than 30 days before the scheduled opening of the regular session of the Parliament, and subject to this section, lay before the Parliament the Commission's Plan of Work for the ensuing year.

(5) In the Plan of Work the Commission shall –

a. include a schedule of the specific social problems to ameliorate which during the ensuing year it proposes to draft bills, and
b. justify on the basis of empirical evidence and rational calculation the schedule of specific social problems.

(6) If—

a. within one week of the submission of the Plan of Work to the Parliament a member of Parliament notifies the Commission that the member objects to the Plan of Work, specifying precisely in what regard the Member objects, and
b. within one month thereafter after public notice and a public hearing on the Plan of Work the Committee on Economic Affairs of the Parliament by majority vote rejects the Plan of Work as laid before the Parliament by the Commission,

the Commission shall amend the Plan of Work to give effect to the objection raised by the Member of Parliament.

a. The Commission shall promptly lay the amended Plan of Work before Parliament in terms of subsection (3).

(7) Upon Parliament's approval of the Plan of Work, the Commission shall implement it in terms of this Act.

5. Powers and duties of the Commission: Drafting bills

(1) In this Act, 'Director' means the Director of Research mentioned in section 7(1).

(2) Except pursuant to subsection (3), subject to priorities established pursuant to the Plan of Work, the Commission may from time to time draft and submit to the relevant Minister or Director of an Agency a proposed bill that purports to achieve the objectives of this Act, and simultaneously submit the proposed bill to the relevant Committee of the Parliament, together with a research report prepared pursuant to Section 6.

(3) Notwithstanding Subsection (2), the Commission may draft a bill out of order, or a bill addressing a social problem not included in the schedule of social problems mentioned in Section 5(a), subject to the following conditions:

a. That the Commission give not less than one month public notice of intention to commence drafting a bill out of order, or a bill addressing a social problem not included in the schedule of social problems mentioned in subsection (4), and inviting comment; and
b. that at a regular or special meeting of the Commission next following the expiry of the public notice mentioned in subparagraph (a) a majority of those present vote to proceed with drafting the bill mentioned in that public notice.

(4) After, pursuant to subsection (2) and (3), the Commission determines to proceed with the drafting of a bill to address a specified social problem, it shall

a. direct the Director to proceed with necessary research and drafting, and
b. simultaneously instruct the Director concerning the procedures the Director shall follow to satisfy the Commission's duties pursuant to Section 7(6).

6. Powers and duties of the Commission: The Research Report

(1) In a research report mentioned in Section 2(3)(c) and in Section 5(2), the Commission shall justify the relevant proposed bill on the basis of empirical evidence and rational calculation.

(2) The Commission shall include in a research report the following:

a. In so far as it has knowledge of them, a description of –

   the specific problematic behaviors that the proposed bill addresses together with empirical evidence of those behaviors;

   the explanations for those behaviors;

   the specific relevant behaviors of an existing implementing agency, if any;

   the explanations for the behaviors of an existing implementing agency;

   the alternative legislative remedies considered;

   the extent to which, if the Parliament enacts the proposed bill into a law, that new law will likely ameliorate the problematic behaviors that it addresses;

the expected social costs and benefits of implementing the new law compared with (i) the present situation and (ii) the most likely alternative legislative remedy;

and

b. the calculations concerning those matters that in the Commission's view justify the proposed bill.

*7. **Powers and Duties of the Commission: Research***

(1) The Commission shall appoint as Director of Research a person with a terminal degree in social science, with a substantial record of publication in the fields either of institutional development, law and development, institutional economics or the use of legislation as a tool for social change, substantial field research experience, and substantial experience as an executive or administrator.

a. After appointment, the Zambian Civil Service Commission shall, after discussion with the Director and the Commission, appoint the Director as a member of the Zambian Civil Service, at a level appropriate to the Director's training, experience and duties..

(2) The Director shall—

a. Under the general direction of the Commission, undertake research relevant to the several tasks of the Commission, and from time to time prepare the draft Plan of Work, draft bills, and prepare research reports as instructed by the Commission;

b. supervise the activities of members of the research and drafting staff;

(3) The Commission may employ as a researcher a person qualified as a researcher by training and experience.

(4) The Commission may employ as a consultant a person qualified as a consultant by training or experience, and who has a substantial record of scholarly or practical publications in the field of the consultant's expertise.

(5) The Commission may employ as many researchers and consultants as reasonably required to accomplish its duties, and as limited by its estimates.

(6) So far as feasible, the Commission shall engage in the research process the stakeholders affected by the matters involved in the research.

8. Powers and duties of the Commission: Rule making.

(1). To carry out the objectives of the Act mentioned in Article 2, the Commission shall make and promulgate reasonable rules including rules for its own governance, and for performing its duties and exercising its powers under this Act.

(2) In making and promulgating a rule pursuant to subsection (1), the Commission shall ensure that the rule prescribes maximum feasible transparency, accountability, and stakeholder and public participation in a decision made pursuant to that rule.

(3) In making a rule pursuant to subsection (1), the Commission shall pursue the following steps:

a. Unless making a rule on the subject at hand reasonably appears to the Commission a matter of urgency, the Commission shall announce in a newspaper of general circulation in Zambia that it has under consideration making and promulgating a rule addressing a specified issue, and inviting submissions from stakeholders and the public at large.

b. After drafting the proposed rule, the Commission shall publish it in a newspaper of general circulation in Zambia, together with a research report justifying the proposed rule, and inviting written comments from the stakeholders and the public at large, and setting a closing date for receiving comments not less than one month after publication of the proposed rule.

c. After the closing date, the Commission shall consider a comment received.

d. After due deliberation, the Commission may reject the proposed rule, adopt the proposed rule, or amend the proposed rule and adopt it as amended.

e. If the Commission adopts the proposed rule or adopts the proposed rule as amended, the Commission shall publish the rule as adopted in a newspaper of general circulation.

f. The Commission shall, when either publishing the rule as adopted or immediately after deciding not to adopt a rule on the issue the proposed rule addressed, publish a summary of each comment received.

g. If the Commission did not amend the proposed rule pursuant to the comment, the Commission shall at the same time publish a statement of the empirical evidence and rational calculations that justify its decision.

h. At the written request of three members of the Commission, or after an affirmative vote of the Commission, at a time and place directed by the Commission or, in absence of direction by the Commission, in the discretion of the Director, the Director shall conduct a public meeting to hear comments from stakeholders and members of the public.

i. As soon as feasible after a public meeting held pursuant to subsection (2), the Director shall report in writing to the Commission about the proceedings at the meeting.

9. Powers and duties of the Commission: Compelling the production of evidence

(1) If a person declines to testify before the Commission about a matter, or to produce a document relevant to a matter, about which the Commission believes that it has a duty or power to inquire, the Chairperson of the Commission may issue a subpoena to require the person to testify or to produce the document.

(2) If the person refuses to obey the subpoena, the Chairperson may petition the High Court for an order requiring the person to testify or to produce the document requested.

(3) After hearing both parties, if the High Court finds that the Chairperson issued the subpoena within the Chairperson's power, the High Court shall order the person to comply with the subpoena.

(4) If the person refuses to comply, the Court shall deal with the matter as for contempt of Court.

10. Powers and duties of the Commission: Submitting a Bill to the Parliament

If the Commission by a duly adopted resolution so directs the Director, the Director shall forthwith submit the bill and its accompanying research report to the relevant Minister, and to the Speaker of the Parliament.

11. Powers and duties of the Commission: Miscellaneous

(1) The Commission shall:

a. on its own initiative or on demand by a person, make available to the public or to that person a document in possession of the Commission;

b. from time to time as necessary to ensure a public reasonably well informed about economic affairs, disseminate to relevant stakeholders and to the public generally information relevant to the achievement of the objectives of this Act mentioned in Article 2;

c. train researchers and drafters for employment by the Commission, and by the national and local governments of Zambia;

d. annually, and not less than 30 days before the scheduled opening of the regular session of the Parliament, submit to the Cabinet and to the Parliamentary Committee on the Economy—

 (i) a report of the Commission's work for the past year;

 (ii) an evaluation of the Parliament's legislative work for the year with respect to enacting laws relevant to achieving the objectives of the Act mentioned in Article 2; and

 (iii) an evaluation of the work of the several ministries in implementing laws relevant to achieving the objectives of the Act mentioned in Article 2;

e. strictly carry out the Plan of Work; and

f. Keep accuate up-to-date records of its financial transactions, which the Auditor General shall audit not less frequently than annually; and

g. generally oversee the work of the Director and the Commission staff.

(2) The Commission may—

a. after public notice of a vacancy and a statement of the qualifications for the post, employ a qualified person at a reasonable salary and terms of employment to carry out the work of the Commission; and

b. do everything necessary and convenient to carry out the duties and exercise the powers of the Commission.

CHAPTER FOUR: IMPLEMENTATION AND CONFORMITY-INDUCING MEASURES

1. Monitoring and Evaluation

(1) Annually, within thirty days after submitting the report mentioned in Section II(1)(d), the Chairman of the Commission shall testify before the

Parliamentary Committee on the National Economy on the work of the Commission.

(2) Annually, the Minister of Finance shall prepare a report on the work of the Commission for the preceding year, and submit the report with the Minister's recommendations to the Chairperson of the Parliamentary Committee on the Economy.

2. Sanctions

A court of competent jurisdiction who finds that, in connection with the Commission's performance of its duties or the exercise of its powers, a person has knowingly made a false statement to the Commission, shall sentence that person to not more than one year in prison or fine of not more than two hundred thousand kwacha or both.

CHAPTER FIVE: MISCELLANEOUS

3. Definitions

In this Act—

'Commission' has the meaning assigned to it in Article 2(1);

'Director' has the meaning assigned to it in Article 8(1);

'institution' has the meaning assigned to it in Article 2(1).

SCHEDULE A: COMMISSION STRUCTURE AND PROCEDURES

1. Appointment of Commissioners; term of office; conflict of interests.

(1) The President shall appoint six members of the Commission, as follows:

a. One member from a list of four persons nominated by the trade union movement in Zambia;
b. one member from a list of four persons nominated by the Zambian Chamber of Commerce;
c. one member from a list of four persons nominated by an organization representing the interests of commercial farmers;
d. one member from a list of four persons nominated by an organization representing the interests of small farmers;
e. One member appointed by the President to serve as advocate within the Commission for the interests of groups or classes in Zambian society not otherwise represented on the Commission; and
f. one member of the faculty of the University of Zambia with an outstanding record of research and publication about the political economy of Zambia.

(2) So far as feasible, in terms of subsection (1), the President shall appoint members of the Commission who reside in different geographical regions of Zambia.

(3) The Ministers of Finance, Trade and Industry, and Agriculture, and the Chairpersons of the Parliamentary Committees on Finance, Trade and Industry, or their nominees, shall serve *ex officio* as members of the Commission.

(4) Unless sooner terminated in terms of subsection (5), an appointed member of the Commission shall serve for a term coincident with that of the President, or until the President appoints a successor.

(5) An appointed member of the Commission may not serve after—

a. the member's written resignation;
b. the member has exhibited physical inability to perform the duties of the office;
c. conviction of a felony, or other misconduct either incompatible with the duties of the office or seriously and significantly affecting the Commission's public image; or
d. failure to attend two or more meetings within twelve consecutive months.

(5) In case of dispute whether a member's term has ended, the Chairperson of the Judicial Service Commission shall on the request of the Chairperson of the Commission appoint a Justice of the High Court to hear and determine the dispute.

(6) A Commissioner may not engage in an occupation or business inconsistent with the duties of the office.

(7) A Commissioner shall conform to the requirements of the Leadership Code.

4. Chairperson of the Commission

(1) With the advice and consent of the Parliament, the President shall appoint as Chairperson of the Commission a person with a strong record of public service and demonstrated expertise concerning issues of social, political and economic development.

(2) The Chairperson shall serve at the pleasure of the President.

(3) The Chairperson shall—

a. Serve as chairperson of meetings of the Commission;
b. in event of a tie vote in the Commission, cast the deciding vote;
c. prepare the agenda for a meeting of the Commission; and
d. ensure that the Commission and its officers and employees strictly comply with rules adopted by the Commission

Meetings

(1) The Commission shall meet regularly once in each month at a time and place determined by the Commission.

(2) The Commission shall meet extraordinarily—

at the call of the Chairperson, or

at the written request of three members of the Commission.

(3) The Chairperson shall deliver a copy of the agenda to members of the Commission one week before a regular meeting and not less than three days before an extraordinary meeting, and at the same time publish the notice of meeting and the agenda in a newspaper of general circulation in Zambia.

(4) By written notice to the Chairperson delivered to the Chairperson before in terms of subsection (3) the Chairperson delivers the agenda, a member of the Commission may require that the Chairperson include a matter in the agenda.

(5) By unanimous vote, the Commission may include a matter on the agenda at a meeting of the Commission.

(6) The Commission may act on a matter after a majority vote at a meeting which a majority of the members including not fewer than two appointed members attend and vote on the matter.

(7) The Commission may not exclude a member of the public from attending a Commission meeting.

Notes

1. Ng'andwe worked in collaboration with a group of colleagues, several of whom accompanied former President Kenneth Kaunda when, in 2003-4, he served as the first African president in Boston University's newly-established African Presidential Archives and Research Center. They included: Mr. Godwin Mfulu, a former senior civil servant in President Kaunda's government, Gabriel Banda, Lori Ann deLucia, Chris Annear, Wei Chen, and Ruth Kerkham.
2. As noted in endnote 4, chapter 1, the Boston University African Presidential Archives and Research Center (APARC) generously financed Ng'andwe's trip.
3. 50 per cent of Zambia's population was aged about 17 years. Central Statistic Office of Zambia, Census of Population and Housing (Nov. 18, 2003).
4. According to the Central Statistics Office of Zambia's results of the census of population and housing, Nov. 18, 2003, the number of unemployed persons had increased by 30 per cent between 1990 and 2000. Of those in employment, 62 per cent comprised unskilled labor with agriculture being the major occupation. *Id.*
5. Oliver Saasa & Jerker Carlsson, *Aid and Poverty Reduction in Zambia: Mission Unaccomplished*, The Nordic Afrikainstitutet Working Paper (2002), at 24.
6. *Id.* at 27
7. See the criteria specified by a South African Parliamentary Committee. Parliament of the Republic of South Africa, Trade and Industry Portfolio Committee and Select Committee on Economic and Foreign Affairs, Report on Public Hearings on Industrial Policy 3 (2002),
8. By definition, *a social problem* consists of repetitive behaviors that somebody characterizes as undesirable. Because they result from undesirable social behavior, Zambia's poverty and unemployment constitute social problems. *See* Ann Seidman & Robert B. Seidman, State and Law in the Development Process:

PROBLEM-SOLVING AND INSTITUTIONAL CHANGES IN THE THIRD WORLD 39 (McMillan, 1994).

9. *See* KLAAS WOLDRING, ET AL., BEYOND POLITICAL INDEPENDENCE : ZAMBIA'S DEVELOPMENT PREDICAMENT IN THE 1980S 116-117 (Mouton Publishing, 1984).
10. Refers to the railroad built under the colonial rule to ship out then-Northern Rhodeisa's exports—mainly copper -- and ship in its main imports: the machineryand equipment needed to expand the mines, and the manufactured consumer goods purchased by colonial managers, administrators and technical experts, as well as the European settlers who, employing low-cost African labor, provided farm produce for the expanding mining labor forces.
11. JONATHAN CHILESHE, THIRD WORLD COUNTRIES AND DEVELOPMENT OPTIONS: ZAMBIA 2 (Vikas Publishing, 1986).
12. In Zambia, independence day brought no substantial changes to the laws that shaped Zambia's institutions. Despite declared populist goals, new governors, not only in Zambia, but throughout the former colonial world, typically left the received law in force, passed new laws that prescribed inappropriate behaviors, or enacted supposedly development-oriented laws that remained rarely implemented and mostly symbolic. *See* ANN AND ROBERT B. SEIDMAN, *supra* note 8, at 39.
13. OXFAM-UK ZAMBIA OFFICE, FIVE-YEAR STRATEGIC PLAN 1996-2001 10 (1995).
14. Many Zambians today are dying at their productive age, with women succumbing more to social and economic pressure than men. Adult survivorship levels have deteriorated between 1990 and 2000, with more people dying at the age of 15 years and over. CENTRAL STATISTICS OFFICE OF ZAMBIA, *supra* note 3,.
15. DAVID REED, ECONOMIC CHANGE, GOVERNANCE, AND NATURAL RESOURCE WEALTH: THE POLITICAL ECONOMY CHANGE IN SOUTHERN AFRICA 74-79 (Earthscan Publication, 2001).
16. 'Law' here means a rule announced officially by the State. *See supra* Box 1-1 of chapter 1.
17. 'Legal order' here means a system in which the State prescribes a range of norms, including parliamentary acts, administrative regulations, subordinate legislation, and government decrees. The legal order constitutes a specialized normative system that defines specific rules or norms, and an associated sanctioning system that enforces them. It remains governmental policy-makers' principal instrument for influencing social behavior. *See supra* ch. 2, at 20.
18. Per-Ake Andersonn, *Foreign Aid, Debt and Growth in Zambia*, Nordiska Afrikainstitutet Research Report No.112 (2002), at 9.
19. HERRICK C. MPUKU & IVAN ZYUULU, CONTEMPORARY ISSUES IN SOCIO-ECONOMIC REFORM IN ZAMBIA: THE MAKING OF MODERN AFRICA 1 (Ashgate Publishers, 1997).
20. At independence, the Zambian government inherited an economy operated by private, largely foreign owned firms.under laws mainly copied from England. *Id.*
21. *See* MPUKU & ZYUULU, *supra* note 19, at 2.
22. *Id.*
23. Andersonn, *supra* note 18, at 9.

24. Mwelwa Musambachime, *Privatization of State-owned Enterprises in Zambia*, 29 AFRICANUS: JOURNAL OF DEVELOPMENT ADMINISTRATION 5, 6 & 16 (1999).
25. *Id.* at 17.
26. *Id.*
27. *Id.*
28. *Id.* at 17-18.
29. John Craig, Evaluating Privatization in Zambia: A tale of Two Processes, 27 REV. AFR. POL. ECONOMY *357, 358* (2000).
30. *Id.* at 374.
31. The countries studied were Benin, Burkina Faso, Ghana, Kenya, Madagascar, Mozambique, Nigeria, Togo, Uganda and Zambia. The data covered events up to the end of 1996. *Id.* at 364.
32. This conclusion has been quoted approvingly by, among others, Musambachime, *supra* note 24.
33. Due to the new economic world order caused by the collapse of communism, the Zambian Government initiated the policy of liberalization and thereafter embarked on the privatization program in 1991. This policy led to the establishment of the Zambia Privatization Agency (ZPA) and the Zambia Privatization Trust Fund under an act of Parliament passed in 1992. The state established ZPA to privatize selected companies.
34. Musambachime, *supra* note 24, at.23.
35. *Id.* at 23.
36. Zambian Privatization Agency 1995: 7, in *id.* at 23.
37. *Id.* at 26.
38. *Id.* at 26.
39. *Id.* at 26.
40. *Id.* at 26.
41. *Id.* at 26.
42. ANN SEIDMAN, PLANNING FOR DEVELOPMENT IN SUB-SAHARAN AFRICA 107 (Praeger Publishers, 1974).
43. More than two hundred years ago, in 1776, in AN INQUIRY INTO THE NATURE AND CAUSES OF THE WEALTH OF NATIONS, economist Adam Smith made what some consider the most famous observation of economics: Household and firms interacting in markets act as if they are guided by an "invisible hand" that leads them to desirable market outcomes. Smith implies that participants in the economy are motivated by self-interest and that the "invisible hand" of the market place guides this self-interest into promoting general economic well-being. *See* GREGORY N. MANKIW, PRINCIPLES OF MICROECONOMICS 9-10 (Harcourt College Publishers, 2d ed. 2001).
44. *See supra* Ch. 2, endnote 35, for an explanation of this term in legislative theory.
45. A long, narrow corridor passing through Copperbelt, Central, Lusaka and Southern Provinces of Zambia, where 'development' concentrates while other rural areas such as Western. North-Western, Luapula, Eastern and Northern Provinces are neglected. Most commercial farms and copper mines are located along this narrow corridor. See map, below at p. 177.

46. In writing this report, Ng'andwe and his colleagues found extensive evidence, some of it cited above, as to the nature and scope of the social problem.. They outline here the considerable amount of evidence they discovered, both relating to Zambia's experience and that in other countries confronting similar problems, to back up their descriptions of the nature of the behaviors that contributed to the widespread failure of law-makers and law-making institutions to introduce transformatory legislation.—The editors.

47. In the 1970s, for example, the Zambian mining firms' managers agreed to pay 20 percent higher prices for all imports of machinery and equipment, purchased from their affiliates abroad. This policy, known as 'transfer pricing' effectively shifted another share of anticipated profits out of Zambia, significantly further reducing the government's share of the mines' real profits. *See* NATURAL RESOURCES AND NATIONAL WELFARE: THE CASE OF COPPER (Ann Seidman, ed., Praeger Publishers, 1975).

48. The second phase of the drafting process culminates either in a memorandum from a public servant, or a 'layman's draft bill' (any draft bill not prepared by the central drafting office) referred to as a 'concept paper'. This may describe the proposed bill in some detail. At this nodal point, policy begins to turn tentatively into its operative, legal form. Typically, the concept paper or 'layman's draft' goes next to a specified government agency for prioritization. *See* DRAFTERS' MANUAL, at 23.

49. These 'entropic' modes of drafting required neither new inputs of evidence nor a theory of legislation. *See supra* endnote 21 in Chapter 2 of this volume.

50. For example, Uate's chapter in this volume provides detailed evidence as to the causes of Mozambican drafters' failure to produce an effectively implemented environmental law.This suggests possible hypotheses as to similar causes for Zambia's drafters' failure to draft more effective legislation to transform dysfunctional Zambian institutions.To confirm these hypotheses, however, will require similar detailed analysis of the available Zambian evidence.—The editors.

51. *See supra* endnote 50 and accompanying text in Chapter 2 of this volume. The ROCCIPI agenda suggests several possible interrelated hypotheses for the problematic behaviors identified for the relevant social actors who comprise the main institutions in each sector of Zambia's economy as well as the law-making institutions.

52. Experience underscores the importance of separating out and analyzing each set of relevant role occupants. Their behaviors, as suggested by the ROCCIPI agenda, may reflect significantly different interacting causal factors. The proposed enabling law's details logically, therefore, might have to include different provisions directed to those different causes in order to make it likely that each set will behave in new, less arbitrary ways.

53. Ng'andwe and his colleagues (*see* note 46, *supra*) gathered whatever evidence they could while in Boston to substantiate the hypotheses included here.For evidence, they drew on their own experiences, published articles and books, as well as on information available on the internet.During his brief opportunity to 'workshop' this report in Zambia in 1994, Ng'andwe also asked the participating legislators, university researchers, and NGO personnel to reflect on those hypotheses in light of evidence as to their own experiences.Self-evidently, however, further debate and research, including focus groups with relevant stakeholders, would help to provide the evidence required to deepen the explanatory hypotheses offered here. That

would help to make it more likely that the enabling act specified the detailed criteria and procedures necessary to ensure that the proposed Law and Integrated National Development Commission will serve as a more effective law-making institution.—The editors.

54. To what extent can the 'law' cause a social problem? Paradoxically, the existing law constitutes part of the explanation for the problem addressed. Proposals for a new law always must change the old law. Problem-solving predicts solutions' likely outcomes based on analysis as to whether they seem likely to alter or eliminate causal factors identified by warranted explanations. It follows logically that the old law constitutes part of the explanation for the problematic behaviors that comprise the social problem targeted.
55. *See supra* note 48 (re memoranda of law).
56. Capacity building in Zambia remains central to development. Here, we consider capacity as the combination of human resources and institutions that permit Zambia to achieve its development goals. Capacity allows people to achieve the objectives they set for themselves. Lacking human and institutional capacity simply implies that Zambia must rely on foreign expertise and resources to perform the elemental tasks of development. Capacity, therefore, must lie at the center of any future development strategy or agenda in Zambia. *See* Saasa & Carlsson, *supra* note 5.
57. The ministry officials usually depended heavily on government institutional procedures inherited from the colonial era. These typically granted civil servants major influence in the decision-making process, confined by inherited rules that perpetuated secrecy. Those rules generally provided neither for public oversight (including that supposedly required of the legislature) nor any form of stakeholder participation in the decision-making process.
58. At independence in 1964, most of the senior ministerial officials remained the same expatriate colonial service officials who manned those posts immediately before independence.
59. Recent evidence has exposed the way, when the second post-independence government resorted to privatizing government's productive assets, a variety of ministry officials took advantage of the opportunity to enrich themselves without regard to the impact on the Zambian economy and people. *See supra* notes 24-38.
60. *See generally* A.L. ADU, THE CIVIL SERVICE IN NEW AFRICAN STATES (Praeger Publishers, 1965).
61. For evidence as to the causes of similar behaviors of drafters in another African country, see Teodosio Uate's chapter 4 in this volume.
62. *See* DRAFTERS' MANUAL., *supra* note 11, Ch. 2, at 30-32.
63. *Id.* at 30-34.
64. *See* id. at ch. 4, on the difficulties of comprehending a bill's detailed provisions without a research report that provides the essential relevant, logically organized evidence ; *see also* ch. 2 of this volume.
65. 'Humanism' built on values that called for government control and use of the nation's assets to meet the people's needs, but offered no guidelines as to the kinds of detailed legislation required to transform inherited institutions in ways essential to achieve its stated goals. *See generally* KENNETH KAUNDA, HUMANISM IN

ZAMBIA AND ITS IMPLEMENTATION (1967) ; HUMANISM IN ZAMBIA, PART II LETTER TO MY CHILDREN (1977); KAUNDA ON VIOLENCE (1980).

66. *See* Musambachime, *supra* note 24, at 5-29.
67. Other authors describe many instances in which other former British-African colonies' new governments essentially granted ministries broad discretion to decide on the details of rules for implementing supposedly transformatory laws. *See e.g.*, YASH GHAI, LAW AND PUBLIC ENTERPRISE IN TANZANIA (1977).
68. A legal writ commanding appearance in court to give testimony or to serve or summon with such a writ. BLACK'S LAW DICTIONARY 1440 (Bryan A. Garner, ed., 7th ed. 1999).
69. Decision-makers justify their decisions publicly, subjecting their decisions to review by recognized higherauthority, and ultimately by the electorate.
70. Officials conduct government business openly so that the public and particularly the press can learn about and debate its details.
71. Persons affected by a potential decision—the 'stakeholders'- should have the maximum feasible opportunity to make inputs and otherwise take part in government decisions. The term 'stakeholders' here includes all persons with a 'stake' (defined as an interest) whom a law may affect.
72. *See* WORLD BANK, WORLD DEVELOPMENT INDICATORS 2003 (2004).
73. For years after World War II, the United States helped to build South Korea as a separate state. Its aid contributed a large share of the government's revenues; a post-war land reform required that former large land holders invest the funds they received as compensation for their estates in the country's expanding industrial sector; the stationing of US military forces in the country provided an assured 'domestic' market for industrial production, while its exports expanded to meet US needs during the Vietnam war. Gaining access to foreign firms' advanced technologies and borrowing abroad, largely from US banks, South Korean business and financial groups rapidly consolidated significant power. *See* ROBERT NILSON, SOUTH KOREAN HANDBOOK (Moon Publications, 1988); PATRICIA BARTZ, SOUTH KOREA (Clarendon Press, 1972).
74. *See* Neva Makgetla's review of the South African case in *supra* Chapter 5 in this volume.
75. Widespread experience underscores the fact that, while the rich and powerful usually have an inside track to both law-makers and administrators, the poor and vulnerable seldom have access to the halls of power; in Zambia, these include the women and families of poor peasants, the unemployed, as well as the workers on the mines and line-of-rail estates. For these reasons, the United Nations Development Program requires that, in proposing development programs in any country, consultants must demonstrate that they have taken into account the concerns of women, children, senior citizens, the poor, and ethnic minorities
76. In addition to adequate budgetary support, that requires specifying the kinds of skills required and, where necessary, the institutionalization of the necessary staff training programs.
77. Ensuring that the legislators acquire the capacity to assess the evidence and logic that underpin the bills may require an additional bill. *See generally* Ann Seidman et al., Assessing Legislation: A Manual for Legislators (2002), available at http://www.ICLAD-law.org.

78. *See* Drafters' Manual, at ch. 7 (difficulties and possibilities of making these kinds of estimates).

79. Engaging university social science students in this process proves valuable in at least two respects: Not only do the students provide information not otherwise available; in the process, they learn a great deal about the nature and causes of social problems confronting Zambians in all walks of life, and gain insght into novel possibilities of more productive use of human and physical resources. *See generally* Denny Kalyalya et al., eds., Aid & Development in Southern Africa—Evaluating a Participatory Learning Process (Africa World Press, 1992).

80. This could help these organizations' members to learn how to participate more effectively in the law-making process.

Chapter 7

Legislating 'Liverpool': The Role of Law in the Development and Conservation of the Mweru-Luapula Fishery, Zambia

By Christopher M. Annear

J. Mulenga, as he is advertised on the signboards of his businesses in Kashikishi, named his third son Bright because he envisioned a radiant future when he relocated north from the urbanized Northern Rhodesian (Zambian) Copperbelt in the 1950s. While many residents of the Luapula[1] region sought employment through labor migration to the Copperbelt, Bright's father trekked in the opposite direction, sure of economic opportunity. He was right. When he arrived with his young wife and family to what was little more than a fishing camp replete with wild animals, he discovered an area literally jumping with fish. His son Bright recalls fish so plentiful that one could use his hat at the shoreline to catch dinner. It was a child's fantasyland that included riding on the backs of enormous catfish known locally as Sampa.[2]

In 1954 when the Central African Federation government erected the first ice plant in Kashikishi, fishing was the domain of colonial interests, secured through a powerful monopoly of mostly Greek fish traders. At that time Africans lacked control over their fishing production, and market demand was driven by regional mining companies. Once more, Bright Mulenga's father envisioned change; he imagined a fishing town run by Africans. Again, he was correct; perhaps more than he expected. The Mweru-Luapula fishery has become accessible to small-scale producers and subsistence level Africans. However, despite these positive changes, the fishery also suffers from unsustainable fishing pressure associated with a proliferation of access.

Today the Mweru-Luapula fishery endures declining fish stocks caused by over-fishing due to atomized enterprise; virtually unmanaged resources; seasonal insecurity and broad fluctuations in catches; and rampant sexual exploitation of the many young women who migrate to the region seeking economic opportunity. Contrary to the colonial era monopolies and restrictions of years past, today's problems consist of too much access; too little management and enforcement; and poor ancillary economic options. Perhaps most telling is that in this region known nationwide for its extensive and delectable fishery resources, Bright Mulenga, the son of Kashikishi's founder of trade, now farms (not fishes) for a living.

This chapter discusses the contemporary ailments of Luapula Province's fisheries, their roots in colonial-era legislation, and subsequent unsustainable, economically-motivated fisheries exploitation. It also reviews the contemporary socioeconomic circumstances and legal structures that continue to encourage destructive behaviors. Although precedents for poor decision-making lie in the colonial era, the contemporary problems of the Mweru-Luapula fishery—as well as the consequences for its possible collapse—are borne by Africans. The fishing industry initially developed along the logic of a British colonial order which demanded the cheapest possible foodstuffs for mine labor at a minimum of infrastructural investment. That demand fostered the unregulated growth of the fishing and marketing institutions, contributing to under-management in an over-exploited fishery: an atomized enterprise that—linked to the Copperbelt (perhaps ironically, a symbol of "development") by efficient daily passenger/cargo transportation network — drains the region's potentially rich fishing stocks.

One of up to six luxury buses, from three competing companies, which departs from Kashikishi daily for Lusaka and the Copperbelt. (photo credit: Christopher M. Annear)

The chapter's first section presents an overview of the ecological and jurisdictional parameters of the Mweru-Luapula fishery, along with a sprinkling of the social and cultural expression that emanates from and sustains it. Section two discusses the socio-economic character and gender of fishing preserve on the Mweru-Luapula. Section three describes the emerging trade in undersized juvenile fish, a consequence of urban markets dictating locally unaffordable prices for certain, highly prized species of fish; and a more general decrease in overall fish stocks. Section four explains the historical roots of today's Luapula fishing industry initially shaped by colonial rule but perpetuated in the postcolonial era. The final section analyzes the influence of law on individual choices and behaviors, which in turn are both reactions to and causes of environmental and economic change in the region. Then, it briefly assesses a draft law currently under consideration by the Zambian Parliament.

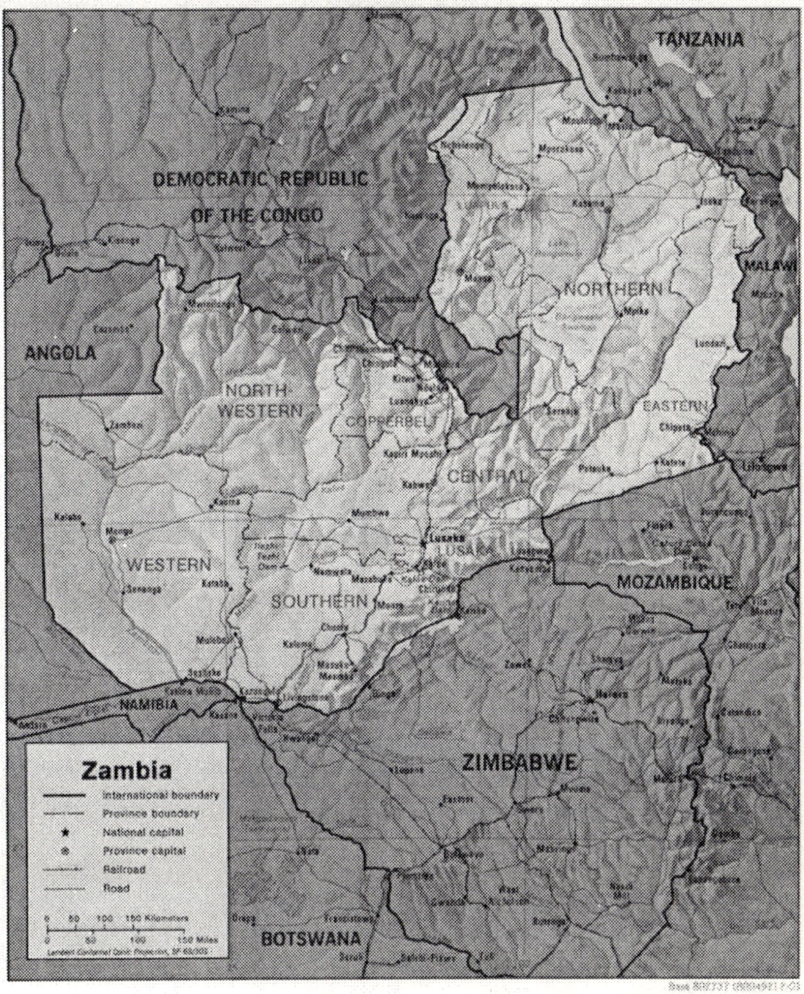

Map 1: Zambia, relief. Luapula Province is located in northern Zambia, west of Northern Province. (map credit: http://www.lib.utexas.edu/maps/africa/zambia_rel01.jpg)

"LIVERPOOL": THE MWERU-LUAPULA FISHERY

Despite being situated over 1,300 kilometers from the capital of Zambia (see Map 1), Kashikishi,[3] the economic and social heart of the Mweru-Luapula fishing industry, is regarded by its residents as a modern, cosmopolitan, and connected place. Locals fondly promote the chic reputation of their fishery through self-endowed names associating it with far-off places of significance. In his 1959 monograph of the region Ian G. Cunnison notes frequent comparison with the mining area of Northern Rhodesia—the Copperbelt—in the quip, 'kuno ni ku migote' ('it is the mines [Copperbelt] here').[4] More contemporary connotations include "Manchester" for Lake Mweru and "Port of Portugal" for the inhabited Potolo portion of the Mifimbo fish breeding area. This remote island offers a seemingly incongruous vision of prosperity composed of bottled beer and blaring recorded music, juxtaposed against the roughshod grass thatch shacks in which the fishers sleep. Although the dreams of modernity and wealth persist, in reality they seem little more than vestiges of past orientations to the former colonial power, Britain. One can easily imagine a certain wistful equivalence intimated by citizens of Luapula to the prestige of their homonymic counterpart Liverpool, England.

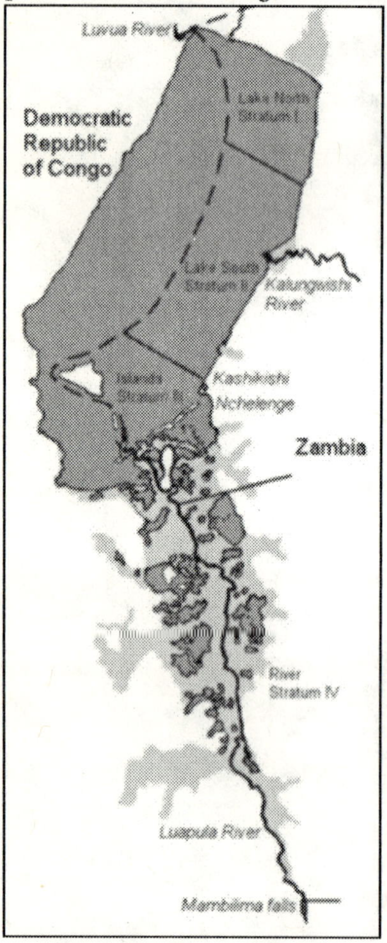

Map 2: The Mweru-Luapula Fishery, divided by Stratum (Map credit: Zambia Department of Fisheries, Ministry of Agriculture, Food, and Fisheries)

Luapula's inhabitants have not composed these visions in a vacuum. Their long history of travel and trade stretches back to the migrations that brought the vast majority of current residents to the region from what is now the Democratic Republic of Congo (DRC). Modern trade links which have evolved in the 20th century continue to be motivated by the desire to buy and sell Luapula fish. Elisabethville (Lubumbashi) via Kasenga in the Belgian Congo (see Map 1) constituted one of the premier early markets for Luapula fish. Over time the Northern Rhodesian—after independence, the Zambian—Copperbelt displaced locales in the Congo both as destinations for making money and conceptual associations that helped migrant workers to build their cosmopolitan credentials. This section describes the ecological environment that gave rise to such flare, style, and trade—and ultimately its capacity to periodically fill a young fisher's pockets with quick money (often, only to be again destitute the next morning).

The Mweru-Luapula fishery comprises two contiguous areas, each biologically different but ecologically, economically and, socially interdependent. These are Lake Mweru itself (Stratums 1, 2, and part of 3) and the Lower Luapula River (part of 3 and Stratum 4; see Map 2). Zambia and the DRC share the fishery; of the 2,748 miles^2 total area of the Mweru-Luapula, Zambia controls 52% (1,594 miles^2; see map 2). Approximately 60 miles long (on a north-south axis) and 25 to 30 miles wide, Mweru is a relatively shallow lake, which gets progressively deeper as it stretches northward (from 10-15 feet to 120 feet at its deepest). Two important rivers flow into Lake Mweru: the Luapula at the south end and the Kalungwishi on the eastern shore; while the Luvua River at the north flows out into the Lualaba and eventually Congo rivers of the DRC. The Mweru-Luapula watershed comprises the Lower Luapula River, which extends 101 miles southward from the lake to Mambalima Falls. The width of this stretch of the Luapula River fluctuates seasonally, from 400 yards wide when confined to its banks in May and June to floods that reach 3 to 11 miles east in December and January. Its depth varies between 15 to 35 feet.[5]

The fishing industry of Mweru-Luapula is almost exclusively artisanal, which is a general definition for small-scale, low-productivity, and low capital-invested fishing.[6] The various methods of 'killing'[7] and marketing fish in the Mweru-Luapula fishery constitute daily and seasonally repetitive behaviors that are bound in ways similar to the institutions described in other chapters in this volume. Unlike these other institutions, however, for the Mweru-Luapula fishing industry to persist into the future requires recognition that as an ecological system it remains vulnerable to unchecked economic exploitation. More so than on the other major fishery in the Luapula region, Bangweulu, Mweru-Luapula is an open-access watershed: Virtually anyone who can travel and even temporarily reside by the lake-river system may venture into its waters to kill, purchase, and sell fish. Unlike other land and water bodies where private owners, traditional rulers, and the government (to name just a few brokers of access) practice restrictive tenure, Mweru-Luapula remains open to any individual or company with the practical wherewithal to exploit its resources. This modern circumstance has developed over the past 50 years as a consequence of a high rate of in-migration, colonial undermining of traditional authority, and improved transport networks that enable anyone to catch and ship fish to industrialized central markets.

Consequently, fisheries law must articulate a set of guidelines to regulate behaviors in an ecological as well as industrial environment in order to safeguard the reproductive capacity of this living system. Greater and more efficient exploitation of fishery resources may contradict their effective conservation and sustainable development. Lawmakers confront two seemingly discrete—even opposing—aspects of any fishery: the economics of fish treated as commodities, and the ecology of this natural system that should sustain and support the reproduction of fish as living inhabitants of a natural environment. The next section reviews the commercial impact of the Mweru-Luapula fishing industry.

Dogfish (or Mbowa) being measured for sale in Muzabwela Market, Nchelenge (Photo credit: Christopher M. Annear)

'LUAPULA IS FISH': A SOCIO-ECONOMY OF FISHING

> *Mwana watemwa ukoba kalaye noko wimona Mweru walala—Mweru ala buluma!*
>
> (Young man who likes paddling, go and get permission from your mother. Don't view Lake Mweru as sleeping—Mweru roars!)
>
> —Fishing song, as sung by a group of fishers and fish traders, Kasheta Village[8]

> *Ku Luapula kwaliwama fwebene minofu yambowa...pe/ Mwaikalila ukutweba ni tubulu imwe mulacula...*
>
> (In Luapula our pride is the flesh of the dogfish[9]...always/ You tell us Luapula people that we are fishing savages, but it is you who are suffering for lack of food....)
>
> —P. K. Chishala, 'Iminofu Yambowa'

In Luapula, the term tubulu is a notorious insult. To defuse its negative potency, P. K. Chishala, the late acclaimed Luapula musician, employs the epithet in his well known song Iminofu Yambowa ('Flesh of the Dogfish,' above). But he also declares that, regardless of its offensive overtones, he and his people remain unrepentant fishers. With a spirit of rebellious pride, he reclaims tubulu as a banner of exultant identity. Literally tubulu means 'someone who soaks his buttocks in water' or 'a dumb fisherman'—in essence he is a person who is unable to take advantage of economic opportunities besides fishing.[10] Chishala insists, instead, that Luapulans should celebrate their distinction as a fishing people. Although only 10% of the overall Mweru-Luapula population actually fish,[11] this song quite rightly implies that the region is economically, socially, and culturally tied to killing fish. This section focuses on the proliferation of fishers and fish traders whose contemporary behaviors have come to threaten the health and future sustainability of the fishery.

The Mweru-Luapula fishery as shown in Map 2 stretches from the Luapula River near Mulundu to the northern border with the DRC at the village of Lupiya. On the Zambian side there are approximately 240,000 people living in this region within the four districts of Mwense, Kawambwa, Nchelenge, and Chiengi, respectively.[12] Out of this overall population, 12,047 fishers (10,152 male, 1,895 female) own gear. Table 1 shows both the total number of gear owners as well as their distribution by ecological sub-region (stratum -see Map 2).

Table 1: Gear Owners By Stratum

	Males	Females
Stratum 1- Open water north	1,738	45
Stratum 2- Open water south	2,054	95
Stratum 3- River mouth, islands	2,610	418
Stratum 4- River, lagoons, floodplains	3,750	1,337
Total	10,152	1,895

Stratum 1, the northern and deepest portion of the open lake, stretches roughly from the villages of Kalobwa to Lupiya. Characterized by low-nutrient content and steep rocky outcrops it makes access to watercraft essential so most of the fishing here remains both commercial and gear intensive. Close to shore, gillnet fisheries target Hump-backed Bream (Ntembwa, *Tylochromis mylodon*,[13] although not classified locally as 'bream'), while long liners seek the member of the large catfish Bagridae family, Imonde (*Chrysichthys mabusi*, also *Chrysichthys sharpii*). Although residents prefer to eat these larger fish, commerecial fishers target the small but lucrative Chisense or *Microthrissa (Poecillothrissa) moeruensis*—a dimunitive sardine, typically maturing to a length of only 7 cm. Although it only recently culturally and commercially accepted as an exploitable food source, fishers effuse that Chisense is "mana from heaven" because of its profitable market price.[14]

Stratum 2, the southern portion of the open lake, stretches from Nchelenge to the Kalungwishi River delta at Kalobwa. Here, fishers also catch Chisense, but supplement it by Green-headed Bream (Pale, *Oreochromis macrochir*), Tiger Fish (Manda, *Hydrocyon vittatus*), Hump-backed Bream, Large-mouthed

Bream (Makobo, *Serranochromis macrocephalus*, again, not referred to locally as bream), and Silver Fish (Misebele, *Alestes macropthalmus*), especially near the Kalungwishi and Mwatishi river mouths.

Stratum 3 includes several of the lake islands; the important Mifimbo fish breeding area, which is off-limits to fishing year-round; the mouth of the Luapula River; and several lagoons. Fishers and fish traders most highly prize the Green-headed bream in this area, although Chisense is also fished seasonally as the schools drift south from deeper areas of the lake.

Stratum 4, the largest and longest sub-section, is home for the vast majority of subsisstance fishers. It includes the Luapula floodplains, large and shallow lagoons, creeks, and areas of dense aquatic vegetation in papyrus swamps. Because the Luapula River bursts it banks annually, Stratum 4 provides a very dynamic ecological environment. Stretching from Mulundu to Kanyembo, it is directly accessible to the many residents who live in villages along it riverine shores. Fishing efforts net spawning tiger fish, and those especially active in the rainy season such as bottlenose or Cornish Jack (i.e., related species: including Lusa, *Gnathonemus monteirii*; Kafutwe, *Mormyrus longirostris*; and the aptly named *Mormyrops deliciosus*), as well as a couple of species of catfish.[15] Subsistence fishers tend to use intensive methods, most of which are illegal. They trap all fish, regardless of size or species, within reach of their nets or baskets. (These small, juvenile fish are known as chibalebale; see pp. 189-192 below).

Outside of the two main groups of fishers and fish traders, a further 60% of the Mweru-Luapula inhabitants depend on fish for employment and/or subsistence.[16] Almost everyone else in the region —from businessmen and transport operators to farmers and civil servants —also connects to the fishery in some way, either as a contributor, beneficiary, or both,. However, this section focuses on those who reap, process, buy, sell, and move fish from Mweru-Luapula. The first group, the fishers themselves, remains difficult to define in a region that, as the section title suggests, 'is fish.'

Fishers—Hands and pockets of the industry

Table 1, on fishing gear owners (p.181) generally excludes 'fish hands'—people who fish, but with equipment owned by others.[17] Young, male, and transient, fish hands hope to acquire their own boats and fishing equipment. Although essential to cost-effective chains of fishing effort, these characteristics make them difficult to quantify. Mweru-Luapula's open access enables these typically unmarried young men to gain a foothold in the industry by selling their labor to established gear owners. At least since the 1950s, older Valley residents have complained that these young men forget their traditions (including those that help protect the fishery) "and care for nothing but fishing on the river [and lake] to make money."[18]

Despite their low economic and social status, fish hands and similarly positioned boat-transport operators nevertheless appear as the fishing industry's public face. Usually adorned in fashionable replicas of American basket-

Young male fish hands (abatiana) and passenger transporters (called "ba-basy" because they travel frequently between the mainland and islands on Lake Mweru) prepare to embark from Muzabwela Market, Nchelenge. (photo credit: David W. Montgomery)

ball and British soccer jerseys, these young men conspicuously represent the modern Mweru-Luapula fishery's underlying economic logic. Known locally as *abatiana,* these laborers typically are family relatives of the gear owners, but simply take advantage of the fishery's open access. They realize minimal profits, however, usually by continuing to fish after ecologically appropriate yields have been exceeded. Sometimes, lake transport operators add extraneous passengers to their already overloaded boats —with deadly consequences.[19] Although they profit little from this often difficult and dangerous work, fish hands and water transport laborers disproportionately jeopardize the fishery because they earn their modest incomes by killing off marginal and vulnerable fish stocks.

Many fish hands dream of improving their earnings through purchase of fishing gear. Such socioeconomic ascension continues, but is becoming increasingly rare.[20] Table 2 shows the previous means of earning capital for those who later invested in gear for the purpose of exploiting the fishery. While these earlier occupations most likely represent the means by which current fishers raised capital for gear, responses also show that they intend to continue such work as a supplement to fishing income. This is especially the case for farmers, an increasing number of whom cultivate agricultural produce during the annual fish ban that runs from December 1 to the end of February each year.

Table 2: Previous Employment To Fishing, Males and Females

Occupation	Stratum 1		Stratum 2		Stratum 3		Stratum 4		Total	
Fish handler (M) / Fish handler (F)	M	F	M	F	M	F	M	**F**	**M**	**F**
	722	12	693	13	804	20	831	87	3,050	132
Agriculture	369	11	430	14	804	137	1,486	486	3,089	648
General work	79	—	126	—	109	—	203	—	517	—
Government work	50	1	90	4	136	4	117	78	393	87
Mining	26	—	70	—	71	—	135	—	302	—
Other	73	3	86	4	163	4	203	78	525	89
Trading	187	14	291	38	212	26	164	18	854	96
School	101	2	154	4	158	48	365	179	778	233
Housewife		2		6		155		435		598
Total	1,607	45	1,940	83	2,457	394	3,504	1,361	9,508	1,883

Source: Adapted from Kees Goudswaard, A Dynamic Fishery in Zambia: A Case of Change in the Mweru Luapula Fishery: Report of a frame survey in 1997 (1999).

Unlike their agriculturist counterparts elsewhere, farmers in a fishing environment cultivate on a schedule and in ways synchronized with fishing.[21] By the late 20th Century, as Zambia's copper-based economy deteriorated, 20% to 25% fishers had left occupations of 'government (of Zambia) work' and 'miner', as well as a significant number of farmers, to acquire gear and enter into the Mweru-Luapula fishery — a recent trend over the last three decades as labor migrants, previously enticed away from rural areas, have trickled back because Zambian urban economies could not sustain them. This in-migration, propelled by an economic rather than a kinship-oriented logic, appears to be a significant factor in the contemporary over-fishing and poor regulation of the fishery.

The number of female fishers with gear rose 23% according to surveys made in 1992 and 1997.[22] However, despite this increase, this group of fishers remains a very small portion of the commercial sector. As an exception to this sexual division of labor, however, women (88% of all those engaged) dominated subsistence basket-fishing. Furthermore, Stratum 4, with direct access from villages to the fishery, provides homes for the vast majority of female basket-fishers.

Table 3 shows a perceptible, if not enormous, growth in boat ownership. The relatively greater increase in plank-boats than other watercraft suggests the continued economic viability (for now) of the open water commercial industry. However, as outboard engines age and remain unreplaced, this increase coincides with what appears to be an 'artisanization' of the fishery as the number of non-boat owners grows.

Women, girls and boys basket-fishing for catfish. Usually, they mix a locally foraged plant-based fish poison with clay to stun the fish before collecting them in their baskets (Photo credit: Christopher M. Annear)

Table 3: Number of Fishers Using Boats and Gillnets, 1955 to 1997

Year	No. of Fishers	No. of Boats	No. of Gillnets
1955			8,750~
1965	2,000~		
1971	5,963	4,155	
1980	7,210	4,004	
1986	7,723	6,640	
1992	8,440	7,707	46,000
1997	12,047	8,696	93,424

Source: Adapted from Department of Fisheries, Toward a Sustainable Fishery: The Need for Joint Action on Mweru-Luapula 3 (1995).

Although the gross number of boat owners continues to edge higher, percentage-wise fewer own more than one vessel. This reflects a reversal of the 1940s-60s era colonial policies that encouraged expatriates to control the fish trade through gear monopolies. Since that time, more Zambians have enjoyed access to gear ownership, and by extension greater capacity to exploit the fishery. Today, most owners possess only one, and few own more than five. However, this trajectory may again be changing direction in the favor of greater consolidation. In 1997 the number of boats recorded in the census was higher than in 1992, but the percentage of fishers without boats also grew by 53.7%. In Stratum 4, the area of the greatest number of subsistence and female basket fishers, 71% of fishers had no direct access to boats.[23] This means that more fishers work as laborers for gear owners in pursuit of less fish. As noted above, since work as a fish hand earns only marginal profit, therefore this increasing percentage of non-boat owners exerts ever greater pressure on debilitated fish stocks.

Gillnet fishers are likewise stockpiling gear to apply their trade. Notably, this is more an ecological issue than one of economics and labor relations, since nets are cheap and widely available. A more significant statistic shows that while the population of gillnet fishers increased by roughly a third in five years, the gross number of nets they used doubled. This indicated the broader trend toward mostly illegal, intensive practices in which several people work together actively to drive fish toward nets. These kinds of aggressive practices tend to entrap juvenile fish and destroy nests—which inevitably reduces the fishery's future potential.

Traders—Heads and legs of the industry

As men and boys dominate the occupation of fish hand and gear ownership, fish trading (at least locally) has become the domain of women and girls. Once transferred from boat to basket and male to female, fish—many still using their auxiliary breathing organs in a struggle for air—become transformed from living organisms to marketable commodities. Interim-distance female traders —known somewhat derisively as banamakupwila —headload the fish to distribution points for sale for local consumption or further preparation — smoked, sun-dried, or frozen —for longer-distance transport to urban markets on the Copperbelt or in Lusaka. This section describes the various duties, profits, and pitfalls of the fish trading chain that stretches from the waters of the Mweru-Luapula to cooking pots over one thousand kilometers away, and a myriad of destinations in between.

In all four strata, banamakupwila, or interim-distance traders, like fishers, comprise a disparate population. Some, well-established residents of fishing villages, have regular trading relationships with fishers. Other young women, with ambitions of living and being educated in the Copperbelt, seek to raise start-up cash. Tilleke Kiewied suggests that in the village of Kasembe near the northern Zambian lake border with the DRC,

> [t]he activities undertaken by individual household members can change seasonally or over the years. A 'trader' can be a trader for a few trips after which he/she has different priorities and activities for all kinds of reasons. A woman in Kasembe manages to buy fish only after she gains enough money from the sale of her agricultural produce. She increases this profit by buying fish and selling it on the Copperbelt. With this profit she buys commodities and returns to agriculture. Other women are involved only when the family situation allows it: when there is someone to take care of the children, when she is not pregnant or breast-feeding a baby, etc.[24]

Not discounting its diversity, a few generalizations may help to better characterize this population: most are female, financially independent from their husbands (if they are married), and at risk to economic and sexual exploitation, (although such risks tend to vary in relation to the degree of their broader social and economic support networks).

Marriage status constitutes a significant delineating factor. Married women, whose husbands have stable employment as teachers, farmers, or civil servants, may work as traders to supplement household income. Some women, married to fishers, remain independent entrepreneurs both financially and in terms of chosen trading partners[25], mainly to earn some extra money.

Unmarried women fish traders, however, face quite different occupational circumstances. With fewer lateral social obligations, potentially they can earn and keep more of their profits than their married counterparts. However, these women seem hardest hit by the annual fish ban. As Robarm Mwape, Chairman of the District Executive Committee of the Mweru-Luapula Fishing Association, says, "they have only their fish;" they are fully invested in buying and selling fish without any reserves or alternative financial support. Many are immigrants without established homesteads where they work; they lack access to land and labor resources for farming during the closed season. Not surprisingly, these women seem most likely to seek or submit to "fish-for-sex" in order to get cheaper fish.[26]

Banamakupwila trade in all fresh, frozen, smoked, and dried fish save one: Chisense. The women who deal in these lake sardines are instead referred to as abakukungwisha or the anglicized nickname banama-bafa after the bathtubs they carry on their heads to transport stocks. Only marginally different from trading in larger fish, their work potentially seems much more lucrative. A recent survey of the chisense fish trade describes some of their activities, as well as the informal chain of command:

> In Kashikishi, towards sunset, buyers employ young boys to run errands and to do the odd jobs for them; they fill the bags with Chisense, they close the bags with threads of mealie meal bags, they print the initials of the buyer on the bags using paint made of disposed batteries and paraffin, carry the load to a storeroom or straight to the truck or bus and lift the bags on top.... One day a young man carried two '90 kg bags' of Chisense on his shoulders from the market to a

> bus. One of the mishanga boys (cigarette sellers) loudly commented with a 'abakali-bakali' expressing his consideration for one of the toughest but relatively well paid jobs being done by a porter.[27]

In 1994, women made up 93% of the total number of 2,929 traders; 43% of those women—almost half—were younger than 20 years old; a further 37% were in the 21-30 age group.[28] The census figures suggest that the potential for earning money makes this activity a popular woman's job, but it involves several pitfalls: "excessive beer-drinking (the fishers always think they will have a good or better catch the following day which makes them spend all their earnings); illiteracy (poor accounting); and payments 'in kind' —which means that when a female trader 'borrows' a bafu [tub] of Chisense from a fisher, in return she may be forced to pay with sex in order 'to avoid trouble'".[29] The latter practice declined with the onset of HIV/AIDS, but, in the past, fishers commonly demanded women be 'gentle.' Some even ganged up, deciding not to sell fish to a particular trader they stigmatized as "difficult."[30]

The category of long-distance traders, those who buy fish from banamakupwila and abakukungwisha for sale in urban areas, encompasses a fairly loose population of people. They may own or operate open-trucks; book vehicles for fish transport; move fish using public transport such as the passenger buses that daily crisscross Zambia; or act as formal driver/buyers for established fish retailers such as Isabi Investments Ltd, Delta/Lusaka Fish Centre, or Chibri Fish Centre of Kitwe in the Copperbelt. Women with startup capital and entrepreneurial spirit engage in long-distance fish trade, and so do male retirees, who seek to supplement their often meager government pensions.

On the whole fish marketers welcome long-distance traders as clients, but they also blame them for driving up fish prices by selling fish in wealthier urban markets. As an outcome of this process—of remote consumers unknowingly dictating the lake-riverside prices of fish— local people, even though they catch and trade the richest varieties, generally eat the less desired species.[31]

This section has described the roles of various operators on the fishery, including their relationships to one another and the underlying ecology. It presented data that shows the mounting pressure on fish stocks as an increasing number of migrants from the Copperbelt have sought employment and subsistence from region's open-access fish resources. Although large scale fishing operations and gear monopolies created problems in the past, today over-fishing reflects atomization (proliferation of individual participants) and artisanization (a trend toward rudimentary and inefficient equipment and increased use of destructive 'intensive' fishing methods). Occupationally, fishing labor remains sexually divided and stratified. In combination, these contemporary aspects of the socio-economy of the Mweru-Luapula fishery coalesce into a circumstance of potential disaster. More people applying pressure on the fishery with diminishing profits translate into greater vulnerability for both the fishery and the individuals engaged in it.

CHIBALEBALE: "DEVELOPMENT" IN AN UNREGULATED FISHERY

> We eat chibalebale due to lack of big fishes. If you buy chibalebale you find it mixed with snails. God made them as food stuffs for big fishes. Maybe big catfish and small catfish eat chibalebale; we just eat what they eat.
>
> —Headman Shinjoni, Shinjoni Village, Kashikishi

The term 'chibalebale' is the recent linguistic invention coined to describe the ecologically destructive product of catching and selling assorted juvenile fish. It refers not to a single species but instead to the quantity of fish being sold. It translates literally as a "thing in a dish," meaning assorted juvenile fish sold by the small dish- or bowl-full for the US dollar equivalent of 10-20¢. It may include various species of juvenile fish, haphazardly collected in nets with illegally small mesh-sizes well before they reach reproductive age. In short, when fishers kill and local customers purchase chibalebale, in effect they consume the potential of future fish stocks.

Filling a market niche previously occupied by adult fish of greater size and prevalence, chibalebale symbolizes the degradedation of the Mweru-Luapula fishery's ecological and economic health. Perhaps as the most telling of the lake-river system's rapid decline due to poorly regulated, uneven fishing practices, local cultural and linguistic concepts contain no adequate definition of chibalebale. Headman Shinjoni expresses ambivalence concerning whether one can classify these juvenile fish, sold cheaply by the bowl-full, as 'food" for human beings. He leaves unanswered the question of how these fish are caught: Are they 'killed' (ukwipaya), 'harvested' (ukusombola), 'snared' (ukutea) in nets, or none of the above? This recent, uncategorized method of scooping up juvenile fish even appears to be a critique of efforts at reducing the malaria parasite among Luapula Valley residents. The most common method of collecting chibalebale is to stitch together a few mosquito nets, which is called kashebondwe when used for this purpose.

Chibalebale perhaps marks the most disheartening sign of the deterioration of a fishery that in 1948 was described as "potentially and extremely rich.... an area in which real development might be achieved."[32] In 1965 when records began to be kept of Catch Per Unit Effort (CPUE), Mweru-Luapula fishers collected 9 kilograms per night for each net employed on a typical outing; in 1992, the same effort yielded just 2 kilograms of fish;[33] and, in 1997, even less[34] (*see* Table 4, *infra*).

More recent fieldwork by the author suggests that a significant amount of this already scanty catch probably comprises chibalebale. A market survey conducted from September 2004 to September 2005 reveals that fishers and fish traders fully understand that catching and selling chibalebale proves extremely harmful to the fishery—the source of their livelihoods.[35] Zambian law clearly declares the use of small mesh-sizes to catch such minute fish illegal.

Why do people continue to practice this and other destructive methods, not only in violation of existing law but in opposition to seemingly commonsense fishery management? After reviewing the evolution of contemporary law, this chapter will revisit that critical issue of fishery resource management. First, it seems useful to explore more fully the nature of the more problematic management behaviors practiced in the Mweru-Luapula fishery.

Fishing down—depleting a fishery

Fisheries biologists use the term 'fishing down' to describe the process of slowly draining a fishery of its fish species through the systematic targeting of the largest individuals of the most desired varieties. Over time the size of the largest individuals begins to diminish until the ones being caught are at the threshold of reproductive ability. With an ever-shrinking population of reproductive-age adults it is only a matter of time until the entire species is fished out.[36] Although fishers recognize declining catches and lament the passing of a species, their 'fishing down' behavior does not tend to change; instead, a second echelon species is chosen as the next favored target, and so on—the cycle continues.

As time goes on in a fishery such as Mweru-Luapula, not only are specific species relegated from dinner plates to the wistful recollections of elderly fishers, but the overall Catch Per Unit Effort declines. This figure's decline reflects a fishery's ecological stress, but, instead of easing fishing pressure, fishers attempt to compensate for their catches' lost volume by intensified effort. This means more aggressive fishing and longer hours on the water—in particular an exponential increase in gillnets and the new destructive methods for catching chibalebale. As an artisanal fishery, Mweru-Luapula provides fishers cash incomes, but also subsistence. As profits go down fishers will not abandon the fishery, especially because it endows them with their only mode of sustenance in a state of increasing impoverishment.

As an additional complication, like open-access natural resource areas the world, over, the Mweru-Luapula fishery confront a tragedy of the commons. Originally people conceived that tragedy as a mathematical ratio that contrasted full individual benefit to the only partially-borne consequences of over-use. Working within a commonly owned resource, the individual views the primary restraint, not as the limits imposed by a diminishing resource, but instead the constraints on his own capacity to exploit it.[37] More recent considerations of the problem, however, suggest that the consequences need not necessarily lead to the limited resource's complete destruction.[38]

In the same way, the Mweru-Luapula case may not end with the fishery's total depletion, nor does the burden of responsibility lie solely with the fishers. As Zambian historian Mwelwa Musambachime suggests,[39] successive colonial government policies, as well as times of notable inaction, have tended to foster over-fishing. He notes that the 1920s, mostly Belgian colonial campaign, to eradicate the Mweru-Luapula crocodile population cleared the Luapula River for total coverage nets.[40] This drive was a major factor in causing the local

Table 4: Total catch and Catch Per Unit Effort (CPUE) Over Time

Year(s)	Total Catch (tons/year)	CPUE (kg/100m net/night)	Source
1911		60-65; 70	de Kimpe; (first figures from fishery, second from experimental gillnets)
1932	1,000		de Kimpe 1964
1940s	4,000		de Kimpe 1964 (DRC side only)
1950s	7,000		(de Kimpe 1964, DRC side only)
1955-1958	15,000 (1955 only)	9.5-13.7; 10.5-11.4	de Kimpe 1964 (both sides of fishery); latter figure from Soulsby 1959
1955-1962		9.6-11.4	Anonymous 1964
1963-1964		8.6-13.8	Allen 1965
1965	15,180	10	DoF 1995 (total catch only) Williams 1972
1969		3	Williams 1972
1970-1974	18,370	4.7-5.0	DoF 1995 (total catch for 1971 only) Anonymous 1975
1980s	16,940	2-3	DoF 1995 (total catch for 1980 only) Reynolds 1991
1982-1985	13,860	1.9-4.2	DoF 1995 (total catch for 1986 only) Van Zwieten and Kapasa 1996
1994		1.8-2.6; 6	Van Zwieten and Kapasa 1995; figure of 6 kg/100m/night is from closed Mifimbo fishing breeding area

Source: adapted from P.A.M. van Zwieten & C.K. Kapasa, Lake Mweru-Luapula: Analysis of the Gillnet Surveys of 1982 to 1985 and 1994 to 1996 (Nchelenge, Luapula Province: Department of Fisheries, 1996).

extinction of the most highly prized and lucrative fish species of the 1940s, the Luapula Salmon.[41] In the same way, as the next two sections describe, governmental focus on economic development to the exclusion of conservation helped to institutionalize patterns of over-fishing that persist to this day.

Despite this contemporary crisis, the Mweru-Luapula fishery has a continued reputation for abundance and fertility. Considering this fishery's importance to the development of both the Zambian and Congolese mining industries it is not surprising that it conjures connections to wealth and development in the minds of Zambians everywhere. To better understand today's threat to the fishery's ecology and economy, it helps to review a brief history of governments' role in the transition from subsistence to commercial production from the late 1800s to the 1940s when the British colonial government initiated efforts to address conservation and development through law.

MINING FOR FISH: THE CREATION OF A COMMERCIAL FISHING INDUSTRY IN MWERU-LUAPULA

> To the people of Mweru-Luapula, the fishery was synonymous to the copper mining industry in Katanga [colonial Congo] and Northern Rhodesia. The river and the lake were mines. The canoes, plankboats and launches were the cages (elevators).... The devices were dynamite and the fish was the copper.
>
> —Chief Kashiba Kalemfu, Kashiba Village[42]

Contemporary international boundaries still divide the Mweru-Luapula fishery between Zambia and the DRC. The emergence of two independent nations has done little to change the socioeconomic and sociocultural relationships shaped over the previous decades. Before British and Belgian colonial forces conquered and politically co-opted the region in the late 19th century, fishery proceeds provided valuable commodities for barter and tribute to local chiefs. Migration, fishing, and trade dovetailed to create a "fishing people", the Shila as products of intermarriage among local indigenous fishers and immigrating Luba peoples from the Congo side of the fishery.[43] The Chibemba term for a member of this ethnic group, mushila, also means a person who fishes. [44]

During the colonial period, the establishment of British South Africa Company (BSAC) administrative centers and several Christian evangelical missions created an early demand for fish. The early 1900s saw the commercial fishing industry begin in earnest upon emergence of the Katangan (DRC) mining sector and a growing demand for fishing as a significant source of protein for mine workers. By 1910, the completion of the railroad link to Lubumbashi stimulated growth of the Union Minière du Haut Katanga (UMHK)mines, accompanied by a growing demand for fish. A 1912 rinderpest outbreak reduced beef exports from Northern Rhodesia, making Luapula fish an increasingly attractive option for the UMHK.[45]

World War I further disrupted meat supplies. The UMHK fomally invited Greek fishermen from Ionedes and Rhode Islands to establish a fishing industry to provide regular rations for its miners.[46] The Greeks dominated the fish trade for the next three decades.[47] Construction of a road in the early 1920s linked Lubumbashi to Kasenga, the fast growing port of sale for transport to the mines on the Congo side of the Luapula River.

The UMHK and Belgian government investments in the fishery exposed the British colonial counterparts' failure to invest in the fishery on the lake's other side. Musambachime suggests this reflected two factors: 1) the BSAC officially classified the Mweru-Luapula region as 'remote;' and, 2) the BSAC remained preoccupied with native hut taxes as the region's primary source of revenue as well as its impact in 'inducing' Africans to work in the Copperbelt mines.[48] BSAC's short-sighted, deliberately exploitative policies, as intended, did force many men to migrate, but many Luapulans left Northern Rhodesia to engage in the expanding activities on the Belgian Congo side – expanding economic traffic that benefited the Congo side to the continued neglect of the Mweru-Luapula of Northern Rhodesia.

Even after 1924, when colonial control passed from the BSAC to the British government, development lagged on the Northern Rhodesian side. That seemed consistent with the British government's declared goal of transforming their inherited colony from a labor and resource reservoir to a financially sustainable entity.[49] The crown government sought to reap profits from existing resources in the country without investing in the infrastructure necessary to make that possible. Only in the 1940s, three decades after the Belgians began regular investments, did British government officials finally begin formally to recognize the fishery's potential.

Initially, this recognition led to the long overdue creation of an agency in part to write the first Northern Rhodesia fishery conservation guidelines. The government gazetted those recommendations in 1930,[50] but only established the Game and Tsetse Control Department ten years later. That agency's first director, T. Vaughan-Jones, asserted his department's stance on the relationship between conservation and development: First, further development would enable the fishery to add to its already impressive output; in 1944 he remarked, "One is mainly struck with great potentialities of a native industry which, with little care in the past, has haphazardly grown so wealthy."[51] Secondly, however, he pointed out that current production already adversely affected the fish stocks' future viability.

A military officer, Cadet Makissack, later a District Commissioner in the region, acknowledged that,

> At present we are doing very little, if any, by way of development as was made clear to me on a recent visit to Kasenga [Belgian Congo side].... On the Belgian side there was a fleet of large motor boats, two established ice factories, one ice factory under construction which contained the latest Americas machinery and numberless

> lorries ready to take fish on ice—(15 tons a day are about to be produced)—to the Belgian Copper miners. On our side which is richer in fish, one saw a few canoes."[52]

As the British colonial authority began to advocate investment in the fishery, calls appeared for implementing conservation regulations to save dwindling fish stocks. In particular, the plight of the Luapula Salmon had caught the attention of colonial officials on both sides of the fishery.

Inspired by the precipitous decline of this elegant pink fish, the call for regulations seemed to reflect at least as much the on-going political struggles over control of the fishing industry as a demand for better management of the ecological environment. The next sections review the nature and impact of past and current fishery regulations, including changes introduced by the independent Zambian state. These uninspired efforts altered the regulations' language but not the unsustainable behaviors that left the region dependent on deteriorating urban centers, its fish stocks poorly conserved, and its people marginalized and impoverished.

MODERN LAW, MODERN EXPLOITATION

Current fisheries law, like the contemporary Mweru-Luapula commercial fishery itself, constitutes an essentially modern institution. In 1955,[53] as a delayed response to a decade of alarming evidence of Luapula Salmon's rapid decline, the Northern Rhodesian government enacted the first comprehensive fisheries legislation. Its 'modernity' still rested on British colonial thinking that prioritized production over sustenance, and short-term exploitation ahead of enduring development.[54]

In terms of fisheries development and conservation, Zambia inherited a colonial legacy of legislative negligence. Although underproductive, Zambian fisheries regulations functioned differently from more heavy-handed, colonially inspired law that shaped other institutions. To succeed, legislation of a fishery and its corollary industry must include not merely a plan for developing human and natural resources but also management of its underlying ecology. Unfortunately, first Northern Rhodesian and then Zambian law tended to relegate conservation to the role of window dressing for market development—always second to political power brokerage and low-cost commercial exploitation of fisheries resources. For the most part, law-makers continued to conceive, write, and enforce fisheries law as an addendum to a primary agenda of low-investment, high return extraction of fish with little regard for the future health of fish stocks, or even the fishing industry itself.

The next section assesses the shortcomings of the successive laws, concluding with a brief review of a recently drafted law that seeks to calm the Zambian fisheries' troubled waters.

DEVELOPMENT OR CONSERVATION?: THE ROLE OF LAW IN REGULATING MWERU-LUAPULA

> Government does not only propose to protect fish...it proposes to move to conserve fish or fisheries so that they are developed to their outmost capacity without...deteriorations in the supplies of the fisheries.
>
> —British Colonial Secretary for Native Affairs, 1943[55]

> Unless the government gives powers to the elders of these places to monitor the lakes and river in traditional ways our young generation shall remain with nothing like fishes from our lakes and rivers.
>
> —Headman Shinjoni, Shinjoni Village, Kashikishi, 2004[56]

In 1929, the first Northern Rhodesia Legislative Council debates on fisheries management viewed conservation primarily as a means of building commercially viable fish stocks. Over a decade later, Vaughan-Jones, the director of the government agency responsible for implementing the resulting regulations still toed this line: Conservation of fisheries, he argued, "is intended to improve the total weight of the economically available fish for consumption. Primarily it implies certain restrictions to preserve the young fish until they have bred" (*sic*).[57] This view seemed in conflict with the typical African perspective reflected in Headman Shinjoni's desire (see above) to conserve fish by traditional means so they would remain available to his future progeny.

The Fish Protection Ordinance of 1929

Issues of conservation, like those of development rarely remain neutral or apolitical. Competing interests drive policy, and political power tends to be the leverage necessary to implement and enforce it. Some claim that a recognition that commercial fishing pressure aggravated the decline of fish stocks[58] led to the first legislation enacted under British controlled Northern Rhodesia.[59] The 1929 Ordinance and the discussions and correspondences that precede it,[60] however, primarily focused on the need to regulate (i.e. generate government revenue) a currently ungoverned industry,[61] as well as a potentially lucrative market for fish for the Northern Rhodesian mines. The Fish Protection Ordinance of 1929, however, did little more than declare the right of the "Governor" to "make alter and repeal regulations." Furthermore, the government waited until 1940 to establish an agency to execute these vague directives.

Fish Control Regulations, 1943 to 1945

The next flurry of legislative activity came in the early 1940s. By this time the fishery had dramatically increased production in order to meet the ravenous appetite of a mining industry, itself propelled by wartime demand for copper. It was recognized that fish consumption had begun to outstrip supply, but lawmakers still apparently believed that fishery regulations must first benefit the commercial capacity of the fishing industry and only then focus on conservation. In practice, this meant the application of consistent pressure to keep commerce moving in the short-term, even if it threatened future fish stocks. Nevertheless, stated policy ostensibly aimed to safeguard the fisheries' ecological integrity. The Fish Control Regulations, 1943 to 1945: Government Notices No. 77 (1943) and No. 40 (1945) reflected these seemingly contradictory ambitions.[62]

'Finishing' the Luapula Salmon—how legislative ambivalence fished out a species

Throughout this period the rapidly expanding Mweru-Luapula fishing industry focused primarily on catching the Luapula Salmon. Praised for its sweetness of flesh, beauty of form, and delicious 'caviar' (roe), the predictability of its movements as a spawning fish made the Salmon extremely vulnerable to fishing pressure. This species's high profits underpinned its (temporary) widely-proclaimed developmental success. Its ultimate demise exposed the disastrous consequences of government's ambivalent policy that depended for implementation on structures beholden to commercial interests. To make matters worse, previous Belgian measures (see above, p. 190) had virtually eliminated the crocodiles that had previously blocked individual African fishers from using nets in the shallows of the Salmon's breeding areas; the fish simply had nowhere to swim but into the nets stretched across their spawning run.

Indirect Rule, the modus operandi of British colonial governance, mandated that chosen 'tribal' political bodies – 'Native Authorities'—implement colonial laws. The Fish Control Regulations of 1943 to 1945' licensing system, therefore, channeled proceeds to the Native Authorities who collected them. This put the traditional authorities in an awkward, comprised position vis-à-vis their own subjects; they felt powerless to restrict the traditional fishing practices of their African support base. Nor did either they or the people ever see the purported benefits of their local political sacrifices on the ground. While colonial officials believed their laws supported both 'development' and 'conservation', the popularity of the Native Authorities among the fishing populace steadily eroded.

Although little positive change was effected, government agents did recognize the difficulties of enforcing the ambiguous regulations of the 1940s. One British District Commissioner reported that destructive fishing by either Greeks based in the Belgian Congo or Africans "cannot be stopped without very serious consequences and breaches of the peace."[63]

Fish Conservation Act, 1955

The next round of fisheries legislation came in the early 1950s, during a heightened atmosphere of political turmoil. In 1953 Northern Rhodesia changed its governing metropole —this time to Salisbury (now Harare, Zimbabwe), the regional capital of the new Central African Federation. This again altered the relationship of Luapula's rural hinterland to government interests.

By then, the Luapula Salmon, now virtually extinct, had dropped from a 1947 high of 43% of annual fish exports to UMHK to less than 5%.[64]

In terms of the political trust and cooperation necessary to implement effective fisheries regulations, the climate could not have been more divisive. Africans on the Northern Rhodesian side of colonial control objected furiously to the Federation's establishment. They viewed the Federation as politically compromised by the role of what they perceived as its 'local faces': the 'fish guards' who enforced the fishery law's iniquitous restrictions; the predominantly Greek middleman fish buyers, whom they saw as favored by the government; and the white Department of Game and Tsetse Control officials whose research called for stronger fishery controls. In 1953, mounting community anger and frustration reached a dramatic climax when the "Kasenga riots" culminated in an assault on a prison to free an African fisherman who had shot a Greek fish buyer.[65]

Given the lack of popular credibility for any government legislative mandate enacted at this time[66] it might seem surprising that the policies put into force in 1955 would be the most comprehensive—and ultimately enduring—to date. After Luapula Salmon's numbers plunged in the late 1940s, the government had rescinded the earlier regulations. It then enacted other far-reaching rules that served as the basis of Zambian fisheries law for the next thirty years.

The Fish Conservation Act, 1955 aimed to "make new and comprehensive provision for the conservation of fish and the control of fishing...."[67] It specified that the Department of Game and Tsetse Control's definition of conservation

> does not mean preservation for preservation's sake, and the powers under the law are intended to serve the main object of increasing fish supplies for the fishermen, to the limit the waters can produce.[68]

Unlike its 1943-5 predecessor, the 1955 law gave the Native Authorities levy-setting control for specific fishery locales (including the subsidiary legislation, Fish Control (Mweru-Luapula Area) Regulations); and power to institute a fish ban annually with less regard to attenuating circumstances such as the "kapata" or the Luapula Salmon spawning period. Nevertheless, implicitly, the 1955 law still underscored the overriding importance of economic development to the detriment of conservation "for preservation's sake."

The Fish Conservation Act of 1955 marked the colonial administration's last attempt to regulate fisheries through the Native Authorities. As a tool of colonial thinking, it envisioned an economically, culturally, and socially stratified fishing industry. As illustrated by the 1953 Kasenga riots, that perspective had contributed to a mounting sense of injustice among Africans in the Mweru-Luapula region. African fishers justifiably felt their opportunities for advancement suppressed in contrast to the Greeks who dominated the export of fish to lucrative regional markets; and their own supposed representatives, the Native Authorities, seemed little more than hamstrung colonial government operatives, expected to enforce the rules without any legitimate decision-making power.

The Fisheries Act, 1974

That the first changes to colonial fisheries legislation came ten years after the official raising of the Zambian flag seems telling. The independent Zambian government may either have viewed the 1955 fishery law more or less adequate, or considered the fishing industry as a relatively low priority. One thing appears clear, however: When they did decide to enact a new law, the law-makers apparently made little effort to reevaluate the earlier law's preexisting concepts and philosophy.

The 1974 Act's first words declared it, too, aimed

> to provide for the development of commercial fishing in the Republic; to control fishing and provide for the registration of fishermen and their boats; and to provide for matters connected with or incidental to the foregoing.[69]

The 1974 Act differs from its 1955 antecedent in three ways: its minor alterations of language; its elimination of an annual closed season; and its implementation structure. For example, the 'Minister' replaced the colonial 'Governor' of the 1955 and previous laws as the highest local official charged with the power of discretion to specific matters such as licensing and penalties. Occasionally, the "Director" or (lower case) "official" now could make decisions. Besides these cosmetic changes, the most fundamental alterations omitted both the annual closed season and the Native Authority structure so prized by the British colonial government. It is not surprising that the Zambian government jettisoned the compromised and symbolically distasteful institutions of the colonially imposed annual closed season[70] and the Native Authorities. Nevertheless, it seems disturbing that such retractions actually translated into a net loss of rights and fish supplies for fishers in Mweru-Luapula. When imposed by colonial legislation— supposedly enforced by uneasy Native Authorities—the yearly fish ban proved highly unpopular among African fishers. The Independence Era government officials might make some short-term political capital by doing away with it; yet, once it was gone chiefs and fishers alike called for its return.[71]

The Native Authorities issue seems less cut and dried. Most, including this chapter's author, would agree that these seemed politically, economically, and culturally untenable institutions. Ostensibly, they allowed chiefs to retain their pre-colonial spiritual as well as political authority over the fishery management, but the expansion of commercial fishing had steadily eroded those controls. Perhaps ironically, it took an African, rather than colonial, government to completely sever this authority.

CONCLUSION: LEGISLATING WHAT'S LEFT

> The success of any management of the fish resource will depend on the participation of the local community.
>
> —Kees Goudswaard

> Confronted by a law, social actors behave within time- and place-specific constraints and resources of the environment within which they live and work.
>
> —Ann Seidman and Robert B. Seidman[72]

As the new millennium opened, legislators writing fishery law no longer had the luxury to choose between conservation and development. More than mere complementary concepts, they prove essential to the survival of the Mweru-Luapula fishery and its corollary industry. Clearly, a commercialized living system, like a fishery, cannot develop without fish to capture and sell. Perhaps somewhat less intuitively, to achieve financially sustainable protection, the fisheries' environment also requires commercial value. This chapter has shown that comprehensive research into the historic evolution of problematic behaviors that comprise today's fishery and associated industry not only can foster a real understanding of the causes of institutional deficiencies, but also reveal avenues for writing better policy.

Mweru-Luapula remains a fishery and a fishing industry in trouble; after so long passively witnessing its demise, can law play a useful role in restoring it? This last section considers this question by reviewing the basic tenets of a draft fisheries law currently under review in Zambia.

Draft Fisheries Act, 2001

The relationship between fishers, marketers and the Zambian government today remains somewhat ambivalent. Instead of the Native Authority implementing the laws enacted in a far off capital, the Department of Fisheries (DoF) is the central enforcer. While by name, creed, and title this department differs from its colonially-imposed predecessors, its *de facto* structure belies significant similarities. Asked to enforce the (now reestablished) annual fish ban, DoF officials remain underfunded, often lacking even fuel for boat patrols.[73] Supposedly, they police the fishery, yet sometimes their relatives, who commit offences, prove difficult to prosecute because of familial obligations. They practically have to use the proceeds from confiscated catches to fund their own enforcement excursions —again placing them in an ambivalent position. Essentially, in terms of conflicts of interest and contradictory alliances, DoF officials appear just as compromised as their Native Authority institutional ancestors.

Although this is the contemporary circumstance, attempts at change are underway. This book proposes a process of researching the ways in which past law perpetuates problematic institutional behaviors, and offers a methodology as a guide for drafting new, more effective law. In the case of the Mweru-Luapula fishery, Zambian law-makers have already begun that process. This presents an opportunity to assess their actual draft in light of the evidence reviewed in this chapter. Specifically, does the draft Fisheries Act, 2001 seem likely to prove effective in changing the causes of the problematic behaviors —the historically-shaped institutions – that to this date endanger the fishery's very existence? Did the drafting process ensure that the fishers and fish traders, most affected by the fishery's conflicting economic and ecological circumstances, had opportunity to voice their concerns? Did that process ensure the drafters heard and took those concerns into account in designing measures likely to prove effectively implemented to help overcome the causes of the fishers' sometimes seemingly perverse behaviors?

Unlike its legal forebears, the draft 2001 Fisheries Act's preamble uses specific, carefully crafted language. Unequivocally, it aims to ensure reinvestment of the benefits of conservation and development, not in the national (certainly not in the colonial) metropole but instead the fishery itself to improve the lives of the fishery communities and those who work in it:

> An act to repeal and replace the Fisheries Act of 1974; to establish the Department of Fisheries and the Central Fisheries Committee; to provide for the establishment of Fishery Management Committees, Fisheries Zonal Management Committees and Fishing Village Management Committees to control fishing in the Republic; to provide for the conservation, management and sustainable utilisation of fisheries resources; to provide for the registration of fishermen, their boats, fishing gears and fish farmers; to enhance benefits from fishery areas to local communities; to provide for the development of aquaculture, to provide for the licensing of fishing, aquaculture and fisheries related activities; to provide for the inspection of Aquaculture facilities; to provide for the control of ornamental fishing and types of fish species and, to provide for matters connected with or incidental to the foregoing.

The Act proposes guidelines to "provide for the conservation, management and sustainable utilisation of fisheries resources"—that is, to find a feasible balance between conservation and development.

After setting out the powers of the Director and the Department of Fisheries the act embarks on balancing industrial growth with 'sound fisheries management.' The contributors to the draft law view conservation, not as an obstacle to "developing" the industry, but as a force to temper unchecked economic exploitation. Each clause that mentions development simultaneously suggests limitations. For example, two subsections under the heading 'General principle of Management' assert the principle that the country's aquatic environments shall be managed as an asset for succeeding generations; the need to apply the precautionary approach to the conservation of the fisheries resources taking account of the best scientific evidence available, so, nevertheless, that the absence of adequate scientific information should not be used as a reason for postponing or failing to take conservation and management measures.

The draft Act's preceeding section emphasizes "community participation in fisheries management." The Act's authors appear to understand the potential dangers of individual interests clashing with community welfare – the tragedy of the commons (see p.190 above). To avoid this, they propose establishing a Central Fisheries Committee, consisting of a broad swathe of actors engaged in exploiting the fishery, who, at least theoretically, have a stake in sustaining it. The Committee, with decision-making power over all the fishery's participants, will comprise twelve members:

- six representatives of local fishery management committees, presumably familiar with the particularities their own locales;
- one from the aquaculture industry familiar with the fishery's unique characteristics;
- one from industrial fisheries who understand those fisheries technical and market realities;

  two 'ordinary members' appointed by the 'Minister in charge of fisheries'; and
- the Director of Fisheries, the Chief Fish Culturist, and the designated Chief Fish Culturist of DoF who understand the DoF's potential for helping to resolve possible conflicts and problems that must inevitably arise in implementing regulations in such contradictory circumstances.

The Committee will have leeway to regulate and develop its subject fishery and fishing industry, but must always take into account the system's ecological well being.

Transforming behavior through law

The draft Fisheries Act, 2001, employing the contemporary language demanded by international donors and non-governmental organizations strikes many of the right chords. Nevertheless, its protocols appear loose and general. Hopefully, the Republic of Zambia's legislative review process will tighten the regulations directly to alter the three interrelated circumstances that, as described in this Chapter, foster the destructive behaviors that currently threaten the the Mweru-Luapula fishery's economic and ecological health: open-access, atomization, and marginalization of fish-hands and young, unmarried fish traders.

Mweru-Luapula's open-access status has fundamentally influenced its constituent groups, labor organization, population structure, and fishing pressure. As this chapter emphasizes, interaction between the fishery and these groups remains dynamic and historically shaped by interacting cultural, political, and economic processes: Precolonial chiefly rule that both regulated and relied upon the fishery for political stability; British co-optation of that authority while prioritizing profits over sustainability; contemporary governmental inaction in the face of problems created by too many fishers killing too many fish; and the migration of more people into the region because it seemed to offer them access to resources they need to survive. To create a bill likely to change these intricately interrelated behaviors, drafters must understand these contemporary circumstances' evolution. At the same time, they must discover how to design legislation to alter these destructive behaviors in the context of a larger legislative program that offers alternative solutions to a large and growing population that has come to depend on the fishery for bare subsistance.

The atomization of the Mweru-Luapula fishing industry has occurred because of its open-access status within a deteriorating national economy. As the national economy prospects declined, growing numbers of Zambians converged on areas like Kashikishi that offered them, if not a prosperous future, at least something to eat. During the colonial era large industrial operators' commercial fishing efforts, profiting first from Belgian mining companies, then Northern Rhodesian Copperbelt contracts extinguished at least one of the fishery's most favored fish species. By the 20th Century's end, increasing numbers of unemployed individuals, taking advantage of passenger buses to transport and sell easily available, cheap fish, threatened the fishery's future breeding stock —a modern-day tragedy of the commons.

As a result of this historically-created circumstance, exploitative (and exploited) fish-hands and young, unmarried, female fish traders, joined the fishery both because of its open access and their own need. When questioned, a young man or woman invariably replied that he or she worked the fishery to make money. Put another way, they did it not only because they could, but because they must. The open-access fishery presented an opportunity not elsewhere available to unemployed, impoverished individuals. However, as more and more young people follow those currently working on the fishery, they found it increasingly difficult to earn a living. Fish hands responded by increasing their fishing effort, often targeting juvenile fish to fill bowls of chibalebale. Female fish traders sought every possible opportunity to purchase lower cost fish and increase their scanty profits—including submitting to risky sexual behavior.

The draft Fisheries Act, 2001 sought to address some of the more pressing ailments currently afflicting the Mweru-Luapula fishery. It proposed to restrict open access through seasonal closure and year round protection of breeding grounds but remained vague on details, committing only to "prescribe areas or periods of the year," and leaving the specific details to future Central Fisheries Committees. It also mandated that all fishers purchase fishing licenses, and outlawed particularly destructive fishing techniques, like the use of explosive and electric devices. Finally, it proposed a much more prominent place for aquaculture in fisheries management in hopes of relieving pressure on wild stocks. Although this latter aquaculture initiative is admirably optimistic, it is not likely by itself to effectively reduce the mounting pressure on the fishery.

In short, the draft Fisheries Act, 2001 grants considerable power and discretion to the Central Fisheries Committee —probably necessary, given the range of issues confronting Zambia's contemporary inland fisheries. The Act presumed a truly participatory committee, all of whose members would reach consensus on the best interests of the fishery – regardless of their divergent interests. Furthermore, any fisheries officer would quickly remind a legislator that regulations mean nothing without funding for implementation; and the financial plan, as it is currently laid out, seems hopeful at best.

Ultimately, no one can predict the success of a law while it remains under review and unimplemented. However, the draft did include submissions from hundreds of people and various vantages across the fishing industry. It seemed to comprise commonsense guidelines, relative checks and balances, and at least a possibility of fundability. Perhaps most importantly, its authors outlined a philosophy that attempted to incorporate both conservation and development in the context of the fishery's realities. Whatever its eventual pitfalls its drafters propose a law designed to *enable* rather than disable the people and living systems that depend on the fishery.

The 2001 draft Fishery Law grants considerable power to the proposed Central Fishery Committee. If enacted, its success will depend in part on the extent to which that Committee's members understand and adopt appropriate regulations to resolve the contradictions which plague the Mweru-Luapula Fishery. In turn, that will reflect the extent to which the detailed criteria and procedures incorporated in the law, itself, ensure the committee members receive the necessary inputs from the relevant stakeholders and act in a transparent, accountable manner. Less apparent, but equally important, is that this process includes feedback mechanisms which enable those affected to report on the law's implementation and social impact as a basis for further revisions to meet the fishery's continually changing circumstances. The success of the 2001 draft law, as ultimately revised – or an alternative law enacted by the legislature —will likely depend in part on other laws, resting on in-depth research of the available evidence, that effectively help to eliminate the underlying institutional factors that have forced so many impoverished Zambians to turn to the fishery for bare survival. Only then will the renowned Mweru-Luapula have a chance to reclaim its reputation as the Liverpool of Zambia.

Notes

1. Pronounced 'Loo-uh-pool-uh'.
2. Interview with Bright Mulenga, in Kashikishi, Luapula Province (Mar. 6, 2005).
3. Kashikishi is located three kilometers north of Nchelenge, the administrative center for Nchelenge District. Nchelenge is indicated on Map 1 on the southeast corner of Lake Mweru.
4. He continues in the same passage, adding:

> There is a feeling that Luapula life is not rural, backwoods life.... In the main settlement areas there is a great chain of stores where most goods available in the Copperbelt African markets can be bought; there are stores and tea-rooms with bread and sugar and tea and milk, beer-houses with daily brews, buses, lorries and bicycles, gramophones, guitars and radios. The town of Kazembe with its hotels, dance-halls, beer-houses and prostitutes is cosmopolitan; it is a Paris of pleasure to which playboys from other tribes come to drink and dance at Christmas and New Year....

Ian G. Cunnison, The Luapula People of Northern Rhodesia: Custom and History in Tribal Politics 25 (Manchester University Press 1959).

5. T.G. Carey, *Lake Mweru-Luapula*, in M.A.E. Mortimer, The Fish and Fisheries of Zambia 62 (Ndola, Zambia: Falcon Press 1965); Sidney Maboshe, Development of the Fishing Industry in Luapula Province: Issues, Challenges and the Way Forward (Mansa, Zambia: Department of Fisheries, 2004).
6. Worldwide there are likely over 20 million fishers in this category. However, such a number can only be approximated as such fishing practice is often overlooked in favor of larger, more mechanized fishing operations. Furthermore, within the scholarship on artisanal fishing industries generally, data and description of inland artisanal fisheries tends to be scant compared to coastal industries. Artisan Fisheries: Characteristics, Problems, Needs, and Relationships to Aquaculture (Nelson Marshall, et al., eds.,1975); T. R. Brainerd, Socioeconomic Research on Fisheries and Aquaculture in Africa, in Fisheries Socioeconomics in the Developing World: Regional Assessments and Annotated Bibliography (A. T. Charles, et al. eds., 1993).
7. "Killing" is the direct and conceptual translation of "ukwipaile sabi," the Chibemban term meaning the act of fishing or catching fish. (Chibemba is the predominant language spoken in Luapula.) This term is used throughout this chapter in places of more familiar English verbs such as "catching" or to "fishing," in order to suggest that locally conceived and articulated ideologies vary from place to place, and have an impact on how such activities are performed and how applicable laws may be interpreted by the fishers themselves.
8. Interview with Ntoto Village fishers and fish traders, Kasheta Village, Luapula Province (Nov. 20, 2004).
9. This is a fish with a rather peculiar façade. It is widely considered a delicacy and such popularity is likely the cause of its demise in Luapula waterways. Perhaps the best description, anthropomorphism included, is provided by P. B. N. Jackson, a fishery biologist who worked in the region throughout the Central African Federation and into Zambian statehood:

> [The mbowa, Auchenoglanis occidentalis] is an odd-looking fish with a heavy truncate head, tapering snout and most mournful expression, accentuated by its capacity for emitting sobbing grunts when captured.... The species is valuable and highly prized by Africans because of the rich, fat, dark flesh.

P. B. N. JACKSON, THE FISHES OF NORTHERN RHODESIA: A CHECK LIST OF INDIGENOUS SPECIES 91 (1961).

10. This term is also used in the more grammatically appropriate constructions, mutubulu, for an individual and batubulu, for more than one. Robert Bates traces the first utterance of this epithet to a 1968 parliamentary campaign in Luapula. ROBERT H. BATES, RURAL RESPONSES TO INDUSTRIALIZATION: A STUDY OF VILLAGE ZAMBIA 229-230 (1976). Two longtime Kashikishi residents recall that the Zambian politician Simon Mwansa Kapwepwe used it to castigate his Luapula Valley audience in frustration at their perceived lack of willingness to diversify their local fishing economy. Kapwepwe first spoke the insult while officially opening Lakes Fisheries of Zambia Limited in Nchelenge, a majority state-owned fishing company. Interviews with Headman Boniface Kabosha, (Jan. 28, 2005), and Bright Mulenga, in Kashikishi, Luapula Province (Mar. 6, 2005).
11. DEPARTMENT OF FISHERIES (DOF), TOWARDS A SUSTAINABLE FISHERY: THE NEED FOR JOINT ACTION ON MWERU-LUAPULA 1 (Nchelenge: DoF, 1995).
12. This figure is based on KEES GOUDSWAARD, A DYNAMIC FISHERY IN ZAMBIA: A CASE OF CHANGE IN THE MWERU LUAPULA FISHERY: REPORT OF A FRAME SURVEY IN 1997 (1999). While more recent census data is available, this number corresponds to statistics of fishers and fishing gear owners recorded during that period.
13. When two terms are indicated, the first represents the species in Chibemba, while the second is its Latin variant.
14. It was not until the 1970s that Chisense was recognized and targeted as a widely edible and marketable commodity. However, longtime fisher and chisense gear manufacturer Mpundu Chishimba suggests that these lake sardines had been supplements to local subsistence diets at least since the 1950s. Interview with Mpundu Chishimba, in Chikonde Village, Luapula Province (Aug. 1, 2005); see also David M. Gordon, The Making of a Hinterland: Environment and Politics in Mweru-Luapula from the 1880s to the 1990s 289 (2000) (unpublished Ph.D. dissertation, Princeton University). Prior to the development of the Chisense industry it was regarded as a low status food source befitting only women and children; men (at least publicly) viewed it merely as food for other fish. Interview in Shinjoni Village, Luapula Province (Sep. 6, 2004).
15. *See* GOUDSWAARD, *supra* note 12; P.B.N. JACKSON, THE FISHES OF NORTHERN RHODESIA: A CHECK LIST OF INDIGENOUS SPECIES (Lusaka: The Government Printer, 1961); PAUL H. SKELTON, A COMPLETE GUIDE TO THE FRESHWATER FISHES OF SOUTHERN AFRICA (Halfway House, South Africa: Southern Book Publishers, 1993).
16. DOF, *supra* note 11, at 1.
17. Tilleke Kiewied, Socio-economic Study of Fishing Communities Along Lake Mweru (LP, Zambia: Rep. ALCOM Field Document No. 21, 1994).
18. Ian G. Cunnison, History on The Luapula: An Essay on the Historical Notions of a Central African Tribe 7 (Rhodes-Livingstone Paper No. 21)(London: Oxford University Press, 1951).
19. Times Reporter, *Three Drown on Lake Mweru*, TIMES OF ZAMBIA, Apr. 7, 2004, at 1; 2004; Patrick Phiri, *"Unsafe" Boats Banned from Lake Mweru*, ZAMBIA DAILY MAIL, Apr. 13, 2004, at 2.

20. See generally GOUDSWAARD, supra note 12; personal correspondence with Musonda Ng'onga, Senior Research Officer of the Department of Fisheries, Nchelenge (Nov. 17, 2004).

21. J. M. S. Allen & C. K. Chileya, *"The Unbaptised": Farming in a Fishing Economy—A Case from the Mweru Lakeshore, Zambia,* 13TH EUROPEAN CONGRESS OF RURAL SOCIOLOGY (Braga, Portugal, 1986); R.H. Kanema, *Nchelenge Agricultural Study: "Farming in a Fishing Environment,"* LITERATURE REVIEW OF AGRICULTURE IN NCHELENGE DISTRICT, LUAPULA PROVINCE (Nchelenge: SNV, 1995).

22. P.A.M. VAN ZWIETEN & C.K. KAPASA, LAKE MWERU-LUAPULA. ANALYSIS OF THE GILLNET SURVEYS OF 1982 TO 1985 AND 1994 TO 1996 (Nchelenge, Luapula Province: DoF, 1996); GOUDSWAARD, *supra* note 12.

23. GOUDSWAARD, *supra* note 12, at 9-16.

24. Kiewied, *supra* note 17, at 18-19.

25. See also Robarm Mwape, personal correspondence, Jan. 13, 2005, Kashikishi Luapula Province.

26. "Sex-for-fish" and some of the tragic consequences that stem from it including sexually transmitted diseases, in particular HIV/AIDS, is a serious and in-depth issue for which space in this chapter is limited. Research and reporting has only recently begun to investigate some of the finer—and frightening—points in the northern Zambia fishing communities. An intriguing piece was recently published in the Zambia Daily Mail, which included the following alarming belief among fishers in Lake Tanganyika:

    > [T]he more sexual relations a fisherman has, the bigger the catch [will be]. His fish business would thrive.... 'It is not easy to be on water alone [one fisher remarked]. We have to protect ourselves from many dangers and our catch also depends on many other things. I know that if I have several sexual partners, my catch is really good. I cannot stop dating women because that would kill my business.

    Wallen Simwaka, Mpulungu: A Breeding Ground for HIV, ZAMBIA DAILY MAIL, Aug. 14, 2004, at 4.

27. P.A.M VAN ZWIETEN, B.H.M. AARNINK, C.K. KAPASA & P. NGALANDE, THE BIOLOGY, FISHERY AND TRADE OF CHISENSE FROM MWERU-LUAPULA: STATUS OF PRESENT KNOWLEDGE 93 (Nchelenge: DoF, 1996).

28. *Id.*, at 97-98.

29. *Id.*, at 112.

30. *Id.*

31. For an extreme example, see the next session on chibalebale.

32. SEC/NAT364, Kawambwa Tour Report for 1948, Vol. IV, DC Kawambwa to Senior PC Ndola, 1/20/48. Credit for this reference, with appreciation, belongs to Mwelwa, Musambachime, although, as always, any errors of citation or content are the author's alone.

33. DOF, *supra* note 11, at 7.

34. *See* van Zwieten & Kapasa, *supra* note 22.

35. Banamakupwila frequently admit that they feel catching small fish is harmful to the fishery. However they blame this practice not on their role in buying and selling it as chibalebale, but instead on the failure of the Department of Fisheries

to eradicate it. Some sample quips: "The Catching of Small Fish attributes to poor catches. DoF [Department of Fisheries] should control"; "Good catch of Ntembwa [hump-backed bream] and Matuku [small bream]; however, there is a big destruction of catching small fish", Shinjoni Market, Kashikishi, Luapula Province (Oct. 27, 2004).

36. Daniel Pauly, Fishing Down Canadian Aquatic Food Webs, 58 CANADIAN JOURNAL OF AQUATIC SCIENCE 51 (2000); Tony J. Pitcher, Fisheries Managed to Rebuild Ecosystems? Reconstructing the Past to Salvage the Future, 11 ECOLOGICAL APPLICATIONS 601 (2001).
37. *See* Garret Hardin, *The Tragedy of the Commons*, 162 SCIENCE 1243 (1968).
38. *See generally* THE QUESTION OF THE COMMONS: THE CULTURE AND ECOLOGY OF COMMUNAL RESOURCES (Bonnie J. McCay & James A. Acheson, eds., Univ. of Arizona Press 1987).
39. *See* MWELWA C. MUSAMBACHIME, DEVELOPMENT AND GROWTH OF THE FISHING INDUSTRY IN MWERU-LUAPULA 1920-1964 393 (Univ. of Wisconsin Madison, 1981).
40. For more information on this campaign also see Mwelwa C. Musambachime, The Fate of the Nile Crocodile in African Waterways, 86 African Affairs 197 (1987).
41. In Latin: Labeo altivelis, local vernacular in Chibemba: Lupumbu or Mpumbu for more than one.
42. MWELWA C. MUSAMBACHIME, DEVELOPMENT AND GROWTH OF THE FISHING INDUSTRY IN MWERU-LUAPULA 1920-1964 313 (1981).
43. *See id.*
44. Whether the implication is that to be Shila is to fish or, to fish is therefore to be Shila remains a matter of conjecture, but the intermingling between cultural identity and occupational livelihood suggests that, in this region, fishing became more an exclusively economic activity. Ian G. Cunnison, a Scottish social anthropologist and Rhodes-Livingstone Institute researcher working in the Luapula Valley in the late 1940s into the 1950s argues that "tribes" introduced certain customs upon immigration to Luapula, which were consequently attributed to them. Fishing is a Shila activity, so therefore by extension one who fishes is Shila. Cunnison articulates this concept with an example:

    > A man who comes to the market to barter his catch of fish for a pot of millet beer does not do so consciously as a Shila trading with a Lungu. The actuality may be the opposite: a Lungu trading with a Shila. But the people are still aware that fishing is the work of the Shila and millet cultivation the work of the Lungu and that it is the diversity of tribal origins that has made this particular exchange possible.

    CUNNISON, supra note 4, at 60.
45. *Id.*
46. D. Paine, *Lake Mweru: Its Fish and Fishing Industry*, 2(I) NORTHERN RHODESIA JOURNAL 7 (1950-52); D.U. Peters, *Visit to Kilwa Island and African Oil Palm*, 31(II) NORTHERN RHODESIA JOURNAL 9 (1953-55).
47. MUSAMBACHIME, supra note 42.
48. *Id.*

49. *See generally* ANDREW ROBERTS, A HISTORY OF ZAMBIA (New York: Africana Pub. Co., 1976).
50. Note that the government had written in and accredited the same recommendations in 1929.
51. DEPARTMENT OF GAME AND TSETSE CONTROL, GAME AND TSETSE CONTROL ANNUAL REPORT FOR 1944 52 (1944).
52. SEC/NAT/364/IV, Kawambwa Tour Report 1948, DC Kawambwa to Senior PC, Western Province (Jan.20, 1948). For both this and the previous citation the author again thanks Mwelwa Musambachime.
53. This was, however, not the first fisheries legislation enacted by the British Colonial government. The Government Order, Number 77 of 1943, entitled the Fish Control Regulation, preceded the Fish Conservation Act by nearly ten years and the Fish Protection Ordinance by almost fifteen, but in the Mweru-Luapula fishery these accomplished little more than to advertise the inaction of the British government in contrast to its Belgian counterpart across the Luapula River in the Congo. See generally MWELWA C. MUSAMBACHIME, DEVELOPMENT AND GROWTH OF THE FISHING INDUSTRY IN MWERU-LUAPULA 1920-1964 (1981); JEREMY GOULD, LUAPULA: DEPENDENCE OR DEVELOPMENT? (1989). These earlier colonial legislative forays into fishery management provided no more than a series of unenforced guidelines since the government did not establish a department to implement them until 1940. Mwelwa C. Musambachime, Problems of Conserving Fish in Shared Fisheries: The Case of Mweru-Luapula 5 (University of Zambia Department of History Working Paper, 1996). More detailed discussion and analysis of these laws follows in the main body of this chapter.
54. In contrast, pre-colonial chiefly rule had emphasized ecological sustainability in concert with the social, economic, and gastronomic needs of human communities. See generally Musambachime, supra note 26.
55. Mwelwa C. Musambachime, Problems of Conserving Fish in Shared Fisheries: The Case of Mweru-Luapula, University of Zambia Department of History Working Paper 6 (1996) (citing Northern Rhodesia Legislative Council, Nov. 20- Dec. 10, 1943, column 123).
56. Interview with Headman Shinjoni, Albert Kalobwe, and Donald Kalenga, in Shinjoni Village, Kashikishi, Luapula Province (Sep. 6, 2004).
57. Mwelwa C. Musambachime, *Problems of Conserving Fish in Shared Fisheries: The Case of Mweru-Luapula* 6 (University of Zambia, Department of History Working Paper, 1996).
58. Musambachime in particular cites comments made by Emile Renaud, a major middleman buyer at that time in the nascent Mweru-Luapula fishing industry, at the behest of the District Commissioner of Kawambwa: The Luapula Salmon, he observed,

> spawns coming back to the lake in April. The majority are caught in small creeks or streams where natives dam the water and put traps. The young ones also are caught. This fish is decreasing in numbers. At Kasenga (on the Luapula) in 1920 a few fishermen would catch 6000. Now it is difficult to catch 1000. But it may be breeding well in the Kalungwishi river (sic). The remedy to check the decrease is

to put restrictions on basket fishing during the breeding season and to close the small streams.

NAZ/ZA1/9/56/Vol 1/35.

59. In 1924 when the British government did not renew the charter that allowed the British South Africa Company (BSAC) to operate in Northern Rhodesia. It assumed control over the territory until October 24, 1964 when it granted independence to the government of the Republic of Zambia.
60. E.g. Northern Rhodesia Legislative Council Debates March 5, 1929, column 65; Secretary for Native Affairs ordered memorandum "A Proposal to Initiate a Native Industry by Catching, Drying & Selling Lake & River Fish for Native Consumption in Mine Compounds and elsewhere (sic)," NAZ/ZA1/9/56/Vol. 1/4; Department of Native Affairs directive entitled "The Native Fish Industry" to Provincial Commissioners nationwide to collect information on their provincial fisheries, NAZ/ZA1/9/56/Vol. 1/5
61. When a European named Maurice Canter applied to export fish from the Kafue River March 29, 1928, the Secretary for Native Affairs' response belied a sense of embarrassment: "I am directed to inform you that no legislation exists at the moment which requires a license to catch or export fish, but the Government intends to introduce an Ordinance at an early date giving power to frame regulations on the subject and Mr. Cantor should bear this in mind if he contemplates undertaking expenditure in connection with this project." NAZ/ZA1/9/56/Vol. 1/1-3.
62. The notices cited and discussed here are those that affect the Mweru-Luapula fishery. It should be noted that during this period the laws, The Fish Control (Protection of Waters) Regulations of 1942 and The Fish Control (Copperbelt) Regulations of 1944, were also enacted. These latter pieces of legislation, respectively, restrict fishing (excepting rod and line) in a stipulated stretch of the Zambezi River and several rivers on the Copperbelt.
63. David M. Gordon, The Making of a Hinterland: Environment and Politics in Mweru-Luapula from the 1880s to the 1990s, 157 (2000) (unpublished Ph.D. dissertation, Princeton University) (citing District Commissioner, Kawambwa to Provincial Coordinator, Northern Province, November 28, 1940, NAZ, SEC 6/191).
64. Gordon, *supra* note 14.
65. *See* Mwelwa C. Musambachime, *Rural Political Protest: The 1953 Disturbances in Mweru-Luapula*, 20 INT'L J. AFR. HISTORICAL STUD. 437 (1988).
66. Since the onset of colonial rule, the majority African population had never had any formal means of expressing political opinion.This particularly divisive and unsettled time, however, reflectedZambians' mounting demands that, in 1964, led to Independence.
67. Notes On Fish Conservation Bill, NAZ/SEC/466/1/FG/3/Vol II/21, at 2.
68. Id.
69. Fisheries Act of 1974, Preamble, 31 of 1974, Cap. 314.
70. This is only in terms of recent popular African imagination. The annual closed season was originally a tool of chiefs and bamwine kabanda (traditional guardians of Mweru-Luapula lagoons) who regulated the fishery for the benefit of fish stock breeding seasons and the nutritive and economic needs of their subjects.

71. *See* e.g. C.K. Kapasa, The Need for Closed Fishing Period: A Review of the Fisheries Management Policy, Objectives and Present Status of Commercial Fisheries, the Involvement of Local Parliament Leadership (Nchelenge: DoF, 1992); Robert Lubilo, Victor Maangwe & Francis Lubasi, Report on the Fish Conservation Seminar for Mweru Luapula Fishers and Traditional Chiefs Held in October 1992 (DoF, 1993); Edward Mafulo, A Study on Management Practices by the Communities in the Mweru-Luapula Fishery During the 1997-1998 Closed Season (DoF, 1998).
72. Ann and Robert B. Seidman rephrased Barth's concept of individual choice within a constrained framework of options (as shown above) in order to integrate it within their broader discussion of how socially and developmentally unproductive institutions can be improved through law. They assert that law has the potential to be 'transformatory,' which means that it can be used instrumentally to direct changes in the various repetitive behaviors that comprise institutions perpetuating circumstances of poverty in specific sectors of the economy of a country. Ann & Robert B. Seidman, Africa's Deadlock of Law and Development (2003) (unpublished manuscript) (citing FREDRIK BARTH, MODELS OF SOCIAL ORGANIZATION (1966)).
73. One official who has worked for DoF for nearly thirty years highlighted one pay cycle when a Luapula district was allotted Zkw 50,000 (US$ 25) for three months of activities. While this may have been a merely a clerical error the misappropriation was never rectified and, he feels, typifies the complacent lack of concern consistently demonstrated by government toward fishery law and enforcement. Interview with Frederick Kafumbe, in Mansa, Luapula Province (Aug. 25, 2004).

PART IV

CONCLUSIONS

Chapter 8

Law-Making: An On-Going Process

The Editors

Too often, the people of Africa have lost the Fatal Race. The old colonial institutions continued, still authoritarian, inegalitarian, arbitrary, sometimes brutal, producing and reproducing poverty, vulnerability, poor governance, constantly changing, but, save accidentally, not in ways likely to foster either good governance or people-oriented development.

The evidence accumulated in the chapters of this book suggests three sets of propositions. First, unless deliberately changed through the use of state power, necessarily exercised through the legal order, institutions tend to reproduce themselves. Over time, they may change—but not necessarily in ways that reflect the wishes of either governors or governed. Africa has ample resources. At least among the first-generation of populist, liberation governors, many, perhaps most, truly aimed at improving the lot of their people. Neither weak resources nor weak leaders, but weak *institutions*, shaped over the years by competing colonial powers, perpetuated African external dependence, poverty, vulnerability, and poor governance.

Second, to ensure good governance, that is, the effective implementation of an appropriate development strategy designed to improve the life of the people, concerned law-makers must learn to exercise state power to transform those institutions. Governors exercise state power through law and the legal order. The widespread loss of the fatal race, the tragedy of the development era, finds an explanation in the governors' want of skill and understanding of the use of law as an instrument of social change.

Third, to provide law-makers with the facts they require to design effective law, social scientists needed to focus research on the kinds of evidence necessary to justify the claim that a proposed law's detailed provisions will likely prove effectively implemented and help to resolve the social problem it targets. This final chapter explores these conclusions and their implications for future efforts to strengthen drafting capacity and law making institutions to enable law-makers to use law to transform dysfunctional socio-economic institutions and foster democratic social change.

INSTITUTIONS AT THE ROOT OF EXTERNAL DEPENDENCE, POVERTY AND VULNERABILITY

The vast African continent houses all the agricultural and mineral resources required to meet the basic needs of its seven hundred million inhabitants. As this book's authors demonstrate, however, interacting government and private sector institutions, that emerged from more than a century of competing colonial powers' rule, blocked the creation of productive employment opportunities and rising living standards for its peoples. Over decades of imperial rule, colonial governments introduced their own laws that shaped the public and private institutions that undergird the export enclaves still characteristic of the divided African nations of today. Unaltered, these institutions—embedded in every country's farming, mining, trading and financial sectors, as well as the law-making and enforcement agencies that still structure them—continued to drain away those countries' rich mineral, agricultural and even human resources. Their persistent presence reflected the unwritten ***'law of continuity of institutions'***: Unless deliberately transformed through conscious human action, an institution may change—but not necessarily in ways likely to contribute to redirecting the development of African resources to fulfill all Africans' basic needs.

More than half century after Ghanaians became the first sub-Saharan Africans to win national liberation, most, if not all, of today's independent African governments still confront a challenge: How to exercise state power through their primary available tool, the rational use of law, to transform their countries' inherited institutions and facilitate their citizens' access to increasingly productive employment opportunities and the continually improving quality of life made possible by 21st Century global innovation? In Ghana, as world cocoa prices tumbled, repeated coups and counter-coups accompanied by neo-liberal privatization measures, clearly did little to improve the average Ghanaian's life. Failure to implement new law to restructure the inherited police force left that institution in place primarily to protect the emerging new Ghanaian elites.

The story of the Luapula fishery (chapter 7) illustrates the likely consequences of failure: In the 19th Century 'Scramble for Africa,' the British and Belgian colonial powers arbitrarily divided and began exploiting Mweru-Luapula's valuable fish resources without regard to the future of either the fishery or the lives of the region's inhabitants. After independence, the new Zambian government merely perpetuated this trend toward decline through targeted overfishing amidst managerial negligence. By the new millennium, as global copper prices tumbled, more and more unemployed Zambians—including growing numbers of women—desperately sought survival by employing ever more destructive means to catch ever fewer viable stocks of fish.

Too many of Africa's new governors seemed to abandon efforts to use law constructively to transform their new nations' inherited dysfunctional institutions. Typically, as Uate describes in the Mozambique case (Chapter 3), institutionalized drafting practices required ill-equipped drafters to design new laws' detailed provisions, supposedly to engage citizens in dealing with social problems like those posed by mega-projects that endangered their country's environment. Too often, drafters drafted by adopting entropic drafting methodologies: They copied laws from other countries, adopted the pluralist myth that political bargains lead to the best possible legislation, criminalized unwanted behaviors, or merely declared those behaviors illegal in broad, generalized terms. None of the entropic methodologies rest on detailed studies of the specific environment within which the new law will function. Without such a foundation, only serendipitously will the law induce the desired new behaviors.

Makgetla (Chapter 3) describes South Africa's post-liberation efforts to bring together disparate groups—trade unions, corporate managers, and civil society leaders—to formulate policies to restructure the socio-economic institutions imposed by *apartheid.* Her story reveals the way the inherited government departments, which under apartheid had long provided social services primarily for the white minority, partially extended them to the black majority. Privatization, adopted by the new government under international financial agencies' pressure, reduced those initiatives' impact as private providers cut back services to those unable to pay for them. In contrast, from the outset, policies to restructure the economy seemed to fall on deaf departmental ears. In fact, by the early years of the new millennium, the percentage of government expenditures to strengthen the economy had fallen to the lowest level since 1946 (when government first published the relevant statistics). Unemployment mounted. A further danger appeared: Unless government could stimulate more effective economic development, providing more jobs and incomes for the poor, as well as increasing tax revenues, it risked not having sufficient funds to pay for the expanded social services it had introduced.

Functioning in colonially-shaped governing institutions characterized by secrecy and non-accountability, in some countries, some new African governors discovered opportunities for corrupt behaviors that enriched themselves and their cronies. Turning cynical, these used their new law-making status, not to advance the public interest, but to enhance their own positions of influence and power. Others, abandoning efforts to transform their nations' inherited institutions, sought to manipulate popular support by mobilizing and even arming ethnic groups to enable them to take over and rule their countries by military force. Too often, these behaviors seemed, almost inevitably, to culminate in the loss of the Fatal Race: Seemingly unable to exercise state power through law to transform the inherited institutions that perpetuated poor governance, underdevelopment, and poverty, too many of Africa's new governors capitulated to those institutions' pressures and illusory promises of wealth and power.

USING INSTITUTIONALIST LEGISLATIVE THEORY AS A GUIDE TO STRENGTHENING LAW-MAKING INSTITTUTIONS AND DRAFTING EFFECTIVE TRANSFORMATORY LAWS

The country experiences described in this book underscore the necessity of strengthening the new African nations' legislative drafting capacity and law-making institutions. Essentially, their law-makers required the theoretical and practical tools to formulate, assess, enact, and implement effective laws to transform their nations' inherited institutions to facilitate good governance and effective people-oriented economic development. This book's second chapter outlined the way institutionalist legislative theory can guide African law-makers in designing and assessing legislation likely effectively to transform the institutions that thwart African efforts to realize the promises of independence. At each of four steps, that theory's problem-solving methodology can assist law-makers in gathering and organizing the relevant available evidence as a basis for designing the details of proposed laws to transform the inherited institutions—the repetitive patterns of behaviors that perpetuate African poverty and vulnerability. These steps require providing the relevant available facts to: (1) describe the social problem the proposed bill targets, and whose and what behaviors comprise it; (2) explain the causes of each of set of those problematic behaviors; (3) design the bill's detailed provisions logically to alter or eliminate the causes of existing dysfunctional behaviors in order to induce new behaviors likely to prove cost-effective in helping to resolve the problem; and (4) after the bill's enactment, demonstrate that the implementation and social impact of the law's detailed prescriptions.

Institutionalist legislative theory offers no easy formula for its use. To the problems of development it brings no treasure chest; it brings a tool-box. In contrast to the 'ends-means' methodology widespread among policy-makers, it does not teach drafters first to search their consciousness for a desired 'end' or objective, and then design the details of a bill apt to attain that end. Rather, problem-solving begins with a detailed description and analysis of the present situation, and then logically designs a solution that, within the means available, addresses those causes of the social problem at issue. What changes law-makers decide to make through law in each particular case depends on a careful weighing of the evidence of the probable social and economic costs and benefits.

The problem-solving methodology undergirds a recommendation that drafters accompany an important bill with a research report that provides the facts, logically organized, to demonstrate that the bill's details will likely help to resolve the social problem targeted. In a real sense, that report serves as a quality control. Just as a judge's opinion serves to justify the judge's decision, so does a research report justify the bill. Just as the judge's opinion constrains arbitrary judicial decision, so a research report, appropriately structured in terms of facts and logic, constrains arbitrary legislative decision. By resting on reasons with which a rational skeptic can be expected to agree—that is, on facts and logic, on what the philosopher John Rawls calls 'public reasons'—it ensures that a bill will likely further the *public interest*. Given a research report resting on facts and logic, rational skeptics on both sides of the political aisle must either agree, or bring forward better facts and better logic. Anyone may make suggestions for improvements in the bill based on better facts and reasons. The requirement of a research report thus serves to make possible increased public participation in the law making process.

In this book's third part, drawing on Zambian experience, Ng'gandwe proposes one possible strategy for improving the law-making process required to produce legislation to transform dysfunctional institutions: The enactment of a Zambian law to establish a national Commission on Law and Integrated National Development. Essentially a new law-making institution, that Commission would study the national economy and the institutions that constitute it, region by region, sector by sector.

Subject to overall direction by the Commission, Ng'andwe's proposed enabling Act requires the Commission's Director of Research to supervise the research. That Act requires that the Director accompany a proposed bill with a Research Report. The Act prescribes in considerable detail the content of that Report. It would provide a description of the relevant facts, logically organized, to demonstrate that the bill's detailed provisions would transform the specified region's institutions in ways likely to ensure the full utilization of that region's human and material resources. Guided by institutionalist legislative theory, those requirements in effect specify the criteria to govern the research.

In addition, specified procedures would require the researchers to encourage participation of those whom the bills would likely affect (i.e., the stakeholders), ensuring transparent, accountable and, as far as possible, participatory decision-making processes. The researchers would obtain inputs and feed-back from relevant ministry and parliamentary staff as well as organized civil society and university personnel.

Annear's chapter 7, describing the Luapula fishery, demonstrates the availability of the kind of detailed evidence required to expose the way, historically, colonial-imposed institutions may contribute to undermining a province's potentially valuable physical and human resources. He mentions that provincial and international donor agency personnel have begun working on a draft bill to try to resolve the resulting conflicts. Institutionalist legislative theory, however, would suggest assessing that bill's details in terms of the kinds of questions raised by considering the four steps of its problem-solving methodology.

FINDING AND ASSESSING THE AVAILABLE EVIDENCE: A NEW RESEARCH AGENDA

As a third conclusion, review of this book's chapters underscores the necessity of encouraging social scientists to work with law-makers to conduct research directed to producing the kinds of evidence required to design effective legislation. Guided by institutionalist legislative theory, drafters need evidence to ensure the validity of their hypotheses at each of problem-solving's four steps. Assessment of current social science research findings suggests that, in general, social scientists rarely focus on the detailed nature and causes of specific sets of social actors' problematic behaviors—the institutions—that tend to thwart good governance and development. Instead, their findings tend to describe the general problems that seem to result from the exercise of individual and state power in policy determination: the nature and extent of police brutality in Ghana; or inherited government departments' apparent failure to formulate and implement policies directed at transforming the institutions that perpetuate external dependence, mounting unemployment, and poverty in Zambia and South Africa.

In contrast, in addition to calling for evidence that describes the surface appearance of the targeted social problem, institutionalist legislative theory's four step problem-solving methodology emphasizes the necessity of gathering facts as to *whose and what behaviors comprise the problem*; the *causes* of those behaviors; the socio-economic *costs and benefits* of proposed legislative measures logically likely to alter or eliminate those causes; and, after the law's enactment, the extent to which its detailed provisions prove effectively implemented and do, in fact—as the drafters (implicitly or, if they provide a research report, explicitly) predict—help to resolve the social problem.

As Annear's chapter illustrates, anthropologists do gather extensive evidence as to social actors' problematic behaviors, like those of the fishers whose unregulated fishing practices threaten the future of the Luapula fishery. Anthropologists less often, however, systematically analyze the detailed facts to describe the nature of the resulting interrelated institutions, or the causes of the relevant actors' problematic behaviors that comprise them. Yet, logically, the design of a law's detailed provisions must alter or eliminate all those causes to induce them to behave in ways likely to solve the social problem targeted. For purposes of designing and justifying legislation, drafters need research on the level of detail exemplified by Annear's research.

Following problem-solving's first two steps, Uate's chapter provides the kind of detailed evidence required to describe and analyze the causes of Mozambique's legislative drafters' behaviors. Those 'behaviors' (shaped by the nation's inherited drafting institutions) produced a law used by the implementing agency—despite a Cabinet's call for public participation in environmental protection—to justify a refusal to publish information essential for that purpose. Although he does not offer detailed proposals, Uate's analysis implies that Mozambique's lawmakers should draft and enact legislative provisions designed to overcome the causes of the drafters' problematic behaviors to ensure that Mozambique's drafting institutions produced more effectively implemented laws to carry out the government's stated intentions.

Ng'andwe's proposed Law and National Integrated Development Commission (chapter 6) suggests one device to remedy a common defect in African law-making for development: The relative absence of proposals for legislation likely to transform problematic institutions. To adopt it—or any other proposal towards the same end—obviously requires much national and local discussion. If established, it will require cooperation of legislative drafters, equipped with institutionalist legislative theory, methodology and techniques, together with knowledgeable ministry officials, social scientists from the universities and research institutions, and non-government organization personnel. It will also require cooperation and participation of stakeholders in conducting the research required to gather and organize the relevant available evidence.

To use law instrumentally to transform societies—that is, to *develop*—requires detailed behavioral research. That research never proves costless. Sometimes donor agencies will contribute. Sometimes, local citizens will participate because of their interest in the outcomes. Experience in several African countries, as well as elsewhere in the developing world, suggests the benefits of engaging university faculty and students, together with members of the relevant community, in the research process.[1] The Commission must try to discover the most cost-effective ways to conduct that research, calling upon whatever human and financial resources seem available.

All the research in this book suggests the necessity of ensuring participation in the law-making process of the relevant stakeholders—and that includes participation in the relevant research. Law can induce new behaviors only when crafted on the basis of the sort of detailed information that Annear and Uate provide. The stakeholders uniquely know the circumstances of their own lives, and hence about the milieu within which the new law will function. Competent legislative research and drafting requires their participation.

In sum, the chapters of this book suggest three conclusions about the use of law to foster good governance and development. First, the impoverishment of most of Africa's inhabitants reflects, not the absence of valuable material and human resources, but the way inherited public and private institutions—shaped by competing colonial powers over centuries—perpetuated their divided countries' externally-dependent socio-economic development. Second, to use law as an instrument of democratic social change requires the development of a theory and methodology to guide the process. This volume offers institutionalist legislative theory and its accompanying problem-solving methodology as a candidate, and urges that, so far as possible, practitioners accomplish that research with the participation of stakeholders. Third, to design effectively-implemented transformatory laws, African law-makers and social scientists need to conduct research on a level of detail more typical of anthropological ethnological description than most other social science research.

Together, in Africa's inevitably changing circumstances, these three conclusions underscore Africa's challenge: To learn what has thus far largely eluded them, how to use law and the legal order as instruments for democratic social change. Africans, like other peoples throughout the world, need to use and improve institutionalist legislative theory. They must also increasingly engage the population and specifically stakeholders in creating an on-going, self-reliant law-making process.

Note

1. For an example of community participatory research in Southern Africa, structured by university faculty members working with senior undergraduate students, *see*

Aid and Development in South Africa: Evaluating a Participatory Learning Process (Denny Kalyalya, Khethiwe Mhlanga, Ann Seidman & Joseph Semboja, eds., Africa World Press, 1987). In the course of a five-year project to strengthen legislative drafting capacity and law-making institutions in Indonesia, Ann & Robert B. Seidman worked together with colleagues from Indonesia and elsewhere to establish on-going research into the behaviors that comprised local and national social problems. These experiences underscore the advantages of encouraging university staff and students in establishing research centers as a valuable asset for institutionalizing an effective self-reliant learning process to improve national legislative drafting and law-making efforts. See http://www.ICLAD-law.org for a review of other countries' current efforts to institutionalize that kind of 'learning process.'

Contributors

Christopher M. Annear is currently a Ph.D. candidate in the Department of Anthropology at Boston University. His dissertation considers human-ecological relationships amidst deteriorating economic opportunities for rural residents in Luapula Province, Zambia. The working title for this project is "Fishing in Decline: The Practice and Politics of 'Killing' and 'Farming' Fish in Luapula, Zambia." He has recently completed twenty-two months of Fulbright (IIE) funded field research in support of this dissertation and is now residing and teaching in Boston. He has also published on the topic of genetically-modified organisms (GMOs) in Zambia. His future research, already under way, will concern mortuary culture and the burgeoning funeral industry in Zambia.

Raymond A. Atuguba is a professor of law at the University of Ghana. A graduate of the University of Ghana, he completed his Ph.D. at Harvard University. He teaches Law and Development, Conflict of Laws, Commercial Law and Administrative Law in the University of Ghana. He helped establish and serves as Director of Ghana's Legal Resources Centre, and is a member of ICLAD's Advisory Board.

Hanson Hu Li, graduated Beijing University in China with a B.A. & M.A.,in international relations and political economy. After taking an M.S. in political economy in the Massachusetts Institute of Technology in the United States, he attended law school at Boston University where he became an editor of the *Boston University Public Interest Law Journal.* Mr. Li has worked as a consultant to the United Nations Children's Fund (UNICEF) Basic Education Program and the World Bank Institute (WBI) Corporate Governance & Social Responsibility Program and co-chaired the Beijing 2000 Conference of the Harvard Project for Asian and International Relations (HPAIR).

Neva Seidman Makgetla, an economist (BA, Harvard; PhD, University of Berlin), has taught in universities in Zambia, the US, and South Africa. She worked for the new South African Government, initially as Chief Director for Fiscal Policy in the Reconstruction and Development Programme (RDP) Office in the Office of the President, and then Director of Research in the Department of Labour. From 1997 to 2000, she served as Deputy Director General for Remuneration and Conditions and Service and chief labor negotiator in the State Department of Public Service and Administration. In 2000, she became co-ordinator of the Congress of South African Trade Union's (COSATU's) fiscal, monetary and public sector policy, and then its policy unit head, responsible for research, policy proposals and negotiations on development strategy. She also writes a fortnightly column in the South African *Business Day*.

Pumzo Mbana holds an L.L.B. degree from the University of the Western Cape in South Africa. He is a Fulbright Scholar (2004-2006), studying towards an MA degree in Sustainable International Development at Brandeis University. Previously he held research assistant positions at the University of the Western Cape and at the Institute for Democracy in South Africa.

Lucian M Ng'andwe, currently enrolled as a graduate student in the M.A./Ph.D Community Economic Development Policy at Southern New Hampshire University's School for Community Economic Development, NH, USA, graduated from Brandeis University, in May 2004 with a Master of Arts in Sustainable International Development. Brought up by his brother, a mine worker on Zambia's Copperbelt, Ng'andwe studied philosophy (1986-1989) and theology (1989-1992) in Zambia. As his main research interest, he aims to identify and, if possible, help to design strategies to alter the inherited institutions that have fostered the misallocation of valuable resources in the economy of Zambia.

Ann Seidman and Robert B. Seidman serve as co-Presidents of the International Consortium on Law and Development (ICLAD). They taught and conducted research for 12 years in African universities, and one year in China, Ann as an economist, Bob as a lawyer. In 1992, building on that experience, they established the Boston University Program on Legislative Drafting for Democratic Social Change to assist country nationals in developing and transitional countries institutionalize on-going programs to strengthen legislative drafting capacity and law-making institutions. In 2004, they, together with colleagues in BU and throughout the world, established ICLAD as an international consortium for the advancement of international cooperation to enhance the use of law for good governance and democratic development.

Teodosio Uate completed his Ph.D. dissertation in the Political Science Department at Boston University in 2005. His dissertation addresses the role played by jurists as bill drafters and advisors to the Cabinet and the Assembly of the Republic in justifying and writing laws and regulations in Mozambique. He teaches law at the Law Faculty of Eduardo Mondlane University in Maputo, Mozambique. He also serves on ICLAD's Advisory Board.

Index